# 9/11 Gothic

# Reading Trauma and Memory

*Series Editors:* Aimee Pozorski, Central Connecticut State University, and Nicholas Ealy, University of Hartford

Reading Trauma and Memory offers global perspectives on representations of trauma and memory while examining the tensions, limitations, and responsibilities that accompany the status of the witness. This series attempts to bridge the gap between trauma studies and new directions in the fields of memory studies, popular culture, and race theory and seeks submissions that closely read literature and culture for representations of traumatic wounding, the limits of memory, and the ethical duty to depict historical trauma and its effects.

Given its breadth, this series will appeal to scholars in a number of interdisciplinary fields; given the specific angle of trauma and memory, it will capture those who see ethics and responsibility as key factors in their scholarship. Such areas include Holocaust studies; war trauma and PTSD; illness and disability; the trauma of migration and immigration; memory studies; race studies; gender and sexuality studies (which has recently had a resurgence with the #MeToo movement); studies in popular culture that take up television and films about witness; and the study of social and historical movements.

We are seeking projects that question how to honor the past through close readings of literature focused on trauma and memory—which would necessarily take on international perspectives. Examples include a consideration of literature, justice, and Rwanda through a postcolonial and trauma lens; recent thinking on the phenomenon of "American Crime Story" and the resurgence of interest in the OJ Simpson trial that parallels the narrative of the Black Lives Matter movement; readings of the attempts of popular culture to address issues of historical injustice as exemplified by *12 Years a Slave* and HBO's *Westworld*.

## Recent Titles in This Series

*9/11 Gothic: Decrypting Ghosts and Trauma in New York City's Terrorism Novels*, by Danel Olson

*Philo-Semitic Violence: Poland's Jewish Past in New Polish Narratives*, by Elżbieta Janicka and Tomasz Żukowski

*Trauma in 20th Century Multicultural American Poetry: Unmuted Verse*, by Jamie D. Barker

*Ethics of Witness in Global Testimonial Narratives: Responding to the Pain of Others*, by Kimberly A. Nance

*The Latinx Urban Condition: Trauma, Memory, and Desire in Latinx Urban Literature and Culture*, by Crescencio Lopez-Gonzalez

# 9/11 Gothic

## Decrypting Ghosts and Trauma in New York City's Terrorism Novels

Danel Olson

LEXINGTON BOOKS
*Lanham • Boulder • New York • London*

Published by Lexington Books
An imprint of The Rowman & Littlefield Publishing Group, Inc.
4501 Forbes Boulevard, Suite 200, Lanham, Maryland 20706
www.rowman.com

6 Tinworth Street, London SE11 5AL, United Kingdom

Copyright © 2021 by The Rowman & Littlefield Publishing Group, Inc.

Copyright © 2005 by Lynne Sharon Schwartz, from *The Writing on the Wall*. Reprinted by permission of Counterpoint Press.

*All rights reserved.* No part of this book may be reproduced in any form or by any electronic or mechanical means, including information storage and retrieval systems, without written permission from the publisher, except by a reviewer who may quote passages in a review.

British Library Cataloguing in Publication Information Available

**Library of Congress Cataloging-in-Publication Data Available**

ISBN: 978-1-7936-3832-8 (cloth : alk. paper)
ISBN: 978-1-7936-3834-2 (pbk. : alk. Paper)
ISBN: 978-1-7936-3833-5 (electronic)

*I dedicate this work to all the victims of the 9/11 attack and their survivors, to the brave rescuers, and to all the innocent victims of wars and refugee crises lost since in its name.*

# Contents

List of Figures ix

Acknowledgments xi

Introduction: Connecting Trauma Theory, 9/11 Novels, Gothic Traditions, and the Unidentified Bones of the World Trade Center 1

1 Don DeLillo's *Falling Man* (2007): Deserting and Impersonating the Dead 25

2 Jonathan Safran Foer's *Extremely Loud and Incredibly Close* (2005): Searching and Disinterring the Dead 53

3 Lynne Sharon Schwartz's *The Writing on the Wall* (2005): Avenging and Resurrecting the Dead 79

4 Griffin Hansbury's *The Nostalgist* (2012): Conjuring and Romancing the Dead 123

5 Patrick McGrath's *Ground Zero* (2005): Abandoning and Angering the Dead 143

Conclusion 163

Appendix 1: Further Reading 171

Appendix 2: Interview at the Opening of the National September 11 Memorial & Museum, New York City, with Its Executive Vice President and Director Alice M. Greenwald (June 16, 2014) 175

| | |
|---|---:|
| Bibliography | 185 |
| Index | 207 |
| About the Author | 217 |

# List of Figures

| | | |
|---|---|---|
| Figure I.1 | Snapshot from Jules Naudet's Footage of United Airlines Flight 175 Smashing into Tower 1's Northern Façade | 2 |
| Figure I.2 | Entering the Smoldering Ruins of Ground Zero with the Fire Department of New York | 5 |
| Figure 1.1 | Richard Drew's Photograph, "Falling Man." | 37 |
| Figure 1.2 | Aftermath of Boston's Cocoanut Grove Nightclub Fire | 45 |
| Figure 1.3 | Pioneering Treatment in Burn Therapy on the Cocoanut Grove Fire Victims at Massachusetts General Hospital | 46 |
| Figure 2.1 | Oskar (Thomas Horn) Beneath Yorick's Papier-Mâché Skull in the Film Version of Foer's Novel | 66 |
| Figure 2.2 | Screenshot of Oskar (Thomas Horn) and His Grandfather (Max von Sydow) from *Extremely Loud and Incredibly Close* | 75 |
| Figure 3.1 | New Yorkers Run for Their Lives on the Streets Surrounding the WTC | 84 |
| Figure 3.2 | Screenshot of Carmen (Marisa Paredes) and Jacinto (Eduardo Noriega) from *The Devil's Backbone* | 86 |
| Figure 3.3 | The First Sighting of Santi's Ghost (Íñigo Garcés) by Carlos (Fernando Tielve) | 87 |
| Figure 4.1 | Screenshot of Tower 1 from *Inside 9/11: Zero Hour* | 124 |
| Figure 4.2 | Screenshot of Missing Persons Sheets in New York City from *World Trade Center* | 131 |
| Figure 5.1 | Screenshot of Ground Zero from *9/11: The Filmmakers' Commemorative DVD Edition* | 151 |
| Figure 5.2 | Screenshot of Firefighters from *World Trade Center* | 157 |

| | | |
|---|---|---|
| Figure 5.3 | Woodcut Illustration of Kim Lee from Her Apartment Balcony as Described in McGrath's *Ground Zero* | 162 |
| Figure 7.1 | Author Standing at What Was New York City's Ground Zero and Now Is the National September 11 Memorial & Museum | 176 |
| Figure 7.2 | One World Tower (Freedom Tower) That Opened Six Months after the 9/11 Memorial & Museum | 183 |

# Acknowledgments

Thanks to director Guillermo del Toro for his intriguing emails on crying apparitions and to novelist Patrick McGrath for reading the first draft and asking after possession ghosts. A bouquet to Joyce Carol Oates for her Gothic friendship and encouragement through it all.

This book would not be possible without the true scholarship, time, and goodwill of Lexington Books' acquisitions editor for Education and Literary Studies Holly Buchanan, editing assistant Megan Conley, senior acquisitions editor Nicolette Amstutz, associate production editor Meaghan Menzel, Deanta project manager Monica Sukumar, the Trauma and Memory Series editors Dr. Aimee Pozorski (Central Connecticut State Uni.) and Dr. Nicholas Ealy (Uni. of Hartford), and the anonymous peer reviewers.

Gratitude to the Lone Star College System sabbatical program, LSCS Employee Doctoral Scholarship Committee, LSCS Board of Trustees, ever supportive dean Dr. Marie Morrison, incandescent vice-president Dr. Laura McMillion, visionary chancellor Dr. Steve Head, and to my stimulating LSCS colleagues & fine student friends like Dustin Bass.

A bow to the generosity of University of Stirling's Impact Scholarship and the Scottish Government's Saltire Scholarship.

Indebtedness to Stirling scholars who kindly enriched draft versions of my 9/11 PhD research with thoughtful questions during its yearly review panels: second supervisor Dr. Adrian Hunter, Professor Kristie Blair, Professor Ann Davies, and Dr. Matthew Foley.

Highest regard for University of Stirling historian of the American Revolution, Dr. Colin Nicholson. In my first semester at Scotland, he shared words about my journey that kept me reading and rethinking, writing and rewriting: "Scholars in one hundred years may look at your thesis for how the American outlook changed at the start of this century, to contextualize Americans' current views of handing over more power to the government, to how they counteracted terrorism, to what were the attitudes towards the threats, to what was the level of both justified fear and baseless paranoia."

Applause for the careful guidance, wealth of knowledge, and many queries from my principal supervisor Professor Dale Townshend (now of Manchester Metropolitan University), who enthusiastically serves PhD candidates in their investigations and fosters innovative ways of seeing the Gothic.

Appreciation to the stellar staff of the University of Stirling Library and Postgraduate Studies; student programs officer Louise Bleakley; Dr. Katie Halsey; Lone Star College Library; Dr. Lashun R. Griffin; Dr. Mari-Carmen Marín; the U.S. Department of Defense for the tour of damaged areas to the Pentagon from American Airlines Flight 77, and for allowing photography; the Smithsonian's Museum of American History for close view of its National September 11 Collection; and director Alice M. Greenwald and her Staff (especially Lynn Rasic) for the warm welcome and interview at the National September 11 Memorial & Museum, New York City.

Some of this book was written while I was teaching undergraduates and graduate students at two campuses of Qufu Normal University in Shandong Province, China. 谢谢 (Thank you) for the conversations with my supportive friends Wanda, Suzy, Lindsay, Cong, Meiling, Beatrice, Ashley, Jonathan, Ray, Andy, Ma Teng, Kelly, Kim, Mike, Amelia, Wei Li, Bonnie, Bella, Jessie, Circle, Tiffany Sophia Echo, Yi Yong, Fiona, Freya, Fire Max, Lily, Cici, Linda, Lucky, Nautilus, Daniel Zheng, Alex, Silivia, Zili Zhang, Vincent, Sunny, Betty, Jelsea Brynn, Aurora, Zoe, and Chen Chenxi (晨曦).

Unbounded love for my family: my giving wife, Professor Catherine Olson, who kindly proofread the whole; inspiring daughters Emily Sophia and Juliana Celeste, who made me smile; soul-siblings David E. Cowen and Susan Musch who shared poetry, feasts, and a Galveston beach; the Cowen Family who showed the art of staying brave before challenges; brothers Gordon and Glen and cousin Bonnie who taught me to love the printed word long ago; and to my caring mother Olga and late father Morrie, who always supported my education.

# Introduction

## Connecting Trauma Theory, 9/11 Novels, Gothic Traditions, and the Unidentified Bones of the World Trade Center

This is a volume interpreting civilian survivors' encounters with the ghostly inside novels set around the World Trade Center during and after 9/11. Another book I envision for the near future will examine how law enforcement and military face the supernatural during the resulting War on Terror (domestic and foreign) in fiction, film, and comics. However, in the midst of writing this calmly scholarly investigation of 9/11 novels, COVID-19 came to America. Suddenly memories and some lessons on instant death, economic shocks, vulnerabilities in national defense, and lingering traumata from the Al Qaeda attacks returned like revenants to me. Twenty years after the World Trade Center destruction, such emotional truths from 9/11 had new relevance and immediacy, as the country faced the horrible tally of over half a million Americans killed by spring 2021, and many more to come. More than that, the lost feelings engendered by 9/11 came back to us and the signs of nationalism were definitely in ascent, but this time the United States was far less unified. Protestors with assault rifles and MAGA caps swarmed state assembly halls leaving governors disturbed and representatives in bulletproof vests, while bathers in bikinis gathered illegally from Miami Beach to Malibu. The Twitterverse was a political cyber-storm, and a presidential election loomed, sure to be contested. Some wondered if there would still be an election in November 2020. Stephen King was wittily remorseful: "Sorry you feel like you're stuck in a Stephen King Novel" (Gross 2020). None of it was make-believe, and none of it was exactly like King's *The Stand* with a virus delivering 99 percent mortality, yet it still had the patina of the impossible, a glimpse of dystopia, and a nudge to the abyss. How could the American economy, which had been roaring, halt? How could so many people get infected in such a short time, and be dying every day, soon eclipsing the American dead from war after war? How could the federal government under President Trump seem so denial-filled, so sluggish to acknowledge the threat and prepare, and so tardy in responding with adequate medical help, tests, and protective clothing? Why was the task force to monitor pandemics and advise the President dissolved as a singular entity in 2018, all akin to the unwise dissolving of the daily briefings to President George W. Bush from a Terror Czar in 2000? How could we have been left in such a fragile position, when one in four New Yorkers was facing food shortages by May 2020 with the CDC warning that "aggressive" rats were hunting now during the shutdown of restaurants and the resulting empty dumpsters (Staff of *The New York Times* 2020; Padilla 2020)? How could our political situation and order so deteriorated that President Trump could, in the midst of pandemic, successfully enflame a mob (largely unmasked) to lay siege on Congress during the January 6, 2021, day of electoral vote count, the worst attack on the Capitol since the War of 1812? We were in a horror story with an ending no one knew, and the White House on that day made it scarier. The largest question that loomed now was the same one that followed the flames of

**Figure I.1    While Filming *A Day in the Life of a Rookie Firefighter* in Lower Manhattan on September 11, 2001, the French Brothers Jules and Gedeon Naudet Became Separated.** Near the North Tower, Jules aimed his camera up as he heard a Boeing 767 Jet screaming overhead at 8:46 a.m. He by chance captured what was thought to be the only footage of the first plane's attack, which is still considered the longest and clearest footage of United Airlines Flight 175 smashing into Tower 1's northern façade. Screenshot from *9/11: The Filmmakers' Commemorative DVD Edition*, Directors Jules and Gedeon Naudet, Goldfish Pictures/Silverstar Productions/Paramount, 2001.

9/11: when will we ever get back to normal, why can't we calm our fears, and how can we mourn when we cannot even attend the funeral? But in a number of respects, 9/11 was singular. One of those aspects is that survivors often had nobody to mourn. The body that is missing and the alarming ways it returns to survivors in fiction become the subject, scope, and significance of this book.

In the early morning of May 10, 2014, New York City fire, police, and port authority vehicles carried from a Manhattan medical examiner's office 7,930 pouches of human remains in American flag-draped transfer cases to their new vault beneath the just unveiled U.S. 9/11 Memorial & Museum at the former Ground Zero (Farrell 2014: 18). Out of the 2,753 people of 115 nations killed on September 11, 2001, at the World Trade Center (WTC) Towers, 1,115 victims or 41 percent were never identified, and the pouches held those bits of bone never matching the DNA from personal items the families of the dead could provide (Staff of *The Encyclopedia of 9/11* 2012; Dobnik 2014). Giving some sense of the gruesome WTC Plaza that day, only twelve bodies found at Ground Zero could be identified by sight alone (Olbermann 2003). To extract DNA from many of the nearly 20,000 other pieces of bodies found near the site, degraded by "fire, sunlight, bacteria and even the jet fuel that poured through the towers," was too difficult a challenge, and the personal identity of these fragments remains a mystery (Dobnik 2014). With the unknown dead situated beneath him in bedrock 70 feet down,[1] President Obama would come the next day to dedicate this space as a "memorial for understanding" (The White House 2014). Despite that, on the morning of remains-transfer a day before, Rosemary Cain, who lost her firefighter son at WTC, cried, "Don't put them in the basement. Give them respect so 3,000 souls can rest in peace" (Dobnik 2014). Another mourner who lost his firefighter son there, a seventy-seven-year-old retired deputy fire chief named Alexander Santora, stood on the ceremonial route on May 10, 2014, wearing his official uniform and a black gag over his mouth: "We had no say in what was going on here. You can't tell me that tour guides aren't going to be going inside that building and saying, 'Behind that wall are the victims of 9/11.' That's a dog and pony show" (Farrell 2014: 18). Adding to the angst over what was "behind that wall" would be a private, black-tie champagne event for sixty fundraising guests (including *Condé Nast* officials and billionaire mayor and 2020 short-lived presidential candidate Michael Bloomberg) at the 9/11 Memorial & Museum the night before its official opening. Joe Kisonas, a retired Fire Department of New York marshal, denied entry to the museum as staff were closing to tidy for the wealthy donors' entrance, left the museum feeling violated: "You don't have cocktail parties at a cemetery" (Sandoval et al. 2014). The bones of the unknown present a quandary to us: as they are of no identified family, they can neither be buried in a hero's or heroine's tomb, dropped over nearby Atlantic waters, nor interred in a particular family's vault, but they cannot be abandoned, either.

Such bone shards without a human name—such trauma falling from out of a blue sky's morning—seem to gothicize survivors' later perceptions in life and in fiction. By "gothicize," I am speaking not so much of the style of Gothic novels, but how their Gothicism's subjects of despair and dread affect and infect minds. I suggest that characters' views of reality that I will discuss become shaded by a new awareness of the sublime and threatening around them. We will explore here how by day and by night the survivors' minds fill with the devastated towers, everything excessively or grotesquely violent, all things diseased, the spirits of the dead, the surrounding elements of the abject and insane, the monstrous and the uncanny embedded in reality, a hatred for the Other, a hatred for the monster inside us as well (and the explosion of repressed violence and sex that finally comes), a new awe for what is transgressive and torturous, and an expanded consciousness of depravity. But how and why does a massive, history-bending tragedy like 9/11 grant some of those enduring it occasional supernatural encounters later? Why do the living start behaving with the personas of the dead? Why does whatever is brooding, dark, and malevolent make a new home in these characters' hearts and minds? How does literature depict and probe this uncanny phenomenon? What is the meaning for literary survivors from their meetings with monsters, doppelgängers, demonic spirits, and human ghosts? What can be unlocked in the novels if we enlist Trauma Theory, psychology, and neuroscience to interpret victims' confrontations with the ghostly? The "ghostly" I address here is the traditional sense of the returning spirit of the suddenly deceased, particularly those suffering a violent demise. And if characters seem to not speak (or to speak nonsensically) about their weird experiences and unhealable wounds is there any key to decode their silences or their seemingly delusional talk? These are questions underlying the nature and the consequences of trauma and haunting and memory of place, but they have not yet fully been explored in 9/11 texts. These eerie facets within novels on the WTC attack written by New York City authors are the focus here. Such narratives have the unique double trauma of creators who are imagining trauma but who also had to live unbearably with the ruins of the Real.

First to name the smoldering six-story WTC site of wrecked concrete, steel, and flesh "Ground Zero" on the night of 9/11 were CBS News' Jim Axelrod and NBC News' Rehema Ellis (Yuan 2011). On the tenth anniversary of the attacks, the owner of destroyed WTC Tower 1 and 2, Larry Silverstein, opined, "Ten years from today, I suspect very few people will remember it as Ground Zero" (Barrett 2011). Such processes of memory and memorializing in fiction are what this book traces. Possibly Silverstein's speculation was a very American tendency at work, or that "the chief business of the

**Figure I.2** Entering the Smoldering Ruins of Ground Zero with the Fire Department of New York. Screenshot from *World Trade Center*, Director Oliver Stone, Paramount, 2006.

American people is business" as President Calvin Coolidge famously said four years before the devastating collapse of U.S. stock market prices in 1929 (Coolidge 1925). One reading of Silverstein's remark is that Americans are, above all, interested in innovating, opening markets, and making money—not in mourning and enshrining tragedies. I doubted Silverstein's surmise, though, when on field research in 2014 I visited the former site of Manhattan carnage and noticed several thousand attendees at the 9/11 Memorial & Museum. An interview I conducted there with the Director of the 9/11 Memorial & Museum (formerly affiliated for twenty-two years with the U.S. Holocaust Memorial Museum in Washington, D.C., where the vow against genocide, "Never Forget," is sacrosanct) seconded the doubt. When I shared Silverstein's prediction with Director Greenwald, her surprised response was: "*I hope they do remember!*" (Greenwald 2014). At least so far, Silverstein's prophecy that Americans will largely forget Ground Zero has not come true. This book investigates those fictions that help us to remember and what about them haunts us and their leading characters.

Several realities emerge from the above-detailed procession of the remains and their interment within the bedrock vault: how precious these bits of unidentified human bone are to families who lack certainty, how contested it is who should possess them or decide where they will reside, and how assuredly their story of nonclosure finds its way into print. Official city vehicles carried the inconsequential physical weight of the remains of these nameless dead with ease, but in attempting to shoulder their emotional weight, people are "overwhelmed," a key concern in the contemporary study of trauma. All this affect, all this problematic carrying of the dead, provides a metaphor for the problems encountered and charted in this study as a whole and reflects prominently in this book's table of contents. Undeclared and undefined human remains breed Gothic meditations. Here the dead are borne away early in each novel, by unimaginable fire and by the blown smoke, but somehow the dead return, time and again, to characters who remain alive, sometimes as dust on their windowsills, sometimes unnervingly as full-blown apparitions on the street corners and subway turnstiles. Resurrected are the desires, habits, and perspectives of deceased colleagues, friends, and lovers from the WTC Towers. It is this weird process of the dead returning to the living, among others, that this book dissects. Why these mourning novels, terrorist tales, memorial narratives, fictions of twenty-first-century tragedy, and convulsion should reach for certain Gothic motifs and structures, in particular, is the uncanny question I raise.

The ways that the dead engage with the 9/11 survivors (and the survivors' memories of the towers burning, some couples falling over a thousand feet hand in hand, and the towers finally corkscrewing down to the ground) is the chief inquiry here. We will trace these hauntings in five novels: Don DeLillo's *Falling Man* (2007), Jonathan Safran Foer's *Extremely Loud and Incredibly Close* (2005), Lynne Sharon Schwartz's *The Writing on the Wall* (2005), Griffin Hansbury's *The Nostalgist* (2012), and Patrick McGrath's *Ground Zero* (2006). So many fine paths to progress through these novels are before us, but I would like to direct the order of the table of contents so that the protagonists' emotions become more intense over the WTC dead, and their relationships more intimate and problematic. We should remember this book as a journey into our grief and our darkness, as well, as we were witnesses on 9/11, too, even if from over a thousand miles away, and we bear our own traumas over it still. We begin our analysis here with a novel where the protagonist has the fewest romantic or familial connections to the dead in the towers, to those novels that have their major characters' hearts tied closely to the WTC dead. We start with a novel where the protagonist's best work friend vaporizes there (*Falling Man*) to a narrative where the protagonist's father is pulverized in the WTC (*Extremely Loud and Incredibly Close*), to a story where the death evokes the protagonist's sister's vanishing, murder, and loss (*The Writing on the Wall*), to the final two novels where one man's wished-for lover suffers her last moments on the 89th floor inside the North Tower (*The Nostalgist*) and another woman's boyfriend, having left her warm bed just an hour before, speaks his last words from the 104th floor of the same tower (*Ground Zero*).

I chose this set of texts out of the many I read for factors beyond simply their uncommonly high level of literary expression and canny representational strategies for what Trauma Theory calls "the unrepresentable." First, they all demonstrate the problem of a vexing Gothic presence not easily explained; second, they are all written by people born, living, or working in New York City, and thus the texts display two levels of trauma—that which is imagined in the narrative and that which is lived every morning by a writer facing the actual wreckage to his or her city and knowing those effects of evil will linger long after the hundreds of tons of debris disappear. The dead seem never to let the living go, as we will explore exhaustively. Horrid and shattering memories of the brutal spectacle from the mass murder irrupt upon the consciousness of the living at any time. Here the conflicted survivors face the challenge of how to mourn, to manage guilt about not dying themselves, and to cope with fear and helplessness, knowing that there is no longer a safe place that terrorists cannot reach.[2] After much consideration, the definition of terrorism I chose to include in my conceptual framework is a wide one, coming from David Punter's *Gothic Pathologies*: "terrorism is not merely a set of activities, reducible to bombings, kidnappings and extortion. . . . It is that which exceeds or combats the existence of a normative space within which society lives, moves, and has its being . . . moving [people] into a world where order will disappear" (Punter 1998: 82, 100). This seems an apt definition borne out by the texts under consideration because, again and again, their characters will find that 9/11 "exceeds" their language, explodes what was once "normative space," and sends them deep into an abyss of fear. These crises will be intense enough, I argue, to create reader-involvement and identification in readers for characters initially distant, unfathomable (in motive) and unforthcoming (of their pasts), as especially evident with the protagonist-lawyer Keith Neudecker in *Falling Man* (2007). Almost every protagonist figured in the novels under consideration evokes the question raised during a 9/11 panel on trauma at Harvard University led by Robert Jay Lifton, a psychiatrist who has studied the survivors of the Hiroshima blasts, the Holocaust, and crimes of the Vietnam War over a very long career: "How can I understand this vastly death-saturated event? And if I can't understand it, I can't understand or deal with the rest of my life. . . . The deeply traumatized person is caught between wishing to talk about nothing but his or her trauma and being unable to talk about it. Therefore, one can be completely stilled" (Lifton 2009). These novels let us into that "stilled" world of catastrophic victimhood, a domain that the discourse and practice of psychotherapy may have difficulty entering. A large number of influential early critics, however, have derided 9/11 literature because its characters seem relentlessly solipsistic, turbid, and unable to heal, caught in a cycle of repeating actions and reenactment that exasperate the interpreters—or that the novels are too interested marriage difficulties and love affairs. I contend that this is an unfair complaint and an impoverished view of literature, one that denies us a deeper encounter with haunting post-9/11 memories in art.

## A GOTHIC INTERVENTION IN APPROACHES TO 9/11 FICTION

As decades pass from the disaster, both scholars and novelists continue to shape the discourse on how 9/11 changed U.S. society, its military, its civil liberty traditions, and its media. With the tacit acceptance (or at least the inability to block) preemptive strikes by President George W. Bush, the passage of the Patriot Act, and the enlargement of surveillance on citizens and massive probing into bank accounts, the post-9/11 world began to form, one where it was promised by the president and Congress that some freedoms would be surrendered for some greater security at home and abroad. My book represents not just one more new piece of the 9/11 puzzle, however modest, but a history of the puzzle too, a retrospective of the leading novels from New Yorkers in the last twenty years that conjure and contend with the startling and unpredictable returns of the dead from Ground Zero. It is as Director/Cowriter Zach Braff put it in his underappreciated film, *Wish I Was Here* (2014): "You spend your whole life wondering if your life has meaning, and then it all comes down to one question: 'What should we do with your bones?'"

As the president of the 9/11 Memorial & Museum Alice Greenwald told me in interview on its opening, fiction is one of the most inviting paths to imagine others' experiences, and I want us to open the pages of six memorable novels written by Manhattanites at the time of its disaster with a critical mind but also a willingness to acceptance the strange shapes and utterances in which trauma comes to us. As hinted at, the book maps patterns in how survivors register their loss of colleagues, best friends, fathers, sons, spouses, suspects, and dream-lovers in the WTC on September 11, 2001. But the book also unlocks secrets that are hard for the survivors to divulge: it asks how the latest ideas in Trauma Theory and Gothic studies can help unbury victims' grief, guilt, and violent memory. This study compares the kinds of ghosts that appear before each survivor and explores why at least one character in each novel seems possessed by the dead (or takes on some of the qualities of the deceased). I am assisted in my insights by psychologists and psychiatrists who published case studies on how survivors' minds react and live with disaster and attack, and how they sometimes succumb to it, taking their own lives.

My book's original through-line is that the ghoulish possessions and ghostly visitations (in night dreams or in waking visions) that 9/11 survivors experience in these novels lead them to articulate Trauma Theory's "unrepresentable event" of violence and collapse in a coded language of Gothic images and situations. Beyond the physical destruction to bodies, we see how terrorism damages survivors' psyches, hopes, futures, memories, relationships, and their vocalizations of harm, grief, vulnerability, and fear. My involvement in the impressive, vast, and growing body of 9/11 fiction studies, however, is to suggest contrary to prevailing wisdom that terrorism does not actually prevent characters from expressing what the attack was. My formulation is to show how, through a close reading of the texts' Gothic images and utterances via Trauma Theory, the characters are expressing the horrors that have been called hidden, a contrary idea to many Trauma Theorists. My other original tack is to analyze only the fiction works by those authors who lived in New York City, those internalizing and releasing the 9/11 trauma in a different way than creators from any other place. To develop my approach, I had to become familiar with two decades worth of scholarly literature on 9/11's burning effect on contemporary literature. I would like to briefly highlight some of the leading early studies on 9/11 novels that began to chart the territory of 9/11 literary discourse.

The two titles most related to mine are below and both from 2012: Professors Georgiana Banita's *Plotting Justice* and Michelle Balaev's *The Nature of Trauma in American Novels*. However, the thinkers I introduce and debate in my book are different than those whom they choose. The motifs they explore are apart from those I do, and the novels I look at are largely separate and more recent, along with side notes on subgenres that they do not address, like the conspiracy and *noir* novel. The books below that originated 9/11 literary studies give us a wall of concepts to build from or to push against. Many of the studies listed, for instance, are comparative, wherein one volume probes graphic novels, reportage, poetry, films (handheld, documentary, or fictional) of the attack, and sometimes popular short stories. They may explore architectural essays and engineers' reports, government studies like that of the 9/11 Commission, and politicians' worrisome speeches. My area, though, is simply the literary novels, and those of a New York persuasion. That said, it is a clear gain to be conscious of what the studies on all media forms are saying, to know the major presses in this field of 9/11 awareness, to see how they redirect the discourse, and to seek how may they help enrich my book. As of publication, I count over one hundred and seventy-five studies on 9/11 literature. I briefly annotate the twenty-five titles I found most helpful on 9/11 literature and cinema from current to oldest:

(1) *Rewriting the American Soul: Trauma, Neuroscience, and the Contemporary Literary Imagination* (Anna Thiemann, Routledge Interdisciplinary Perspectives on Literature, 2018). Intrigued by the place where ideas of neuroscience, Freud, and trauma meet, this work (which was begun as a thesis at the University of Münster) concentrates on six recent fictions, one chapter of which looks at a book I do, *Falling Man*. Many of the other novels investigated make no mention of 9/11, though,

including Hustvedt's *The Sorrows of an American* (2008) and Cole's *Open City* (2011).

(2) *British and American Representations of 9/11: Literature, Politics, and the Media* (Oana Celia Gheorghiu, Palgrave, 2018). Gheorghiu shows how 9/11 fiction never dwells "in the tower of high literature, but has mingled with other discourse of contemporaneity" (3). She wonders why that tendency makes the fiction not only more popular but more memorable.

(3) *9/11: Topics in Contemporary North American Literature* (Ed. Catherine Morley, Bloomsbury, 2016). Some of the essays by the scholars are interested in the religious and the prophetic natures of the works, from novels to comics to movies. Many people had an end-of-the-world reaction (for a short time) to 9/11. These essays try to measure how those eschatological instincts appear in or are transfigured by the arts.

(4) *A Poetics of Trauma After 9/11* (Katharina Donn, Routledge, 2016). A critical theory-invested author, Donn enquires how the latest Trauma Theory can accommodate "the digitization and virtuality of present day realities" (6). She is interested in whether 9/11 was a new kind of terrorism because of how it was broadcast around the world in real-time. As with Petrovic's book below, Donn asks if there are limits to what fiction can do in comparison to the most intense journalistic storytelling. What are the borders between the overwhelming trauma and its representation?

(5) *Transatlantic Fictions of 9/11 and the War on Terror: Images of Insecurity, Narratives of Captivity* (Susana Araújo, Bloomsbury, 2015). Araújo's polemic illustrates "white Western middle-class captivity," and how fiction reimagines what terror, insecurity, and "futurity" are after 9/11 (61).

(6) *Representing 9/11: Trauma, Ideology, and Nationalism in Literature, Film, and Television* (Paul Petrovic, Rowman & Littlefield, 2015). Authors from many disciplines widen and complicate the post-9/11 canon, giving some range to the ways that different world media has interpreted the attacks and their aftermath. The authors express the limits of art to represent terrorism and show why that is.

(7) *Fictions of the War on Terror: Difference and the Transnational 9/11 Novel* (Daniel O'Gorman, Palgrave, 2015). This book has questions about how we look at people's difference in another way after 9/11. O'Gorman places his critical lens on five novels to indicate where the books are "blurring the boundaries between the domestic and the foreign in a way that draws attention to the element of the Other within the self, as well as the self within the Other" (6).

(8) *Narrating 9/11: Fantasies of State, Security, and Terrorism* (Eds. John N. Duvall and Robert P. Marzec, Johns Hopkins UP, 2015). An

extension of Banita's arguments, this anthology is interested in how fiction understands twenty-first-century terrorism, the public and government responses to it, the workings of surveillance and secret agencies, and the reformulation of American identity post 9/11. The shoring of American Exceptionalism and false fantasies of security are examined, as well as how fiction incorporates the expanded surveillance state, the Bush Administration's preemptive war push, as well as extraordinary rendition and torture.

(9) *Narrative Innovation in 9/11 Fiction* (Magali C. Michael, Brill, 2015). Michael's effort is one of the more lucid attempts to show how 9/11 authors feel compelled to experiment in their forms to match the new reality the world faced after 9/11. He will discuss the fiction of Foer, Beigbeder, Walter, DeLillo, and McEwan. Michael asks how narrative fragmentation and types of genre fiction (like *noir*) insert themselves into realist fiction to register what it is to live in the face of the attacks.

(10) Writing a review of *The American Imperial Gothic: Popular Culture, Empire, Violence* (Johan Högland, Ashgate/Taylor & Francis, 2014) for the University of Stirling's "The Gothic Imagination," I was taken by Högland's idea of how cataclysm and end-of-the-world moments in American life and fiction become creation stories. Such works offer "a new frontier landscape where conflict is regenerative. New champions appear, revitalized by this new frontier" (165). Some of my analysis of the behaviors of the preemptive striker Pres. Bush are shaped by Högland's perception.

(11) *The 9/11 Novel: Trauma, Politics, and Identity* (Arin Keeble, McFarland & Company, 2014). This analysis probes the extent to which fiction mirrors American realities in the face of disaster. Like the U.S. population, 9/11 novels were split on whether we should meditate on mourning, then asking why the disaster happened and working to prevent more conflicts—or whether we should avoid introspection and concentrate on finding and killing the enemies of the state.

(12) *Transatlantic Literature and Culture after 9/11: The Wrong Side of Paradise* (Kristine A. Miller, Springer, 2014). Miller challenges the American Exceptionalism that 9/11 ushered, asking, How does American Exceptionalism reinforce the paradoxes and myths of America as the place of "never-ending bliss and everlasting death" (4)? Miller contends that 9/11 can be both an American tragedy and a global one. She commendably shows the weakness of America not more fully searching for peaceful solutions to long-simmering conflicts that eventually exploded on its own soil.

(13) *The Nature of Trauma in American Novels* (Michelle Balaev, Northwestern UP, 2012). This book elegantly poses memorable questions

about how the traumatized create and move through mythic landscapes in novels, though none of them deal explicitly with 9/11.

(14) *Plotting Justice: Narrative Ethics and Literary Culture after 9/11* (Georgiana Banita, U of Nebraska P, 2012). Where are themes of "ambiguous resistance" emerging in 9/11 literatures from around the world, *Plotting Justice* asks. Banita queries what are the "imperatives and responsibilities" of fictional narration contending with terror in the twenty-first century. Her concerns are ethics in fiction, and she meditates on quite a range of concerns, from "ethical spectatorship, psychoanalysis, race, transnationalism, and surveillance" (5).

(15) *The "Image-Event" in the Early Post-9/11 Novel: Literary Representations of Terror After September 11, 2001* (Ewa Kowal, Jagiellonian UP/Columbia UP, 2012). This is a comparative study based on her PhD thesis that cites movies, graphic fiction, news reports, and to a lesser extent, novels, which belies the title. Kowal is interested in the surreal frameworks or "architecture" of the first 9/11 fictions, and how they make the works successful or not. She maps the collapse of borderlines between fiction and reportage after 9/11 between nonart and art.

(16) *Literature After 9/11* (Jeanne Follansbee-Quinn, Routledge, 2011). All the chapters explore "the incommensurability" of 9/11. The study interrogates all kinds of media that reacted to 9/11's unprecedented, incomparable, and cataclysmic nature. Follansbee-Quinn determines that the fictions severely suffer from "the impossibility of knowing or conveying what actually occurred that day." I will be arguing the opposite in my book: the fictions are telling us what happened on the day of the attacks in shocking and lengthy detail, but in a Gothic shrouded language that covers memory like a winding sheet over a body.

(17) *After the Fall: American Literature Since 9/11* (Richard Gray, Wiley-Blackwell, 2011). This is a seminal work that tries to expand the canon of 9/11 novels but is also largely dismissive of them. Many studies appreciative of 9/11 fiction like mine end up contesting his thesis. I do disagree with Gray's central point—that 9/11 books are largely a failed effort, as they are too inward and interested in conflicts within families, rather than U.S. policies and the international causes behind the attacks. Still, Gray's observations are so cunning, and his voice is so commanding, clear, and compelling, that he has convinced many. I have to question myself every time I read it about my own ideas, which is just one mark of this book's power.

(18) *Ground Zero Fiction: History, Memory, and Representation in the American 9/11 Novel* (Birgit Däwes, Universitatsverlag Winter, 2011). This scholar finds that 9/11 novels like *Falling Man* are counternarratives to the initial stories of 9/11. The first narratives from media and

the U.S. government were of loss, victimization, color-coded threats, consumerism, and a (rather militaristic) march to recovery. However, Däwes warrants, the fictional perceptions are still transforming our beliefs about 9/11 in radical ways,

(19) *Out of the Blue: September 11 and the Novel* (Kristiaan Versluys, Columbia UP, 2009). Versluys looks at "fiction as a place of resistance to brutal reactions in Realpolitik." He scrutinizes how the 9/11 writers affirm the humanity of the disoriented individual, "as opposed to cocksureness of the killers, give voice to stuttering and stammering as a precarious act of defiance" (13). Above all, the book tracks the wide variety of ways that traumatic memory is formed into a narrative/storytelling memory.

(20) *Portraying 9/11* (Véronique Bragard, Christophe Dony, and Warren Rosenberg, McFarland & Co., 2009). This is another wide treatment looking at "historical, political, cultural, and personal meanings of the disaster . . . [the] crisis of sensibility in American life and values" (8) through examining comic books, novels, plays, and movies on both sides of the Atlantic. The editors are attentive to how cultural products make memories of 9/11 for us.

Beyond these monographs and anthologies on 9/11 literature above, five penetrating studies of 9/11 cinema below inform and enlarge the ways I understand how an act of terror disrupts memory and affects our expression of an attack's grotesqueries, attendant fears, and the wounds that will not heal: Linnie Blake's *The Wound of Nations* (Manchester UP, 2008), Editor Matthew J. Morgan's *The Impact of 9/11 on the Media, Arts, and Entertainment: The Day that Changed Everything?* (Palgrave, 2009), Kevin J. Wetmore's *Post-9/11 Horror in American Cinema* (Continuum, 2012), Editors Aviva Briefel and Sam J. Miller's *Horror after 9/11: World of Fear, Cinema of Terror* (U of TX P, 2012), and Glen Donnar's *Troubling Masculinities: Terror, Gender, and Monstrous Others in American Film Post-9/11* (UP of Mississippi, 2020).

All of this scholarship engages the 9/11 cultural/political/social/literary aftermath admirably, offering varied, satisfying, and notable ideas. Yet not one connects Trauma Theory, 9/11 novels, and Gothic traditions. I suggest in the following that the Al Qaeda killings, posttraumatic stress, and the Gothic together triangulate an emotionally resonant space in recent American fiction, and that this space needs critical processing.

A brief description of the survivors' relationship with the dead is already mentioned in the chapter titles. To give a sense of the fiction's changing reception and reputation, as well as what aspects critics are belatedly growing to value, I survey reviewers' appraisals at the book's release in popular media at the beginning of each chapter, as well as scholars' later and longer evaluations of the novel in professional journals and monographs. Here are capsules of each chapter for readers who may want to focus on a particular one first.

Chapter 1 interrogates what happens when the frightened protagonist from Don DeLillo's *Falling Man* flees the struck North Tower on the morning of 9/11 without helping to dislodge the injured, leaving to the flames his coworker/best friend to die. This experience ushers in self-contempt, guilt, haunting for the lawyer, suffering even a kind of soul-possession by his dead friend. Starting with a summary of Freud's ideas on mourning and the uncanny (and the insights of Freud's predecessors and his later notable interpreters including Derrida and Slavoj Žižek), I move to discuss the meaning of "disaster ghosts," the erotics of 9/11 or the appeal of "terror sex," and representations of the attack in art. Here I dissect how festering mental wounds affect sex drive, and I plot the viral transmission of trauma from one New Yorker to another. I also illustrate that if one can empathize with another's pain and reveal one's shared trauma (as do Oskar in *Extremely Loud and Incredibly Close* and Renata in *The Writing on the Wall*), then one can have a united, if still unfinished, mourning with others. Such open characters tend to stay in New York City despite all the reminders of loss, and keep their roots, maintain contacts, help victims, and become those for whom others will someday mourn. If one is not open to others' pain (as with Keith in *Falling Man*), one tends to become physically violent toward others and oneself, leaves New York City, and loses family and lovers. Such shadowed characters as these live the contradiction of being dead (as their family members say they actually are) while still alive.

Chapter 2 establishes that there are Gothic tendencies within the quest structure of Foer's Manhattan 9/11 novel where a son's father dies in the North Tower. I argue that behind every trauma in this novel there stands another trauma and they inform on each other (a pattern seen in the other novels in our table of contents). I apply the critical and recurring debates about memory in Trauma Theory that show in Foer's young protagonist Oskar and his traumatized Jewish grandparents from World War II. I suture incomplete mourning in this novel to the ghostly arrivals coming to the living. Such visitations are a symptom of guilt whose precedent is often seen in Western literature before, especially in Shakespeare's tragedies. I expand concepts that keen Shakespearean critics developed on the ghosts of dead fathers to *Extremely Loud and Incredibly Close*. Closer to home, these 9/11 novels are tied to a larger storytelling tradition embedded in our American literary canon: the injection of brutal and graphic violence, the fear of the Other, and retribution coming for our repression as seen from one of our earliest novelists born before the American Revolution: America's first Gothicist and Romantic, Charles Brockden Brown.

Chapter 3 is curious about the vexing problems of traumatized 9/11 survivors seeing doppelgängers (literally, "goers before") in the days following the attack. It meditates on the incestuous and murderous traumatic past for a family overlapping the traumatic present of 9/11. The protagonist Renata in Lynne Sharon Schwartz's *The Writing on the Wall* had a molested twin sister who died years before by either murder or suicide; later the sister's daughter (the offspring of incest) goes missing. Then on 9/11 a young mute woman wanders rubble-filled Manhattan streets fitting the description of the missing daughter. Is she the vanished one returned, or some doppelgänger? In Schwartz's narrative, the undeclared remains of the dead feed the unresolved mourning of the living. The man who molested is found to still be alive, and the Gothic impulse enters her novel again and again as stealthily yet constantly as the smoke, ash, and dust of the WTC dead drifted into the residences of the New York City authors composing these narratives after 9/11. I meditate on the purpose of doppelgängers and ghosts that materialize or even possess Schwartz's characters. I develop a Gothic formulation about contamination in terrorism texts, one infiltrating memories of lovers' meetings in the past, connecting to terrors of the future, and infecting characters' hunger for revenge in the present. I determine that the persistence of such ghosts and doppelgängers is not just a spectral reminder of the instant vaporizing of thousands at the WTC, or the hundreds from the towers taking their lives by jumping out windows, sometimes hand in hand with another. The arrival of ghosts in this novel, and the others, is perhaps the greatest externalized trace to a concealed but corroding vault of traumatic memory of a previous trauma. The buried secrets are leaching out.

Chapter 4 meditates on a shocking and obscene lie that lives at the heart of *The Nostalgist,* the only volume here written by someone who is not a professional novelist, but instead a New York City psychoanalytic therapist. We will probe the erotic pathology of Griffin Hansbury's Robert Crumb-lookalike protagonist Jonah who perversely fabricates a romantic relationship with a woman who worked and died at the towers on 9/11, Rose Oliveri. The protagonist Jonah, a man in his thirties who has never had a girlfriend, invents the affair after the last poster reporting Rose's disappearance is taken down from New York City streets six months following the disaster. From an untruth spun to her parents and his friends, this alternative romantic-history Jonah concocts is complicated by the ghost of the deceased terrorist victim eventually haunting this man's apartment, and then disrupting his later, more authentic romantic relationship with a (live) woman. I explore how ghosts are not immune to romantic and sexual jealousy, and how ghosts are notably less choosy in a "mate" than the living. Discovered in the analysis are the meanings and necessities behind such dastardly lies the narrator tells and follows, or the extreme introvert's assumed emotional safety of loving the dead. I evaluate, in Trauma Theory terms, how the "necessary ghost" becomes both his therapist and a self-imposed retribution. I also explain why Jonah is not alone, and suggest psychological reasons for why some survivors post-9/11 developed impossible infatuations with the dead, those love affairs never to be consummated with the alluring but impossible visages smiling out from the missing persons posters of Manhattan in autumn of 2001.

Chapter 5 teems with erotic obsessions and "catastrophe sex" amid a love triangle of a New York City artist Kim Lee (and sometime prostitute) and her local customer Daniel (a civil rights lawyer) and the lawyer's therapist. This psychoanalyst wants to possess Daniel herself. In the traditional Gothic, castles and mansions were suggestive of human minds, with lower reaches and dungeons related to the unconscious, and the visible floors to consciousness. I argue similarly that the Twin Towers, the "Hole," and all the destruction surrounding them, become an extension of the novella's male lovers' lives. From the protagonist-lawyer's life to that of the artist-prostitute's dead boyfriend Jay who apparently jumped from the South Tower as she watched it fall (adding Oedipal energies to the tragedy, Jay's father lives and is also one of Ms. Lee's clients). Dead Jay's ghost appears to her at least three times to her later—always after she makes love—but the question becomes why does his spirit keeps manifesting, and what is his message? I look at Derrida's multiple essays on ghost appearances and how one trauma serves to instruct on another, all to help explain what the spirit is saying and wanting of the woman, and how that is connected to the living characters' evolving understandings of the disaster. This chapter is also fascinated by what happens when seven years of psychoanalysis do not seem to particularly help a client, and when a psychoanalyst is disturbed herself, and the client decides to start becoming an impromptu therapist for someone else, namely for his traumatized lover.

## CRITICAL CURRENTS

The overwhelming response to 9/11 fiction, especially not only in journalistic circles so far but also in some more rigorous scholarly treatments, is that it has not delivered what it was to be alive in those times. The appraisals, again and again, are negative, some even entirely dismissive. On the other hand, in many of the critical accounts, evaluators present few criteria as to how a "successful" 9/11 novel might read, perhaps because no model has yet had its qualities indexed, or its undeniable power largely agreed upon. Here, a number of pressing questions present themselves is the novel supposed to capture what it was to walk through smoke and ash, and face the dread that more violence was to come? Does the ideal 9/11 novel analyze the destabilizing effects of terrorism on relationships (the arrival of "burning-skyline sex," domestic abuse, an increase in separation and divorce)? If so, then the set of novels considered in my book would possess the basic operating obsessions and should be evaluated seriously, rather than be quickly disregarded, as they all too often have been. A key reason for this study's existence is to counter the tide of negative evaluations that have stained 9/11 novels since they first arose.

Roland Merullo was the first American writer to allude to the 9/11 terrorist attacks, according to *Commentary* critic D. G. Meyers (2011). In a 2002 novel-as-memoir of growing up in the 1960s, *In Revere, in Those Days*, Merullo observes in passing that "people did not bomb airplanes in those days, or fly them into buildings" (Merullo 2002: 30). By the tenth anniversary of the plunge of planes into the WTC complex, the Pentagon, and an abandoned field in Shanksville, Pennsylvania, media sources commenced to hunt, track, and tout the great 9/11 novel, or even a moderately impressive one. From around the world, critics appraised the body of 9/11 novels, finding 2006 and 2011 to be peak years of 9/11 novel production (Kohari 2011) and articulated, with depressing regularity, a range of negative assessments for a wide variety of reasons, not all of which seem to be warranted. Besides giving some historical record of the unease Americans in the press felt about the novels that contended with the monsters of terrorism, the initial reaction in the press is worth examining because it affects later scholarly research and public expectations alike.

Jimmy So, in *The Daily Beast*, for instance, judged that "even the best 9/11 novels only deal with 9/11 in oblique ways" (So 2013). D. G. Meyers seconded that and concluded that Claire Messud in *The Emperor's Children* "is more interested in the drama of a romantic breakup, which she dramatizes very well, than in the trauma of 9/11" (Meyers 2011). More complaints from Meyers followed: Joseph O'Neill's *Netherland* "is more absorbed with cricket than terrorism"; too much of Nicholas Rinaldi's [*Between Two Rivers*] "is padding," and, while there are "provocative connections between political terrorism and violent crime" in Ian McEwan's *Saturday*, the book shows an "implausible ending" (Meyers 2011). Despite the implausibility from the historical record that she invites in, Meyers concludes the best novels about 9/11 actually took place *before* 9/11, namely, "Joseph Conrad's *Secret Agent* and Philip Roth's *American Pastoral*. The 9/11 books add little that cannot be learned, and more memorably, from them" (Meyers 2011).

On the other end of the spectrum, however, critics fault the novels under discussion not for their drama, but for their dullness. An editor for *The New York Times Book Review* determines that of the thirty 9/11 narratives his paper reviewed, none can "stack up to nonfiction," and "none has seized the public imagination." There are "pretentious ones (Don DeLillo's *Falling*

*Man*) and sentimental ones (Jonathan Safran Foer's *Extremely Loud and Incredibly Close*). But sorting through the pile of so-called 9/11 novels is a sad exercise, one that grows more pointless by the day" (Garner 2008). The *New York Times* editor still awaits "the bracing, wide-screen, many-angled novel that will leave a larger, more definitive intellectual and moral footprint on the new age of terror" (Garner 2008). Besides desiring a novel to be more open-ended akin to a Christopher Nolan film (say, the brilliant *Inception*), as Dwight Garner would appear to wish, other critics find that the novels lack a focusing drive. Others find the novels not only turgid but also turbid, somehow paralyzed by the momentous need to memorialize, and in the process losing a narrative that compels readers. Yvonne Zipp "dutifully read [the novels] and wished they hadn't felt so duty-bound to say Something Important. None of those novels had that tuning-fork moment that comes when reading something great. And none seemed to grab the public imagination" (Zipp 2011). Ruth Franklin in her ten-year review of 9/11 fiction in *The New Republic* blasts John Updike, noting the author "admitted that his research for the novel was superficial—he even consulted a book called *The Koran for Dummies*" (Franklin 2011). Anis Shivani disagrees with Franklin, but only up to a point: "John Updike tried very, very hard, and we were grateful to him at the time, but now his earnestness on the topic wears ill. They were all just flailing and failing, and we were making excuses for them.... 9/11 has become filler, agitprop candy, drama's rape, the magician's cap (and cape) we all put on when we don't know what to do. Its default mode run amok, secondary input masquerading as primary insight" (Franklin 2010). Thus, the critical contention here is that famous authors felt obliged to write on the tragedy of 9/11 and readers felt obliged to buy the books out of a reverence for what headlines called "the Day that Changed the World," but both parties were wearied by the ponderousness of the prose.

Arguing in the opposite direction, critics sensed that the fatal flaw in the 9/11 novels were that their authors could not make the losses distinct, so ended up pursuing the trivial. Laura Miller, in *Salon*, for instance, finds 9/11 simply to be "kryptonite to novelists": "Charged with looking beneath, behind and around such images [of the WTC towers collapse], the novelist comes up against the question of what makes these particular violent deaths so very different from every other violent death. That isn't easy to answer, and any answer you do come up with is likely to sound disrespectful, cynical, unfeeling and insufficiently solemn" (Miller 2011). Very influentially, Richard Gray complains that in this cataclysmic fiction, "all life here is personal: cataclysmic public events are measured purely and simply in terms of their impact on the emotional entanglements of their protagonists ... [and this] reduces a turning point in national and international history to little more than a stage in a sentimental education" (Gray 2009: 135). In assent with this much, Michael Rothberg notes that in American 9/11 fiction, "epochal change remains separated from individual lives" (Rothberg 2009: 1469). Again, more charges of unearned emotion are leveled at the authors of the novels to be analyzed in this book: "A novelist may decide to push onward anyway, whether into sentimentality (*Extremely Loud and Incredibly Close*) or smarmy self-aggrandizement (*The Good Life*), but in such cases, the results feel thin, vaguely false and meretricious" (Miller 2011). Art and culture critic Kevin Canfield in *Salon* concurs and may issue the most blistering cry:

> Forget the best Sept. 11 novel—there are far more contenders for the most shameful and embarrassing. . . . There's also been some embarrassingly bad prose—lots of it by authors who should know better. For some writers, 9/11 offered an excuse to write about the anatomies of sexy Western temptresses or the siren song that is rock 'n' roll performed by men in spandex. For others, it was simply an obligatory and careless plot point tossed into the mix, a cynical narrative device meant to energize a flagging story line. (Canfield 2011)

The worst offenders, Canfield alleges, are also some of America's better known: Andre Dubus III's *The Garden of Last Days*, Tom Robbins' gonzo *Villa Incognito*, and Jennifer Haigh's and Nicholas Sparks' terrorism-romances *The Condition* and *Dear John*. Citing multiple damning lines from each of the fictions, Canfield (echoing Meyers) laments that their endings were less a resolution than a concession: "I don't know how to finish this novel, so I'll add a dash of 9/11 and call it a day" (Canfield 2011). This claim of Canfield's seems the least evidenced. In actuality, the endings for the narratives interrogated in this study tend to be of three kinds: the weary protagonist (1) has a vision, (2) leaves a marriage or a home having had big doses of "terror sex" beforehand, or (3) collapses, crying out in his or her forlorn state. Nevertheless, continuing with the charges, Canfield levies most of the blame on the two literary lions of the group, finding myriad examples of how they lose their way. Both Dubus and Updike, it is said by Canfield, trip over giving too much luscious detail to the exotic dancers in their novels.

Although not literally stated as such by Canfield, the implication of his critique is that these fictions, considering that their remit was the impending death of civilians, fell unwisely into an unintentionally and erotically obsessive and comic sphere. *Terrorist*, for example, "spent a lot of time leering at ladies [at sexually oriented businesses]. Updike's main character is named Ahmad. He's a devout Muslim—and a big-time breast man . . . taking note of 'the tops of her breasts, exposed by a loose-necked springtime blouse.' . . . [They] 'bounce' and wing'; they're 'white as soap' or 'dark as eggplants'; they're 'freckled' and they 'have crescents of shadow beneath their rounded weight'" (quoted in Canfield 2011). It is a point well taken that Updike, who died in

2009, has been enthralled with women's bodies ever since Harry "Rabbit" Angstrom commingled with part-time prostitute Ruth Leonard in *Rabbit, Run* (1960), and he may be in thrall to women's bodies in this posthumous fiction. However, he was also reflecting the record of club forays by the so-called "Hamburg Cell" of terrorists who came to America, so he might be excused of this charge. Dubus, similarly, in *The Garden of Last Days* features an Al Qaeda operative named Bassam who holds up 160 one-hundred-dollar bills when he visits "the Puma Club for Men" (Dubus 2008: 16). Of course, odd connections *are* made in Bassam's head, which Canfield objects to, including this deduction: "This dancing woman upon the stage wears nothing but the hat of cowboys. . . . The singer David Lee Roth [front man of Van Halen], an American Jew, [who] wore a cowboy hat like this [stripper]. . . . This David Lee Roth, if there was time, Bassam would find him and kill him" (Dubus 2008: 90). On the one side, this is quixotic, bizarre, nearly too absurd; on the other, a number of sources report that, in order to blend in, but possibly for the less mission-related reasons of tasting and re-tasting the forbidden "evil place one last time" (Dubus 2008: 26), the terrorists of 9/11 did in fact visit sexually oriented businesses frequently (*The 9/11 Commission Report* 2004). Thus, it seems reasonable for a novelist to conjecture on what incongruously erotic thoughts the terrorists may have had at the clubs and how their experiences "in country" may have made them detest American culture all the more, its strange blend of attraction and repulsion, its almighty dollar and impossible fantasy, all the rusted tin beneath its promise of Las Vegas gold. Indeed, if foreign actors in American films have come under Al Qaeda targeting, as the FBI warned Russell Crowe as he was about to accept an Academy Award for *Gladiator* on March 21, 2001 (Staff writer of *The Scotsman*: 2005), then it may be no more patently absurd for a fictionalized David Lee Roth to be in the crosshairs, too. Though my study primarily exams the victim's perspective, it is noteworthy that Hammad, the hijacker pilot of American Airlines flight 11 in *Falling Man,* also frequents "gentleman's clubs." An answer to Canfield is that both Updike's novel and Dubus's would be amiss if they did not feature this lurid, liberated, seemingly ironic activity of the fundamentalist terrorists' American lives. Certainly, the women who dance and strip at the parlor for Bassam in *The Garden of Last Days,* who in his misogyny he blights as "these dirty kufar who would laughingly pull him between their legs straight to the eternal fire" (Dubus 2008: 25), form a foil to the virgins that, he is told, will await Bassam and his fellow attackers. What reviewers may dismiss, then, as mere decadence in 9/11 fiction, mere titillation, may actually be closer to the historical record of terrorists' activities and quite necessary to dwell upon in order to begin to understand them.

In none of the ten-year or twenty-year critical retrospectives that surfaced on literary 9/11 are any 9/11 fictions described as "superlative" or "destined to be read in the next fifty years." None are given hoped-for Gothic adjectives either, such as "sublime," grotesquely "abject," or hauntingly "endarkened." Yet, as we have seen, it seems the criteria used to rate them so far seem questionable: narrow, unusually subjective, unaware of how trauma manipulates a text, and unforgiving of the formal and thematic experimentation needed to register trauma. Shoring the bias against 9/11 novels is this last reason cited for the novels' failures: time—not enough of it to digest the events and make a masterwork from them. This argument is well summed up by literary editor Erica Wagner of *The Times*: "Ten years is not a long time from the standpoint of fiction. . . . If you look at Dickens's novels, for instance, they appear to be contemporary to his times. But often he was writing about his childhood—that in itself is a distance of about 40 or so years" (quoted in Kohari 2011). Mohsin Hamid (author of *The Reluctant Fundamentalist* in 2007) seconds the view that a great terrorism novel's redwood-paced growth is necessary: "Fiction is a long, rambling encounter with many things. Fiction re-complicates what politicians wish to oversimplify. . . . Events should have as many definitions as the number of people who experience them. Pearl Harbor was many other things also: it was a kiss, it was a swim in a lake, it was a fisherman wondering what the commotion was, it was a flock of birds taking flight" (quoted in Kohari 2011). This seems an ironic finding considering Hamid's Camus-inspired *The Reluctant Fundamentalist* took only seven years to write, and yet was Booker-Prize shortlisted and an international bestseller, a novel which *The Guardian* called "decade-defining" (Hamid 2011).

Still, the fallacy in the "mass-murder is still too close in time" argument (Kohari 2011) is that it ignores the presence of highly influential works that have appeared in the midst of the terrors they covered. Conrad's *Heart of Darkness* (1899), Henri Barbusse's anti-WWI novel *Le Feu* (*Under Fire*, 1916) and Graham Greene's *The Quiet American* (1956) all critiqued the respective terrors contemporary to the hour of their publication. Announcing the death of the 9/11 novel, too, seems premature and unwise, but that is no less than Anis Shivani's point. He delivers the eulogy:

> By now every variation of the 9/11 novel has been exploited. . . . The most exploited variation was this. Dysfunctional family, grieving over all sorts of superficial things, split up over non-issues, maybe with children and parents inhabiting opposite coasts. Somehow 9/11 brings them all together. . . . The image of people falling off towers, flying to their death, somehow puts petty family grievances in their true perspective. A lot of novelists tried their hands at this genre, and no doubt will continue to do so until at least 2020. Or maybe until environmental collapse finally makes it into the novelist's imagination. (Shivani 2011)

It is true that dysfunctional families arise in all the novels surveyed here, and part of the investigation is to show the patterns of dysfunction. However, in none of the novels does "9/11 [bring] them all together." Instead, 9/11 is a splintering force, causing wounds that people can barely understand or articulate as the memories of trauma intrude without warning, and usually compelling characters to go inward to an unhealthy and isolating degree. Shivani's analysis may too easily condemn the novels' inner lives, plots, and conflicts before making a sustained or authentic attempt to understand them.

It should be acknowledged that some noteworthy evaluators of fiction recently apologized for their minimizing of 9/11 novels, and we may sometime witness that change of judgment in relation to DeLillo's novel and the others covered here. With disarming honesty, Ruth Franklin of *The New Republic* expressed regrets for her premature critical scorn in 2004, namely that "no important fiction dealing with that day had yet appeared" (Franklin 2011). As she later confessed in the same journal, "Every critic, I'd venture, has written something that he or she would like to take back. . . . Blame it on the fever for documentation that arose in the wake of the attacks, perhaps" (Franklin 2011).

Surveying the majority of critical viewpoints above, we see trending several strains of complaint to these novels' approach to catastrophe: either the 9/11 novel has been too serious or too flippant, too sexual or too asexual, too earnest or too ironic, or too weak for the challenge of understanding and capturing even a part of what is called, in Trauma Theory, "the Unrepresentable." Considering the daunting task and the resulting damaging reviews over the last thirteen years, we may see Martin Amis's comment, less than a year after the disaster, to be prescient: "After a couple of hours at their desks, on September 12, 2001, all the writers on earth were reluctantly considering a change of occupation. I remember thinking that I was like Josephine, the opera-singing mouse in the Kafka story: "Sing? She can't even squeak." A novel is politely known as a work of the imagination; and the imagination, that day, was of course fully commandeered, and to no purpose" (Amis 2002).

The compulsion to write about the terrorism was irresistible for writers, Amis suggests, yet capturing the complexity of the story was too much of a challenge.[3] Readers and initial reviewers were reluctant to accept it because the fiction could not create "the unrepresentable." As Elizabeth Anker in *American Literary History* pronounces it, 9/11 is "a, if not *the*, paradigmatic postmodern event, given that it casts open the competing desires mobilized by the spectacle, lays bare the intimacy between art and terror, and reveals the violent underside of the postmodern sublime" (Anker 2011: 476). Still, the reaction is, as Director Alice Greenwald mentioned to me in the 2014 interview, that very little within this fiction leaves us awestruck or challenged, and the event was already witnessed in real-time on screens by an estimated two billion people which she noted in an earlier interview (Greenwald 2010: 118), all of which limits the impressions these texts can make. Likewise, Anker continues to make the case that 9/11 texts ruin themselves largely through their simplicity.

If such consistently negative appraisals from the popular press on both sides of the Atlantic are representative and critically accurate, then either (a) 9/11 fictions have systematically failed in their powers to move and involve readers, to register terror, and to present a time and its outer manifestations of characters' anxieties, or (b) reviewers' evaluative schemes are limited, or (c) a combination of defects in 9/11 fiction and its criticism exists. As I will discuss in chapter one, some of these popular assumptions and value judgments work their way into more formal, academic literary discourse.

Like the bones of the unknown dead from America's worst terror attack, our appreciation for 9/11 fiction seems sealed in a crypt, just as the horrors of its imagined characters' pasts appear envaulted or encrypted, too. What is more, for the first time I will be teaching college students this year who were born *after* this tragedy. Thus, the traumatic misery and our unhealed wounds are doubly hidden from young adults, as it is not a lived history with the pain that many of us still vividly remember. I want to show now how such fictional witnesses may not always render the attack linearly and in conventional speech, but that they do express the 9/11 cataclysm through Gothic forms that can be interpreted in the most haunting ways. Sooner or later in Gothic fiction, if something pries from the outside—*or something pushes from the inside*—the casket, coffin, tomb, or vault breaks open. Like the falsely assumed dead and envaulted sister Madeleine Usher, white-robed and bloody and in moaning cry, something there is that will rise and fall upon us yet from this fiction, leaving us "a victim to the terrors" (Poe).

## NOTES

1. It would be hyperbole to say that every museum has bones hidden in its bedrock that visitors walk over (as with the 9/11 Memorial & Museum), yet a recent illustrated study shows just what has been stashed from view—because of its frail state, controversy, holy powers, or echoes of an unacceptable past. Molly Oldfield in *The Secret Museum* goes around the world to fifty specimen rooms behind closed museum doors (where usually "nobody ever goes in, nobody ever comes out") and finds that "usually there is more hidden away than there is on display" (Oldfield 2013: 12). The U.S. 9/11 Memorial & Museum may well have objects presented for view in the coming years that challenge or reinforce some of the conclusions in this book.

2. In a September 19, 2016 book launch and signing of the novel *Here I Am* in Houston, Texas, that I attended, Jonathan Safran Foer remembered back to 9/11 and told me that the worst part of surviving 9/11 was dread and hopelessness. In as small

an island as Manhattan, nothing was safe anymore: "If you took the subway, you could die, but if you walked to work, you would probably die, too."

3. There may be no tragedy in the last quarter century causing writers to so doubt their imaginative powers. At some point in their careers, many writers, if their memoirs speak true, face excruciating crises of confidence, but 9/11 was a communal, simultaneous, and sustained crisis of creation that seemed to lay waste their powers. What Amis admits as "a feeling of gangrenous futility" overtaking him about his own work or his "pitiable babble" also infected a number of major writers (Amis 2002): Jay McInerney reports "a period of intense self-examination and self-loathing after the terrorist attacks on the World Trade Center. . . . I worked as a volunteer for a couple of months, feeding the national guardsmen and the rescue workers near Ground Zero, listening to the rumours and the strange paranoid lore of the place" (McInerney 2005), while Norman Mailer told him "to wait ten years" (2005). Mailer's advice would appear to fight his practice as he wrote the novels *Why Are We in Vietnam?* (1967) and *The Armies of the Night* (1968) with the Vietnam War in full fire. Following McInerney's feeling, Ian McEwan claimed in an interview to have found it "wearisome to confront invented characters" post-9/11 (quoted in Mishra 2007). Last, America's most prolific literary novelist Joyce Carol Oates, who wrote no novels about 9/11 (only a short story "The Mutants," featuring a woman trapped in her Lower Manhattan apartment on the day of the crash), admitted the unsayable, "Words fail us" (Oates 2001): "This does seem to be about the right time for these novels to be coming out" (quoted in Wyatt 2005). Interestingly, Oates, perhaps America's most influential living Gothic novelist (Oates 2014: 103), admits that novels may not even be the medium of choice for this disaster: "But the greatest art form to deal with this might be film, because it can capture the hallucinatory nature of the long hours of that siege" (quoted in Wyatt 2005). Film will be a media we examine in connection to *Incredibly Close and Extremely Loud*.

## Chapter 1

# Don DeLillo's *Falling Man* (2007)
## Deserting and Impersonating the Dead

### CRITICAL RECEPTION

*Falling Man* is largely the story of Keith Neudecker, a middle-aged business lawyer who escapes from the high reaches of the burning WTC North Tower on 9/11, but not before helplessly trying to remove his best friend Rumsey from the next-door office. Its three subplots, like the main plot of Neudecker's trauma and dissolution, all revolve around memory. In the first, Neudecker's sympathetic wife Lianne works, counseling those who are losing their memory (primarily early Alzheimer's disease sufferers). This job is understandably nearly unbearable for her because Lianne's father fatally shot himself in the head after a diagnosis of Alzheimer's. Alongside the triggers of that traumatic memory comes another: Lianne keeps walking down streets where above her a heavily harnessed performer named David Janiak[1] reenacts WTC jumper photos by hurling himself off Manhattan buildings.[2] Though always appearing in the daylight, Janiak resembles her now traumatized and Gothicized imagination "a trump card in a tarot deck" with his "name in Gothic type, the figure twisting down in a stormy night sky" (DeLillo 2007: 221), a "falling angel" and a "beauty," albeit "horrific" (DeLillo 2007: 22), which to Jerrold E. Hogle shows a trauma-born "displacement of [Janiack's act] that is itself incomprehensible" (Hogle 2014: 80). The second subplot has Lianne's German father-in-law, once suspected of Red Brigades guerila actions decades before, wondering if the current Mideast terror against New York City equates with the German terror in the 1960s. And in the final subplot, Hammad, a terrorist on the plane that crashes into Neudecker's building, keeps remembering his early unease and disagreement about killing civilians with the true-believer ideologue who was his teacher in terror. Hammad is a barely disguised version of the leader of the so-called Hamburg cell,

Mohamed Atta,[3] who finally shows an "allegiance of the living to those who were dead and defeated" throughout Arab history (DeLillo 2007: 78). Jerrold E. Hogle perceptively calls Hammad this novel's "Gothic primal destroyer," committing the Gothic "primal crime" (Hogle 2014: 80).

As the narrative begins, two jets crash into the towers. Dust and ash cover all, bits of once-important paper float throughout Manhattan, and the odor of burned flesh sickens Neudecker. He is estranged from his wife for a year and a half, but in automaton-like fashion he plods to her apartment rather than his own on that killing day. She later describes guiding him to the hospital "step by step, like walking like a child" (DeLillo 2007: 9). The rest of the novel concentrates on their attempts to restore their marriage and improve his strained relationship with his ten-year-old son Justin. However, with Neudecker's visit and a brief affair with a fellow survivor named Florence,[4] his wife Lianne's new way of seeing violence and peace after the terrorism, and Neudecker's inability to confront, reveal, or heal from what he has undergone, he will damn all his attempts at reconciliation. The secret agony stemming from his moments in the burning North Tower reveals itself to no other characters, only to the reader at the book's end. A growing incapacity to function at work, an inability to feel and to mourn, a detachment, and a dissociative fugue and identity crisis befall him as he wanders about like a drifter. At the novel's finale, this once successful and motivated New York lawyer languishes in Las Vegas, relentlessly playing and losing at poker, the very game he used to look forward to each weekend with the only friend he was "intuitive" with, the dead office mate Rumsey (DeLillo 2007: 121).

Moving away from the lashing, blustery short reviews of *Falling Man* that greeted its publication—of which Anis Shivani's seems the most dismissive—we find that Andrew O'Hagan, a novelist himself, notes positively in *The Good of the Novel*, that DeLillo succeeds mostly "at male dissociation, especially the kind that can thrive in certain domestic environments, and he can be as forensic as Saul Bellow" (O'Hagan 2011: 36). O'Hagan concludes that the descriptions finally become "the best things in the book: they have the force of felt life" (O'Hagan 2011: 37). Curiously, when seasoned critics do find elements to praise in the novel, they are often keyed to what could be called the symptoms of the trauma novel, like the dissociative states just mentioned from which Neudecker will suffer. Kristiaan Versluys, one of the earliest to apply insights gleaned from trauma theory to this narrative, mentions DeLillo's technique of having shattered sentences mimic the chaotic movements of a ravaged Manhattan as the book's strength: "The very texture of the prose itself reflects the raggedness of experience, whilst the splintered composition of the novel is the most telling proof of the indelibility of trauma and its shattering impact" (Versluys 2009: 40). Drawing skillfully upon Freud's work on melancholia, Versluys calls the book and its "anti-redemptive" ending "the most devastatingly pessimistic novel among the 9/11 narratives" (Versluys 2009: 14). Beyond its distinctive fatalism and dissociative states, though, this novel may distinguish itself in its exploration of misaligned temporality. Certainly, Linda S. Kauffman is aware of that dimension as she probes *Falling Man*'s narrative structure and time, and she is impressed at its design: "*Falling Man* portrays the contradictions between present and past; life and death; time and eternity. It records, moreover, the precise moment when these contradictions collide with deadly impact" (Kauffman 2008: 368). Conte regards the contradictions, as well, noting: "Temporally, the novel ends slightly before it begins, with Keith fleeing the North Tower, so that by violating in his fictional narrative the inexorable forward thrust of events that comprise history, DeLillo can reexamine the motives of the terrorists and the experience of the survivors. . . . [The narrative of terrorism] can move in only an inexorably linear fashion; totalising and enclosed, it can move only deathward" (Conte 2011: 568). However, this reading seems forced and somewhat restrictive. Time among the traumatized victims slides however it may—to the past, to the present, and back again. Versluys' follow-up seems more convincing by dramatically illustrating how this "reading experience [of *Falling Man*] itself mimics the violent lurching back and forth between the (imperfectly engaged) present and the (vividly relived) past, which is typical of traumatic memory" (Versluys 2009: 40).

Still, despite this linkage to one of North America's towering and Nobel prize-winning novelists and its accurate display of the lurching testimony of witnesses diagnosed by trauma theory, the fault-finding soon comes. O'Hagan, strongly contradicting another appraisal he makes of the same book elsewhere, undercuts all when he writes that DeLillo is unable "to conjure his usual exciting prose" (O'Hagan 2007: 37) and cannot make us imagine the horror any better than "the astonishing pictures on television" (O'Hagan 2007: 37). Not being able to compete with what everyone already saw on TV must cause a sense of severe defeat for people who make their living with silent words, as Amis predicted, and O'Hagan avers. In *The American Prospect*, Laura Frost echoes the flaw identified by O'Hagan, despairing over *Falling Man*'s "staged artfulness" and "compromised ambitions" (Frost 2007). *Falling Man* was also faulted stylistically for its overuse of "monosyllabic speech," "stilted diction," and lack of "wisdom": its characters were a mere "amalgamation of strange habits" (Constant 2008). Reviewers at *The Garfield Review* simply found the characters "dull" (Staff of *The Garfield Review* 2011).

Perhaps Sonia Baelo-Allué accounts for the poor estimation of *Falling Man* most reasonably by noting that "Since DeLillo had previously written about global capitalism, terrorism, conspiracies, death and the media, some readers and critics expected him to write an epic, panoramic, political novel that would illuminate the cultural zeitgeist following 9/11. However, *Falling Man* deals with the domestic and intimate rather than the panoramic and public" (Baelo-Allué 2007: 64). Again, expectations thwarted or disappointed figure in Chris Cumming's low ranking from *The Paris Review*. Cumming points out that politics in DeLillo's "fictional treatments of terrorism and mass shootings" (Cumming 2013) are usually filtered through the killer's consciousness [apparently referring to novels like DeLillo's *The Names* (1982), *Mao II* (1991), *Underworld* (1997), and *Cosmopolis* (2003)]: "Throughout DeLillo's work we encounter young men who plot violence to escape the plotlessness of their own lives. He has done more than any writer since Dostoevsky to explain them" (Cumming 2013), but in *Falling Man* we do not have that to a great degree. The Al Qaeda terrorist Hammad's account is at the very end, and we are not seeing the problem and the violent "solution" through his eyes as much as the disbelief and thwarted attempt to understand motivation through the eyes and minds of the survivors. Thus, faulted expectations—but not diminished literary energies and conflicts and styles—may occasion the first cause for reservation with critics.

A short piece of nonfiction DeLillo wrote may have both lifted the critics' early hopes, and then expanded their reservations later once they read *Falling Man*. DeLillo's affective and effective "Ruins from the Future," a prophetic essay published by *Harper's* just three months after 9/11, demonstrates a Whitmanesque tone, celebrating American diversity, energy, phoenix-like abilities despite loss, cataclysm, and war: the voice is a floating one, easing over the American landscape (especially in the first section) as the voice does in sections of Whitman's *Leaves of Grass* or in "The Sleepers." Whitman, the often-cited "Father of American poetry," served as nurse throughout the war of greatest numbered dead in American history. Considered the greatest threat to the Republic in its first hundred years, the Civil War killed over 2 percent of the U.S. population at the time: 620,000 soldiers and 50,000 civilians (Faust 2008: xi, xii; McPherson 2002: 3, 177, n. 56). Accordingly, in DeLillo's essay, there is not only a fear of what the attacks will do to the Republic but also a modicum of hope, and a defense of the Western World and especially America: it is American "diversity," "freedom," and "technology" that are most feared by the mullahs, his essay opines. As DeLillo sees it, the supernatural has been replaced by the technological, and that is an affront to the radical Jihadist: "The materials and methods we devise make it possible for us to claim our future. We don't have to depend on God or the prophets or other astonishments. We are the astonishments" (DeLillo 2001: 37). In short, the technology, presumably offered by computers, the Web, and mobile devices are a "threat," as "less scientifically advanced cultures" would no longer "need to rely on a God in whose name they kill the innocent" (DeLillo 2001: 36–37). This essay may seem brash, defensive, and uncritically positive about America now, but considering how early it was written (not long after headlines in Frances's newspaper *Le Monde* declared "Nous sommes tous Américains"), and before the post-9/11 wars against Afghanistan (beginning October 7, 2001) and Iraq (beginning March 20, 2003) commenced, it may well reflect the spirit of the times, and even the sensibility of the reviewers of his future novel. Thus, this widely read, praised, and cited essay of DeLillo's promised one thing: an indictment of religious zealotry and the primitive, irrational, and broken barbarity of the "past made into the present" (often a key interest of the Gothic). It was such a cruel past "that humanity had to overcome to produce the Enlightenment," DeLillo argues in the essay, and now it is the present outrages that must be defeated, those Taliban and Taliban-like cultures returning to "the old slow furies of cutthroat religion" and "Medieval experience" (DeLillo 2001: 37). An expectant reader for his coming fiction *Falling Man* may have assumed it to be a novel crying out against that regression into an older time and intolerant value system, but what *Falling Man* would offer was much different, almost a counternarrative, and its key terrorist Hammad a much more sympathetic character than the essay's position toward fundamentalist murderers would portend. If the novel fails on showing what it was to be alive on 9/11, gives too little for readers to care about the characters or their dilemmas, or has nothing in terms of style to distinguish it, then the critical panning is warranted. However, some appraisers may mistake unfulfilled expectations from DeLillo's famed essay with presumed absences in the novel's art, feeling, or depictions of an anxious age.

Alice M. Greenwald, the founding director of the 9/11 Memorial & Museum (who has meditated on trauma before, as the associate director for Museum Programs for the U.S. Holocaust Memorial Museum), sees more potential than the earlier reviewers do for 9/11 novels, but less for DeLillo's. Greenwald noted in interview that "fiction often provides a form of access to interior realities that are not as evident in more documentary forms of expression. This in turn provides a reader with a sense of personal investment in the narrative, creating a sense of immediacy and fostering an awareness of the familiar" (Greenwald: Interview in Appendix). Yet she thought "DeLillo's [*Falling Man*] was compelling but also struggling itself to come to terms with the history and so not quite as powerful as some of his other works" (Greenwald: Interview in Appendix). Perhaps more clearly echoing Shivani's claim that *Falling Man* is "pancaked [art], like the dust of the towers, unable to rise up and assert [its] concrete and steel narrative volume" (Shivani 2010) is James Wood, a Princeton University critic who has breached the academic/popular critic divide. Wood complains that the DeLillo narrative is "all limbs—many articulations and joints, and artful map of connections, but finally no living, pulsing center" (Wood 2007: 50). As a counterargument to

Wood, we might argue that there is a detectable "pulse" in the novel but that it is a traumatized one, weak at times yet still beating.

Another figure who straddles the academic/popular divide is Michiko Kakutani, senior fiction reviewer at *The New York Times*. For her part, she concedes that DeLillo's novels, from *Players* and *White Noise* through *Libra*, *Mao II* and his massive, panoramic *Underworld*, "not only limned the surreal weirdness of the waning years of the twentieth century, but somehow also managed to anticipate the shock and horror of 9/11 and its darkly unspooling aftermath" (Kakutani 2007). Yet her verdict on *Falling Man* falls like a death sentence: it is "spindly," "small and unsatisfying and inadequate," "a terrible disappointment . . . [never] illuminating the zeitgeist in which 9/11 occurred" (Kakutani 2007). Its chief flaw is that "Mr. DeLillo makes no effort to situate these two very self-absorbed characters within a larger mosaic of what happened that September morning; they remain two not very compelling figures adrift in the anonymous sea of humanity." Keith, the main character, is "a pathetic, adolescent-minded creature . . . [who] decided to spend his foreseeable future playing stupid card games in the Nevada desert" (Kakutani 2007). This critique by one of New York City's best-known literary judges is a problematic appraisal of trauma's effects in the novel. Besides the problem of omission—the blind spot in which she fails to reference the multiple traumas of Neudecker's wife and his lover, which are draining in themselves—Kakutani judges as "paltry" the suffering of both the jumper Janiak and lawyer Neudecker. Yet we see in the novel that suffering has actually torn out their reason for living. Nonetheless, in her impoverished view of *Falling Man* may rest on a word waiting to launch the book's recovery and that word above from Kakutani is "zeitgeist."

Beyond suggesting the spirit of the age, zeitgeist in German literary translates as "time-ghost." Curiously, a time-ghost takes readers to the edge of *Falling Man*'s deepest abyss of trauma and Neudecker's PTSD. There is a spirit (both in the sense of a corpse, and also an *oeuvre* of dark knowledge) from the trauma of murder that may not go away. It may not stay in its own time but intrude upon ours and enter the survivors' minds.

It would be useful to chart the Gothic appearance of traumatic wounds in this novel, including the Gothic's emphasis on the grotesque and unwatchable (in this case, falling bodies and dead ones scattered on the avenues and the breathing of dead flesh in the smoke for weeks after the attack). We will also explore the uncanny or Neudecker's searching for images of himself in that most photographed and filmed day of disaster in world history, and the finding of no photographs of himself on the familiar streets. Second, we will diagnose his paranoid physical violence—with no acknowledged violence before the terrorism, Keith now hits men for looking aslant at his lover and confesses wanting "to kill without penalty" (DeLillo 2007: 214) while his wife grinds objects into the faces of women who play Mideast music. Moreover, we will examine death-play in sex (Keith commences sex with his wife after she strikes a position of a falling body first), and track disease (especially in the shape of the impossible sickness of nostalgia for what was before the destruction),[5] and probe Keith Neudecker's complete dissolution, his becoming something "other" as the novel puts it, his possession by a disaster ghost.

The Gothic impulse in this novel and other 9/11 texts erupts, I argue, like the fugue states, ontological uncertainty, nightmares, memory loss, self-destructive behavior, and identity changes erupt among the traumatized victims themselves. Such impulses repeat, reenact, dissociate, disjoin, intrude, and contaminate. A means to decipher these 9/11 texts now, to see them as more than mere "death imprints" (Lifton 1980: 170) or chronicles of numbing or helplessness, is to understand and expand notions of the uncanny, and for that we turn to Freud's concepts. In this chapter, we will probe the ways that trauma's guilt and shame and secrets destroy a protagonist and his relationships, and how some trauma survivors start to show signs that they are possessed by their dead loved ones and friends.

## FREUD, THE UNCANNY, AND DISASTER GHOSTS

*The impression [the traumatized] give is of being pursued by a malignant fate or possessed by some "daemonic" power.*
—Sigmund Freud, *Beyond the Pleasure Principle* (1919a)

Sentence for sentence, Freud is the thinker most mentioned by the seminal trauma theorists and interpreters from the 1990s forward in their discussions of PTSD and literature, including Michelle Balaev, Judith Butler, Cathy Caruth, Dominick LaCapra, Ruth Leys, Robert Jay Lifton, Roger Luckhurst, and Anne Whitehead. Freud's observations are extended, reacted against, and affirmed by these and other critics, and ought to be raised here. Ironically enough, though, Freud did not treat through psychoanalysis the exact trauma wounds that we observe in *Falling Man*, nor the wounds from most of the novels that this publication examines, except for the sexual abuse that is meditated upon in Lynne Sharon Schwartz's *The Writing on the Wall*. Moreover, Freud did not technically treat the mental afflictions of those physically attacked, or from the mass war trauma of his time: Luckhurst goes as far to say that Freud "wrote little on the war [World War I] and treated no shell-shock cases himself" (Luckhurst 2008: 56).[6] Consequently, recourse will be made to the theories of Alexandra Adler, Erich Lindemann, Lifton, and Caruth, as well as others who studied survivors of sudden cataclysmic attack like Neudecker. One of Caruth's insights is a towering one for Falling Man, namely, that a trauma's return makes us wonder how it is that we are alive: "What one returns to in the flashback [or nightmare] is not the incomprehensibility of one's near death, but the very incomprehensibility of one's own survival. Repetition [is] . . . the very attempt *to claim one's own survival*" (Caruth 1996: 64). Survivors not being able to fully accept they are alive is a confusion and condition akin to a ghost not realizing that it is dead and circling the abode it had while alive or reenacting its last moments. A similar bewilderment befalls *Falling Man*'s protagonist Keith Neudecker and may explain some of his numbed reactions to his post-9/11 life, which somehow never moves into the postlife stage. For Neudecker, there is no exhilaration in surviving cataclysm because he still does not comprehend passing through the disaster.

Keith Neudecker (a gambling pun of a surname evoking a "New Decker," suitable for a rambler looking for fresh cards and better luck) who "used to want more of the world than there was time and means to acquire. He didn't want this anymore" (DeLillo 2007: 128). Neudecker now listlessly watches gambling on TV or drifts off to poker matches around the United States, though apparently not making as much money as he did while working in the WTC tower. DeLillo himself points out in an interview the power of poker's escape: "You have to give the game concentration, and for that reason, a game of poker helps you forget, for a couple of hours, all the problems you've got" (Amend and Diez 2008). Neudecker, however, cannot concentrate, yet cannot stop searching for a way to forget or be forgiven for his abandoning Rumsey at his hour of death. A once-prosperous lawyer for over ten years (at a firm where most employees have now been killed by the Al Qaeda attack), he currently has no interest in gaining a livelihood outside of gambling.

Neudecker no longer contacts friends, and he seems monosyllabic at best to his wife and ten-year-old son, Justin. Only in his brief sex affair does he give the sense of some energy and personality. At other times, he just seems in another state, nearly half dead, and it is more than his soulful, long-suffering wife can withstand near the book's end: "Week after week . . . catching planes to go play cards. I mean aside from the absurdity, the total psychotic folly, isn't there something very sad about this? . . . Like a séance in hell. Tick tock tick tock. What happens after months of this? Or years? Who do you become?" (DeLillo 2007: 216). Like the meaning of his first name "Keith," originally a Scottish surname indicating woods, wilderness, or one dwelling in the forest (Zaczek 2007), he is truly bewildered in action. If he does attend metaphoric séances throughout the book, as Lianne suggests, it has been a numbing form of communication: Keith "looked at her [Lianne] and nodded as if he agreed and then kept nodding, taking the gesture to another level, a kind of deep sleep, a narcolepsy, eyes open, mind shut down. There was one final thing, too self-evident to need saying. She wanted to be safe in the world and he did not" (DeLillo 2007: 216). Exactly who is inside of him now, experiencing these somber misadventures of a nearly dead man, is what may keep much of the narrative drive going. On examination of textual evidence, the interpreter finds disquieting evidence that Keith is not *anyone* alive anymore. The proof is faint at first but grows: Keith is becoming his dead friend Rumsey.

The first unease that readers have toward Keith should come by page one. The South Tower has just fallen, the North Tower will implode any minute, and all around him are first responders and fellow businesspeople running, and yet the protagonist is *walking* away. Keith has no foot or leg injury, and only minor glass cuts to his arm and very superficial ones to his face. He is in no greater emotional shock than any of the people running by him. This first page marks the book as enigmatic and it will never lose this cipher-mark. Walking away is such an unexpected act that even the shrewdest critics see something that does not happen: they misremember that Keith *runs*. This is not a small point, and its oddness has yet to be fully realized. Sonia Baelo-Allué observes, "Time and space seem to have collapsed in the opening pages where we see how Keith, a lawyer who has worked in the North Tower for a decade, has just escaped and is running through the smoke and debris" (Baelo-Allué 2012: 70). However, that is not the case: "Runners" and "Run," are mentioned once, and "Running" is mentioned five times in these first seven pages, but for Neudecker, there is only "walking" five times and "walked" twice. This mistaken but understandable perception that he runs when he only walks away from the swaying North Tower is made by other critics, too.

Like a somewhat clichéd *Twilight Zone* scenario, Neudecker is in another dimension as all other life capable of movement almost flies. The fact that Keith does not quicken when he can raises a number of unsettling ideas, foremost being that he doesn't fully want to leave, that he is somehow fixed to the place of death, that he cannot cross to the boundary to the escaping and alive, that he could be, as Helene Cixous writes of the victims of the Uncanny, "dead while living . . . in a dubious state" (Cixous 1976: 545). When Keith does arrive to shelter, he goes not to his apartment, but to his estranged wife Lianne's home (they have been apart for a year-and-a-half). Something of the uncanny greets her, she says to her mother, when she opened the door and sees not Keith, the man who fathered her son, but only the burned traces of someone once alive. She says to her mother, "It was not possible, up from the dead, there he was in the doorway. It's so lucky Justin was here with you. Because it would have been awful for him to see his father like that. Like gray soot head to toe, I don't know, like smoke, standing there, with blood on his face and clothes" (DeLillo 2007: 8). She also says that her husband was no longer really the same man, but something that seemed not older, as we would expect, but younger, "I didn't know what to do. I mean with the phones out. Finally we walked to the hospital. Walked, step by step, like walking a child" (DeLillo 2007: 8–9). He is not her husband; he is some other. This is one way to explain the cryptic lines that issue from the mind of Neudecker: "Things inside were distant and still, where he was supposed to be" (DeLillo 2007: 3). His thoughts turning ever more enigmatic, ontologically questioning, and existence-doubting, Neudecker muses: "Maybe this is what things look like when there is no one here to see them. He heard the sound of the second fall, or felt it in the trembling air, the North Tower coming down, a soft awe of voices in the distance. That was him coming down, the North Tower. . . . He tried to tell himself he was alive but the idea was too obscure to take hold" (DeLillo 2007: 5). In many ways, he never leaves the North Tower and is unable to run away from the dead, and that is severely problematic for his marriage, the guidance of son, the holding down of his job, and the savoring of whatever life he does have left.

Ideas of the uncanny, unhomely, or "unheimlich, that species of the frightening that goes back to what was once well known and had long been familiar" as Freud understood it (Freud 1919b: 124), are those we can unreservedly apply to Neudecker and others in *Falling Man*. In an astute reading, Avril Horner helpfully characterizes the feeling of the uncanny as "the fear which derives from the helplessness experienced by one who continually finds himself confronting that from which he desires escape," which goes a long way to describe Neudecker's predicament (Horner 2009: 250). There are three common occurrences of the uncanny, and they are part of the Gothic foundation in this novel: people can no longer orient themselves in Manhattan because the towering landmarks have vanished, people don't recognize spouses or lovers or their ways of moving as they come home in dust, and their loved ones are eerily becoming someone else, someone no longer alive, yet not fully dead.

That grimness observed, something neglected about the uncanny albeit remembered by specialists on humor and the Gothic, such as Avril Horner and Sue Zlosnik, is that the uncanny first holds surprise that also has a farcical and ironic edge, something Freud calls "irresistibly comic," as we see early in *Falling Man*. Later in this novel, the uncanny becomes unrelentingly dark. Every one of the 9/11 novels examined in this Lexington monograph contains at least one unexpectedly amusing or befuddling moment, one wintry smile, as the uncanny introduces itself. The feeling of the Uncanny is the equivalent of having "lost one's way in the woods, perhaps after being overtaken by fog, and, despite all one's efforts to find a marked or familiar path, one comes back again and again to the same spot, which one recognizes by a particular physical feature" (Freud 1919b: 144).[7] True to this example, *Falling Man*'s endarkened protagonist recalls to his wife a story of farce and bewilderment in the midst of disaster. A repairman's service van pulls up to rescue Neudecker from the street of terrorist wreckage. The problem for the driver (who is either a plumber or an electrician) is that his radio has been stolen *eight* times, a ridiculously high number, and he cannot tell what has happened to New York City within the last two hours. This recalls one of the most satisfying commentaries and deconstructions of Freud's "The Uncanny" from Helene Cixous's "Fictions and Its Phantoms."[8] Cixous asks: "How many repetitions are necessary before distress turns into comedy?" (Cixous 1976: 540). In the case of *Falling Man*, it is eight: one stolen radio is sad, two seems a cruelty, and eight gone is just carelessness: he is forever parking on the wrong streets of New York City. If repetition pivots calamity to comedy, then the sudden disappearance of a massive building turns a morning into a head-shaking mystery for the driver, and the dramatic irony mounts for readers. The repairman does not know what has happened on the morning of 9/11 in Manhattan, only that his two towering landmarks are hiding, seemingly moving, and he cannot orient himself. He cannot entertain that the unthinkable has happened, or that 110 stories have vanished: "He saw the smoke. He drove east a ways and looked again and there was only one tower. One tower made no sense. Then he turned uptown because that's where he was going and finally he saw me and picked me up. By this time the second tower was gone" (DeLillo 2007: 25).

On a crisp blue morning come sky-clouding explosions and the largest loss of life from any terrorist attack in history on American soil. Neudecker and the rest of the city look for some explanation, shelter, comfort, affirmation, or wisdom during these moments of sublime terror, but the service driver only volunteers two sentences of dubious worth: "Eight radios in three years, he said. All stolen" (DeLillo 2007: 21). This homely, unfathomably trivial detail in view of the catastrophic loss garners snorts. Unexpectedly grim humor, absurdity, and irony have a deep place in this process of defamiliarization, this process of "making strange," but DeLillo has more complicated plans for the uncanny.

Much of the uncanny for Freud and for Otto Rank, whose study "Der Doppelgänger" Freud references, is in a mix of simultaneous recognition and nonrecognition of ourselves. Rank and Freud mention seeing ourselves in mirrors yet not recognizing ourselves. Freud, in his final note to "The Uncanny," leaves readers once again with what we could term the comic uncanny. He writes of a rude man stumbling from out the water closet and into Freud's train carriage compartment, to whom the coinventor of psychoanalysis sprung up to shove back out of door, before freezing himself and the intruder abruptly with a look: "[T]he train lurched violently. The door of the adjacent toilet swung open and an elderly gentleman in a dressing gown and travelling cap entered my compartment. I assumed that on leaving the toilet ... he had turned the wrong way and entered mine by mistake. I jumped to put him to right, but soon realized . . . the intruder was my own image, reflected in the mirror on the connecting door" (Freud 1919b: section III, note 1). What *Falling Man* does is the reverse of this mirror story: Neudecker longs to see himself reflected and cannot see himself at all. On the day of the most still-photographed and motion-filmed terrorist attack in history, Neudecker cannot find himself in one image afterwards, though he was walking and not running from the falling buildings, and he pores over the news for one sign that he was there on the familiar streets, alive. As if brush stroked out of the crowd of 9/11 survivors, Neudecker feels the terror of being missing, or what David Punter in his definition of terror calls "being confronted with 'absence' . . . which threatens our illusions of a fullness of being" (Punter 2009: 244). By itself, this omission of Neudecker's presence from any media-captures could be forgotten by readers, but DeLillo will leave us with a wealth of even more uncanny realizations.

Trauma comes for Neudecker not only from what is mysteriously missing in space, but also from what is shifting in time. Indeed, this misaligned perception of time a victim suffers is important to a school of trauma theorists, as well, as it is consistently returned to in their conceptualizations, from Freud in "A Project for a Scientific Psychology," to Caruth in *Trauma: Explorations in Memory*, to Lifton in *Death and Life*, and to Laub and Felman in their *Testimony*. As Aimee L. Pozorski cogently summarizes it: the aforementioned thinkers' "idea of trauma comes more from a theory of time—a kind of skewed temporality, . . . [a] repetition of the key aspects of the event . . . in search of that missed encounter with death" (Pozorksi 2011: 71). Horrors witnessed are not fully taken in at the moment of traumatic crisis, all the above theorists suggest, but return like an intruder at unwarranted hours: in its splintered and compulsive replay and physical repetitions, this process seems to express the death drive. More traumatic is how this fearful recognition/nonrecognition of 9/11 terror and death produces angst in Neudecker. Angst, according to Dylan Trigg's interpretation of Freud's "The Uncanny," is the central feeling created by the uncanny, and it is tied to time's flow and a disruption of that temporal current: "Angst establishes a correspondence between a subject haunted by his or her self-discontinuity and a world that persists despite that discontinuity" (Trigg 2012: 319). To the most threatening depths, Neudecker descends; so far he falls that he "becomes co-owner of the other's knowledge, emotions, and experience. . . . [He may] identify himself with another and so become unsure of his true self; or he may substitute the other's self for his own. The self may thus be duplicated, divided and interchanged" (Freud 1919b: 141–142). Paradoxically, by walking away from the site of disaster, Neudecker has literally *run out of time*: from now on, he is in another time and place, more a comrade with the dead than the living.

Figure 1.1 Rushing to the Disaster on an Express Subway from Times Square to Chambers Street in Front of the WTC, Photographer Richard Drew Looked up and Saw Both Towers on Fire and Captured Images of People Falling Out of the North Tower, Including This Image from the Video. Tom Juneau from *Esquire* came up with the name, "Falling Man." Courtesy of the Boston Public Library, Leslie Jones Collection.

A Gothic strangeness, compelling in its takeover of personality, begins in earnest. Caused in part through extreme identification, the living start to take the place of the dead: the living becoming a specter of the deceased. Readers witness a ghosting of the living man, a phantomic rendering, a bizarre entwining of who Rumsey was and who Neudecker is. A recount of basic details suggests that Neudecker is no longer in the world that we are in: he says he did not leave the North Tower, that his wife at first seeing him postattack is doubt-struck and thinks of him as dead ("It was not possible, up from the dead" [DeLillo 2007: 8]), and that his son no longer speaks to him and vice versa. More than that, we might notice how little physical description of Neudecker's face and body there is anywhere in this novel (fewer details than in any DeLillo novel or novella that comes to mind, save for his *The Body Artist*), and how few highly visual passages there are of Rumsey. Either one of them can look like the other in the reader's mind, and there is little to prevent them from merging in other ways, as well. One of the first signs of this merging is, fittingly enough, a rise in repetitive behaviors. For instance, Rumsey was a self-declared counter of anything and an obsessive-compulsive sufferer. This behavior was uncongenially combined with an inability to stop fantasizing about women. As the novel progresses, though the protagonist never exhibited this behavior pre-9/11, Keith now seems to be counting more. More to the point, Rumsey had started an affair with a darker-skinned woman just before the disaster. Neudecker will start an affair with a darker complexioned woman just after 9/11. His friend Rumsey loved watching women take their clothes off almost more than anything else, and now Neudecker (for whom there is no evidence of an extramarital lover before) visits his 9/11 paramour Florence Givens in her apartment, and growls, "Come out wearing something, so I can watch you take it off" (DeLillo 2007: 53). I do not remember him anywhere more alive in this novel than in this one passage, and it seems a welcome release of constant strain for a reader. Rumsey had another delight: he confessed to loving when women would start wearing open-toed sandals in springtime. It apparently became a chief recreation for him, so much so that Neudecker would tease his tabulating friend, back in those days, before he himself became aroused by women's feet. Neudecker mocked Rumsey for the love of toes: "But what if the digits don't always total ten? You're riding the subway, . . . and you're absently scanning the aisle, and you see a pair of sandals, and you count and count again, and there are nine digits, or eleven?" (DeLillo 2007: 123). But now, post-9/11, Keith who only pulled the legs of foot-fetishists before, cannot help pondering the divinely naked feet of his angel Florence Givens.

## THE EROTICS OF 9/11

*I don't know why, but I feel like going out and having sex with strangers.*
—9/11 Respondent, *Everything You Know
About Sex Is Wrong* (Schwartz 2001)

The Gothic has frequently obsessed over sexuality in a time of fear, showing mad desire and the often-lost battle with the internal censor since its first novel *The Castle of Otranto* showed the sexual designs of a father-in-law-to-be on his intended daughter-in-law after his son is mysteriously smashed to death on their wedding day. Later Gothic writers would focus on a demonic and violent sexuality: the attraction/repulsion of vampires, witches, and werewolves; the sinister secrets behind clerical rapes and murders in abbeys and monasteries and cathedrals; the aristocrat's sadism over subjects, and the coitus that would beget monsters.[9] Novels of 9/11 plunge into sexual obsession, too, and we could ask if they are inspired by actions of the New York City survivors. All novels in this book feature "Armageddon sex," and much of the 9/11 fiction read outside here shows it as well. Trauma, as represented in the 9/11 novels, displays an illicitly sexualized dimension. Cole Kazdin in a feature at *Salon* coined a term for it in New York ten days after the disaster: "terror sex." Kazdin wove her article around anecdotal reports of her New York friends experiencing a yearning to connect intimately with shaken strangers under the "Manhattan skyline, still burning." Kazdin quoted a University of Washington professor of sociology, Pepper Schwartz, as saying, "You want some kind of homage to a life force. 'I'm alive, I'm functioning, I'm real.' There's an euphoria, a triumph in sexuality that [sic] you can see why someone would want to do it as a very profound act" (Kelleher 2001). It was followed another ten days later by a *Los Angeles Times* article discussing the "most primal post-disaster reaction: Sex. The impulse to sleep with someone, even a stranger, comes from an instinctive place, and may have nothing to do with attraction" (Kelleher 2001). Sex took away the fear people had for a little while. Indeed, the New York City love-shop Toys in Babeland "reported a 33 percent increase in sales that fall" (Baker 2011), and some New York hospitals "were reported to have seen a 20 percent increase in births nine months following 9/11" (Baker 2011), neither of which may necessarily involve sex with strangers.

The novels surveyed here commonly depict trysts at comfort stations for rescuers (including fire and police department forces) among near strangers. Many accounts in New York magazines and newspapers reported them, as well, but some of the journals were renowned for exaggeration and sensationalism with an accompanying disregard for facts, studies, reputable sources, and statistics (*The New York Post* and *The New York Daily News* being chief examples of the yellow press). Thus, there may have been much more terror sex unfolding among two or more people on the printed page than in real Manhattan. However, sources with more reliability than those of the popular press, polling from sociological and psychological methodology and published in the *Archives of Sexual Behavior,* suggest there was a terror sex phenomenon. One of that journal's first post-9/11 studies was of 2,915 men who have sex with men (with twenty percent of the participants reporting sex with both men and women), trying to detect different patterns of sexual practice in the three months before and three months following 9/11. Men from all fifty states completed the survey, and exposure to the attacks varied: "11% lost a friend or relative; 5% witnessed the attacks in person [with eight of the respondents inside the WTC]; and nearly all saw the attacks on television within one hour of their occurrence" (Chiasson et al. 2005: 527). In brief, the social scientists found that a "significant proportion of men reported an increase in UAI [unprotected anal intercourse] and an increase in the number of partners following the attack" among study participants who were near the WTC collapse or Pentagon attack than those who were not (Chiasson et al. 2005: 532). Their conclusion sheds light on the erotics of trauma in

9/11 novels. As Chiason and team understood it: "The powerful need to connect with another person experienced by many after September 11 may have motivated some to seek comfort, security, and affirmation of life through sex. The sense of fatalism prevalent after the September 11 attacks, however, may have exacerbated reduced concerns about high-risk sexual behavior, particularly within the context of drug and alcohol use" (Chiason et al. 2005: 532). If substance abuse, along with random sex, becomes a constant in 9/11 novels, it is perhaps understandable for characters facing the continuing threat of additional air attacks and bioterrorism-related anthrax mailings following the fall of the towers. In *Falling Man*, reckless terror sex occurs. Neudecker, who has no history of sexual liaisons before 9/11, suddenly has at least three physical intimacies with his fellow survivor Florence Givens, and it seems a therapy for both, though also Gothically fraught with memories of the burning towers, where they first met. In the other novels, the experience of "end-of-the-world sex" is even more frequent but more menacing than in *Falling Man* (as it is tied to threats of spousal rape, especially in Kalfus's *A Disorder Peculiar to the Country* and McInerney's *The Good Life*). In *Falling Man* terror sex seems largely, but not exclusively, an escape from a spouse who cannot understand the horrors (or for whom the spouse cannot share the splintered memory of them)—but no evidence stands that it arises out of hope for a new and longer relationship borne out of the rubble with a fellow survivor. It signals in *Falling Man* a hunger for risk, an attempt to have one's consciousness fully held by something sublime and to deliver forgetfulness of all the terror around them for a few hours. Yet terror sex is not restricted only to outside lovers; it can occur occasionally in these novels with one's spouse. In *Falling Man*, on the first occasion post-9/11 when Keith and wife Lianne first make love after the bombing, the event contains an unmistakable death drive in its eroticism. It is a silent and strange testimony, but it also suggests a weird third figure with the lovers in the afterglow. Post coitus, Lianne rises and with her hands raised, presses herself against the cool surface of their tall mirror, leaving a full body trace. When Keith comes out of the bathroom, he may experience a shock at seeing the impression of her thighs, bust, hands, and face against the looking glass. Something in him pauses, and it could be an image that may recall instantly the falling man himself and all the tortures of that day.

Providing a screen that separates them from unbearable horror, their lovemaking is as potent an affirmation of desire and life as can be made by two people who recently assumed the other was dead in the exploded towers. Still, something of the taboo of the dead is still raised here. Their Gothically inflected sex seems at first to indicate, as Fred Botting similarly notes in a discussion of Gothic film, that "horror cedes to romance, and revulsion to attraction" (Botting 2008: 5). However, here we can also accept that the "Gothic genre's usual trajectory is reversed: a flight from figures of horror and revulsion is turned into a romantic flight towards them, now figures of identification" (Botting 2008: 5). Why does Lianne make love to her husband and then take the position of a tower-jumper against the mirror, leaving a body trace in the steam? Lovemaking may be often thought as a way of clouding terror, but Lianne presses against the fog and leaves the reminder of the falling man from the burning tower, a reenactment as discussed in trauma theory. This act in steam reimposes the terror and the ominous ruin as witnessed in earlier Gothic fictions. Sex, here, does not obliterate fear and dread for long, as some may assume terror sex may do. The falling dead, unknown and unmourned, form mental ghosts in the bedroom. For sixty pages before this, Lianne had watched again and again the "Falling Man" performance artist Janiak strike his dying leap poses from edges of New York buildings in the days after 9/11, but she had never mimed him until now, after the sex. And her pose is uncannily like Janiak's, with hands raised to head and body collapsing. Janiak and the deceased are the first thing on Lianne's mind after intercourse, as demonstrated by her making their body-form on the mirror, instantly and wordlessly reminding Keith of them. This is the visible evidence that Lianne is identifying with them, posing as them, becoming them, inviting them deep inside. In the post 9/11 days, the living are honoring the dead even in after-moments of ecstasy. Though the dead (in particular, Keith's colleague Rumsey) are initially left behind in the burning towers, they are not missing from the apartments of the living (even their burned particles in the air waft inside to the rooms and are breathed): reminders of the murdered are so numerous that survivors are forced beyond memorializing into misery. Revealingly, in the next moment after sex, we see Neudecker going into a repetition cycle, staring long at her falling image in the fogged mirror, and then invoking the symptoms of trauma of his last moments with Rumsey. His physical wound is outwardly healed—he has thrown way his wrist splint, stopped applying ice to his fist, and says he is fine—but he cannot *believe* it so, as the wound to his mind remains an open one. Moreover, the trace of a WTC falling body on the mirror reawakens Neudecker's suffering, signified by his physiological reactivity. The body outline is a cue that, as the *Diagnostic and Statistical Manual of Mental Disorders* recognizes in its discussion of PTSD, "symbolizes or resembles an aspect of the traumatic event" (*DSM-V* 2013: 468). He falls back into repetitive states, reenacting his old physical therapy for a hand already healed, a compulsion perhaps attributable to the intrusion of memories of using and injuring his hand in the North Tower.

Neudecker leaves his friend behind in the tower with the defense that Rumsey is probably already dead, though he has no stethoscope or other device to check for a heartbeat, however faint. Jumpers must be flying by his window[10] as he leaves the burning tower, but he does not see them as people, the sky is not "set among strangers falling down"; he only sees white shirts sailing "out of high smoke" and "falling again, down toward the river" (DeLillo 2007: 4). Internal defense mechanisms must be forbidding the complete registering of the grotesque and completely unpredictable deaths of that morning, but much of the repressed memories will break into his consciousness by the novel's last pages. By not taking Rumsey down the stairs with him, Neudecker violates a rule: never leave your partner, your "fellow soldier" behind in the slow-motion warfare that is the business world, whether he is dead, alive, or wavering in between. Neudecker makes his decision to abandon Rumsey, walking away from a WTC plaza presumably littered with human legs, arms, torsos, and heads, and now he must face the posttraumatic havoc that comes of it.

It is instructive to consider a contrasting case from Neudecker's, venerated at the 9/11 Memorial & Museum with photographs and emotionally resonant artifacts on display. According to the founding director of the 9/11 Memorial & Museum, moments after the South Tower fell, Abe Zelmanowitz, a computer analyst on the twenty-seventh floor at Empire Blue Cross and Blue Shield in the North Tower, would not heed the evacuation order and would not abandon his coworker and long-time friend Ed Beyea, a wheelchair-bound quadriplegic. Captain Billy Burke of Fire Engine 21 (which itself is now parked inside the 9/11 Memorial & Museum) encountered Zelmanowitz on the stairs with Beyea, and Zelmanowitz still would not leave Beyea behind. The captain ordered all his men to head downstairs to safety below as he and Zelmanowtiz began to assist Beyea down the stairs. Phone contact with a close friend of the Captain was made and, Burke was heard as saying, "This is my job. This is who I am." Minutes later at 10:28 a.m. the North Tower fell killing all three (Greenwald 123). This presumably would have been a much-discussed true story in the newspapers during Neudecker's convalescence, and Captain Burke's selfless action toward strangers is an unspoken yet constant reminder to Neudecker that he did not make the sacrifice to a man who was his friend.

## THE VIRAL TRANSMISSION OF TRAUMA

Many trauma theorists speak of the virus-like transmission character of traumas (Butler 2004; Caruth 1995, 1996; Leys 2000, 2009), as when sons or daughters of genocide survivors exhibit some of the same angst, fear, dread, and depression as their parents, though their parents understandably chose not to share the details of their years in concentration camps or interrogation/torture centers with their children. Affirming this pattern to a degree, Lianne demonstrates some of the uncharacteristic violence shown by her husband who is driven to Gothic excess. No evidence exists to suggest she would smash objects into women's faces before 9/11, she runs a support group after all, but her violent ways start mirroring her husband's after this unnatural disaster. Nevertheless, the contagion of violence is less pronounced in this novel than the Gothic power of possession of the dead over the narrator. Even Neudecker recognizes something peculiar in the trend of possession: "The persistence of the man's [Rumsey's] needs had a kind of crippled appeal. It opened Keith to dimmer things, at odder angles, to something crouched and uncorrectable in people but also capable of stirring a warm feeling in him, a rare tinge of affinity" (DeLillo 2007: 122). This affinity goes too far, though, when Neudecker identifies with the dead, as is felt in one the most soulful moments of the novel when Keith returns to Ground Zero days after the attack. He hangs on the hurricane fencing wrapped around the disaster site for a period, and gazes at the "skeletal remnant of the tower where he'd worked for ten years": "The dead were everywhere, in the rubble, on rooftops nearby, in the breezes that carried from the river. They were settled in ash and drizzled on windows all along the streets, in his hair and on his clothes" (DeLillo 2007: 25). It is indisputable that the dead *are* everywhere as DeLillo says, but most crucially they are also breathed, in minute amounts, directly into Keith's lungs.[11] He has mixed his essence with theirs, and a curious switch in perspective happens when Keith goes to his own apartment on the next page: "He stood and looked and felt something so lonely he could touch it with his hand.... Maybe he was thinking of the man who used to live here" (DeLillo 2007: 27). It seems the view has changed: mentally he is outside, closer to the ruins, magically looking at the man in his apartment who once was him, and yet he is also physically inside the apartment.

The uncanny stresses repeated encounters with a thing, and in this novel that repeated encounter is with falling white things—again and again Neudecker finds falling white paper, or sheets stuck to windows in his apartment, and the vision of a white shirt falling and floating over Manhattan from the morning of 9/11 replays in his mind each time he sights white paper. They are the same figure that each of these novels will see and turn away from, and later repress, then have reemerge: the falling bodies of 9/11, the ones seen but shut away, and the overwhelmingly gruesome aspect that this trauma must include, the bodies meeting with the ground. This is the grief that cannot be expressed, the wound that will not heal, the view that was too violent to take in and too shattering to remember, but like these white sheets descending and sticking to surfaces, the bodies of the dead exist no matter how diligently witnesses may look away. The clinging paper represents an inevitable return of the corpses to the minds of the sufferers much as Freud reflects, "The frightening element is something that has been repressed and now returns. This species of the frightening would then constitute the uncanny ... something that should have remained hidden has come into the open" (Freud 1919b: 147). The twisted and burned bodies from that morning come back into Neudecker's consciousness with each nearly weightless, singed scrap of twenty-five-pound cotton bond floating by or stuck in the gutter.

Neudecker's symptom presentation—heightened reactions, flashbacks, dissociation, and identity change (seeming to metamorphosize into a living-dead man)—suggest the PTSD syndromes from the DSM-V. In much of the recent research of trauma theory from Caruth, Felman, Laub, and Lifton, it is often pointed out that the arrival of PTSD as a category in the DSM-III (1980) was in large part a result of research on afflicted Vietnam War soldiers, and activism by health professionals, peace groups, and veterans themselves. The attempt by these four groups was to help the psychic wounds from war gain legitimacy and, it was hoped, much more and sounder psychomedical help (Caruth 1996; Leys 2000; Luckhurst 2008). However, a number of sources outside the arena of trauma theory point out that the effort to recognize PTSD has much deeper roots, particularly in the first studies of acute grief as a "remarkably uniform" syndrome (Kastenbaum 2008: 354). The first such study was by neurologist Alexandra Adler (born in Austria in 1900, the daughter of Alfred Adler, Freud's psychoanalysis colleague, and the founder of Individual Psychology). Psychiatrist Eric Lindemann (born in Germany in 1901) led the second study. Before World War II broke out, both Adler and Lindemann settled in America, and with the War's advent, both ended up interviewing and studying survivors of what is yet the largest nightclub fire in world history, and still the third deadliest building fire in American history, following the WTC with 2,666 deaths and Chicago's Iroquois Theater in 1903 with 602 deaths (NFPA 2016). In 1942, the Cocoanut Grove nightclub blaze in Boston would kill 492 people, and leave traumatized survivors reenacting, and at other times repressing, memories of "being choked and trampled upon" (Adler 1943: 1099). It was these two landmark hospital studies that paved the way for more reports of how trauma affects survivors, enabling George Engel's ground-breaking medical model of grief in 1961 which asked if grief was a disease (Kastenbaum 2003). Engel would argue that one could have a disease (like grief) and still not require medicine: to claim the opposite would only follow a social, not a medical, definition of disease.

In listening to patients from the fire and encountering them later, Adler repeatedly detected "anxiety neurosis" (Adler 1943: 1100). Adler noted in the *Journal of the American Medical Association* that they "complained mainly of fears and anxiety which they were unable to control and which prevented them from readjusting to normal activities." Their prognoses were not good, as "two thirds had hardly improved when re-examined after nine months" (Adler 1943: 1100–1101). In a psychiatric journal a year later, Lindemann would draw an even more startling pattern, sketching a portrait of possession

**Figure 1.2 Boston's Cocoanut Grove Nightclub Blaze Remains the Most Lethal Nightclub Fire in World History, with Almost Half of Its 1,000 Visitors That Night Perishing.** On the night of November 28, 1942, rescuers moved the injured, the dying, and the dead onto the street in front of the club. By day, it was clearer to see that exits were deliberately blocked at the building, a traumatic memory that would seek expression from its survivors. In 2017, two of the eight survivors (Joyce S. Mekelburg, 93, and Marshall Cole, 92) joined with families of the victims along with a former mayor of Boston at a special ceremony, marking its seventy-fifth commemoration and showing the close bond that develops between witnesses. They mused on their trauma, their escape, and survival since. Used with permission from the Leslie Jones (1886–1967) Collection, Boston Pictorial Archive, Boston Public Library. Courtesy of the Boston Public Library, Leslie Jones Collection.

that is eminently like Keith Neudecker's symptoms, especially in what Lindemann termed the "sixth characteristic":

> These five points: (1) somatic distress, (2) preoccupation with the image of the deceased, (3) guilt, (4) hostile reactions, and (5) loss of patterns of conduct, seem to be pathognomonic of grief. There may be added a sixth characteristic, shown by patients who border on pathological reactions, which is not so conspicuous as the others but nevertheless often striking enough to color the whole picture. This is the appearance of traits of the deceased in the behavior of the bereaved, . . . especially symptoms shown during the last illness, or behavior which may have been shown at the time of the tragedy. A bereaved

person is observed or finds himself walking in the manner of his deceased father. He looks in the mirror and believes that his face appears just like that of the deceased. He may show a change of interests in the direction of the former activities of the deceased and may start enterprises entirely different from his former pursuits. A wife who lost her husband, an insurance agent, found herself writing to many insurance companies offering her services with somewhat exaggerated schemes. It seemed a regular observation in these patients that the painful preoccupation with the image of the deceased described above was transformed into preoccupation with symptoms or personality traits of the lost person. (Lindemann 1944: 189–190)

It is hard to see which portions of this distressing diagnosis of morbid grief and overidentification with the deceased that Neudecker does *not* have. For the survivors to go from meditating on the loved lost one to transforming into that lost one, or at least taking up his or her interests and believing they appear just like the deceased (even if of another gender), is an extreme bond of, in Gothic terms, the living becoming a ghost of the dead. Neudecker's spectral condition provides a traumagothic model to compare to the other

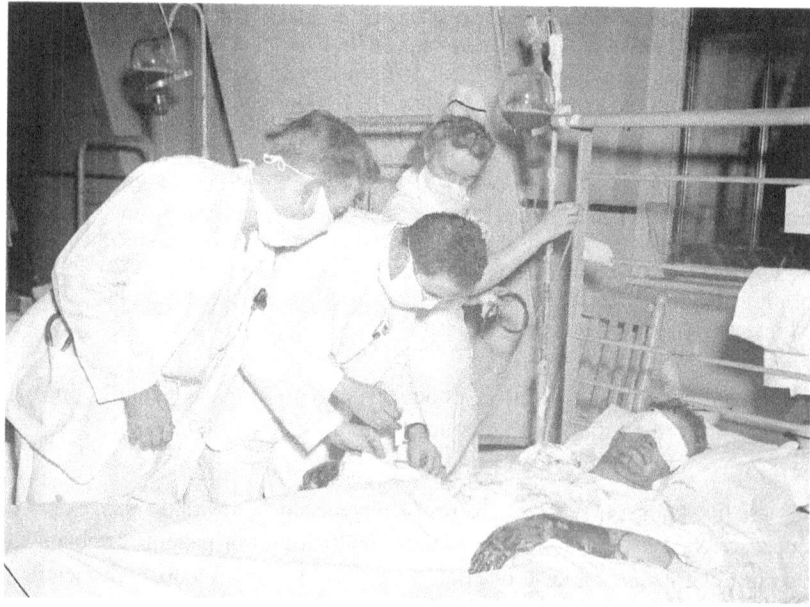

Figure 1.3 **Pioneering Treatment in Burn Therapy on the Cocoanut Grove Fire Victims at Massachusetts General Hospital (to Be Applied in the Ongoing World War II) Would Be Followed by Adler's and Lindemann's Psychiatric Studies of the Survivors.** Used with permission from the Leslie Jones (1886–1967) Collection, Boston Pictorial Archive, Boston Public Library. Courtesy of the Boston Public Library, Leslie Jones Collection.

novels here, though his possession by the dead, starting subtly at first, may well grow to be the most extreme of any of the novels herein.

A question arises as to whether these ghostly possessions or pathological identifications are still happening after recent disasters, and if their depiction in fiction resembles that in life. Exploring another cataclysm, British journalist Richard Lloyd Parry has had a large number of encounters in the wake of the Japanese tsunami in 2011, when 20,000 people died (Kastenbaum 2011: 338), of which he has written of at length (Parry 2014). Through these accounts, we begin to see that what happens to Neudecker in *Falling Man* happens elsewhere in contemporary "real" trauma. Parry describes his research in a bereft Japanese inland town named Kurihara, where the local chief Zen priest noted that the survivors "didn't cry. There was no emotion at all. The loss was so profound and death had come so suddenly. . . . They couldn't understand what they should do, or sometimes even where they were. . . . I couldn't really talk to them, to be honest" (Parry 2009). Though the number of lives lost on 9/11 was just over a tenth as many as those lost in the Japanese tsunami, the Al Qaeda strike was also swift and left survivors speechless with the many bodies of friends and loved ones never recovered, the living often not knowing how to mourn such a catastrophic loss (Kastenbaum 2011: 338). Like the tsunami in Japan, the day in September in New York was "Impossible . . . insupportable, soul-crushing, unfathomable. . . . Television images failed to encompass [it]" (Parry 2014). What the Zen priest and residents started noticing in Kurihara was a rise in the number of family members not acting themselves, as in *Falling Man*. People began seeing "sightings of ghostly strangers, friends and neighbors, and killed loved ones. They reported hauntings at home, at work, in offices . . . and on the beaches in the ruined towns" (Parry 2014). A case in point was a local builder Parry calls Takeshi Ono.

Continually revisiting the shore where multitudes were swept away, Ono later exhibited behaviors of some of these dead that he claimed were within him. Ono's family took him to the local Zen priest Kaneda to have the invading dead possessing him exorcised. Many other examples of disaster ghost possession follow in this memory from Kaneda, twenty-five over the summer for the Zen priest, leaving him "overwhelmed. . . . [I] found myself listening to the voices of the dead" wherever he would go (Parry 2014). As with the thousands of mental health workers sent to New York to help after 9/11, often the burden of hearing and empathizing was too great to bear, and "the therapists developed reactions that were characteristic of trauma," including exaggerated startle reflex, avoidance, flashbacks, fear of attack or collapse, feelings of failure at their job and helplessness" (Seeley 110–11). Despite the rash of disaster ghosts and supernatural possession in Japan, Parry insists on a resolute rationality in the Japanese character which typically might reduce credulity or over-receptiveness to the paranormal, and be at odds with fanciful sightings and symptoms of occupation in the living by the dead. When "opinion polls put up the question, 'How religious are you?' the Japanese rank among the most ungodly people in the world" (Parry 2014). This rationality, despite the intrusion of the uncanny, recalls Neudecker, who pays no heed even once in the novel to gods or devils, angels or demons, and spirits or ghosts, yet seems inhabited by his dead friend.

## CONCLUSION

*Let the Dead bury the Living.*

—Nietzsche, *Untimely Meditations* (1876)

One of the least examined Gothic elements in 9/11 novels is how the living are possessed by the dead. Moreover, walking in the manner of the deceased, cultivating new interests "in the direction of the former activities of the deceased," believing one's face to resemble the dead individual, and channeling the "personality traits of the lost one," into oneself are not the stuff of fiction alone, but pathognomonic among survivors of sudden disaster in psychiatric and medical journals (Lindemann 1944: 189–190). However, though distinct characteristics of PTSD in life and in fiction are outlined in the key post-1990s texts on trauma, possession by a dead friend is not one of them.[12] Out of all the protagonists encountered in the novels discussed in this book Neudecker does the least grief-work and may be the most shattered trauma-sufferer. He barely talks with his wife of his panicked moments in the North Tower, never attends a 9/11 memorial, and never joins a therapy group of survivors to share his memories with people who could understand. He never seeks professional psychological help, never conducts a ritual of any kind in the name of those that he lost, never tries to help the many children of the dead, and never has an imaginary dialogue with his lost friend. Ominously, Keith Neudecker never cries, either. This victim may have had some temporary relief and control by suppressing grief, but this grief resisted or ignored ends by dissolving him, corroding all connections with family and friends and even his lover, until he floats away to the hazy, smoke-filled gambling dens around the United States. His mishandling of trauma is a pattern to revisit as this monograph probes the traumas and responses from the remaining fictions.[13] There is little indication from Neudecker on how or when he has dealt with bereavement before—no mention of his parents or siblings dying sometime before 9/11, or any other lovers or friends who died before planes "were coming out of that ice blue sky" (DeLillo 2007: 134), so the reader has no sense of his former capacities to heal. This makes Keith

Neudecker a cipher, certainly. Yet the chorus of critics affirming that he is "not very compelling" (Kakutani 2007) may have misjudged him. Holocaust Research Centre director Robert Eaglestone finds *Falling Man* fails along with other 9/11 novels because they continually "fetishize a lack of communication and understanding of events and contexts, . . . show[ing] an inability to address the terror that is their proclaimed subject, and indeed perform their own failure and collapse of voice" (Eaglestone 2007: 22). Yet, Neudecker, a ghost-man in Gothic isolation who reveals to what extent being possessed by the dead is incompatible with living, is a patient as tortured, fascinating and instructive as Freud's Rat Man or Wolf Man. Though dismissed by scholars for showing a "lack of communication" between spouses and even between fellow survivors—when so much agony, fear, grief, and rage yearns to be expressed, *Falling Man* is yet a terror-entity unto itself. More to the point, Keith Neudecker is not *one* being, as critics have heretofore assumed, but weirdly *two*: he is "*double* in himself [emphasis added], coming and going, [in his] walks across the park and back, [in his] deep shared self, down through the smoke" (DeLillo 2007: 157).

## NOTES

1. Sonia Baelo-Allué identifies a real individual claiming he inspired the character David Janiak for DeLillo with leaps that occurred two years before the novel's publication, the "Brooklyn photographer Kerry Skarbakka, who staged a number of jumps from the roof of Chicago's Museum of Contemporary Art on June 14, 2005" and exhibited his photos as *The Struggle to Right Oneself* (2007: 73). A key difference not acknowledged is that Skarbakka lived, and his moments in suspended peril did not take place in front of New Yorkers in the days following the attacks. Skarbakka's photos are often instead over fairly short distances (e.g., a stairwell) and his face shows an almost comic expression of surprise, rather than fear of impact.

2. The leaps profoundly disturb most viewers in *Falling Man*, except for children beneath the jumper, who yell "Jump, Jump!" and for the Mayor who simply dismisses him as "moronic." However, Marie-Christine Leps incisively concludes that Janiak makes a "fictional stillness designed to give memory and provoke new modes of knowing . . . a different form of relation to the other, born of ethical responsibility rather than reason alone" (2010: 187).

3. Born in Kafr el-Sheikh, Egypt (September 1, 1968), considered the ringleader of the terrorist cell, and attending the same university at the same time as myself in the late 1980s, the American University in Cairo, under pressure by his father to learn English (the staff of *The 9/11 Commission Report* 2004).

4. Though it seems to be overstating it as the affair takes up few pages of the book and does not appear on each of the lovers' minds all the time, Joseph Conte calls the "bond between survivors . . . the counter-narrative" (Conte 2011: 567) of the entire novel: through it, they meditate on their place in the catastrophe and in "the world

narrative in which they are now engaged" (Conte 2011: 567). This raises the question of whether every novel of terrorism covered here has a counternarrative inside it.

5. Lianne's Basho-like sentence after the attack summarizes everyone's nostalgia well: "Even in New York, I long for New York" (DeLillo 2007: 34).

6. Despite not psychoanalyzing them, Freud did ponder the shattering, uncoded, and unmediated dreams of war neurotics carefully, as their suffering challenged his theory on dreaming from *The Interpretation of Dreams* (1899), considering that none of the dreams of the traumatized veterans seemed like wish fulfilments, as his theory of psychoanalysis vowed they would. This interest in explaining the threat to his theories is evidenced by comments in the second section of *Beyond the Pleasure Principle* (1919a), which he began as he was finishing his short essay that this volume has recourse to later, "The Uncanny" (1919b). It should be noted that Freud wrote with more compassion than I have seen anywhere else in his work, save for on the death of children, over the veterans' state and attacked the physicians' cruel treatment of them, as apparent from a 1920 memo. Asked to give expert opinion by the Austrian War Ministry after World War I on treatments of the shell-shocked by army doctors, Freud wrote very sympathetically and rather heroically against the electrotherapy they were administered:

> The war that has recently ended produced and brought under observation an immense number of these traumatic cases. . . . [Their] therapeutic procedure, however, bore a stigma from the very first. It did not aim at the patient's recovery, or not in the first instance; it aimed, above all, at restoring his fitness for service. . . . The strength of current, as well as the severity of the rest of the treatment, were increased to an unbearable point. . . . In German hospitals there were deaths at that time during treatment and suicides as a result of it. . . . I am in a position to bring forward conclusive evidence of the final break-down of the electrical treatment of the war neuroses. (Freud 1920)

7. Freud noticed that often for his neurotic patients, "There is something uncanny about the female genitals. But what they find uncanny ['unhomely'] is actually the entrance to man's old 'home,' the place where everyone once lived. . . . 'I know this place, I've been here before,' this place can be interpreted as representing his mother's genitals or her womb." Dylan Trigg unpacks this repeated observation well, noting that "constant work modifying memory is required in order to fend off the unhomely shadow that lurks within the longing for home" (Trigg 2012: 46).

8. In Cixous's boundary-pushing analysis and characterization of "The Uncanny," she defines it as "less a discourse than a strange theoretical novel [with] . . . something 'savage,' . . . a breath or a provocative air which at times catches the novelist himself off guard, overtaking him and restraining him. Freud and the object of his desire (i.e., the truth about the Unheimliche) are fired by reciprocal inspiration, . . . [and] the psychoanalyst [is] psychoanalyzed in the very study he is seeking to develop" (Cixous 1976: 540).

9. See Marie Mulvey-Robert's illuminating *The Handbook of the Gothic* (2009, 2nd edition) and Ann B. Tracy's *The Gothic Novel 1790–1830* (1981) for more occasions of "taboo" and "perverse" sexuality in Gothic novels. For book length studies of the sex, see Ruth Bienstock Anolik's *Horrifying Sex: Essays on Sexual Difference in Gothic Literature* (2007), Joseph Andriano's *Our Ladies of Darkness: Feminine*

*Daemonology in Male Gothic Fiction* (1993), George Haggerty's *Queer Gothic* (2006), and Judith Halberstam's *Skin Shows: Gothic Horror and the Technology of Monsters* (1995).

10. Horribly, Neudecker may have seen many more plummeting "white shirts" than he can recall. *The New York Times* notes "some researchers say more than 200 people most likely fell or jumped to their death. Others say the number is half that, or fewer" (Flynn and Dwyer 2004). *USA Today* estimates "that at least 200 people jumped to their deaths that morning, far more than can be seen in the photographs [and motion film] that morning. Nearly all were from the North Tower, which was hit first and collapsed last. Fewer than a dozen were from the South Tower. The jumping started shortly after the first jet hit at 8.46 a.m. People jumped continuously during the 102 minutes that the North Tower stood. . . . For those who jumped, the fall lasted 10 seconds. They struck the ground at just less than 150 miles per hour—not fast enough to cause unconsciousness whilst falling, but fast enough to ensure instant death on impact. People jumped from all four sides of the North Tower. They jumped alone, in pairs and in groups" (Cauchon and Moore 2002). Less reported is the belief that the North Tower jumpers, like the ones Neudecker represses, saved many lives by their act. As *USA Today* reports, "Many South Tower survivors say the sight of people jumping created an urgency that caused them to leave immediately and ignore announcements that it was safe to return to their desks. About 1,400 people evacuated the upper floors before the second jet hit" (Cauchon and Moore 2002).

11. All of the novels in this book meditate on the dust characters inhale in lower Manhattan and what is left of someone's body therein from the towers and plaza. It should be noted that out of the dust breathed by these characters in this part of New York City, a very small amount of it contained human remains. One of the most detailed studies of dust of the WTC concludes from its samples that only 1.4 percent of the dust produced from the towers' fall was human (Schuppli 2012: 132).

12. The studies consulted include Anne Whitehead's *Memory* (2009), Colin Davis's *Haunted Subjects: Deconstruction, Psychoanalysis, and the Return of the Dead* (2007), Maria del Pilar Blanco and Esther Peeren's *Popular Ghosts: Haunted Spaces of Everyday Culture* (2010), Ruth Leys's *Trauma: A Genealogy* (2000) and *From Guilt to Shame* (2009), Roger Luckhurst's *The Trauma Question* (2008), Dominick LaCapra's *Writing History, Writing Trauma* (2001), Michelle Balaev's *Nature of Trauma in American Novels* (2012), Judith Butler's *Precarious Life: The Powers of Mourning and Violence* (2004), and Judith Herman's *Trauma and Recovery* (1997).

13. In his patterns of grief-work, nothing Neudecker does—except for time spent with an extramarital lover who went through the horrors of the WTC collapse—expresses mourning and a movement toward healing. A number of books meditating on patterns of approaching loss suggest where he could start, including Karen M. Seeley's *Therapy after Terror: 9/11: Psychotherapists, and Mental Health* (2008), Naaneen Interland's "How Do You Heal a Traumatized Mind" (2014), Doug Manning's *Don't Take My Grief Away* (2011), Peter McWilliams' *How to Survive the Loss of a Love* (1993), Dixie L. Denis's *Living, Dying, Grieving* (2008), Kathleen Fischer, "When Grief Won't Go Away" (1991), and Edna B. Foa et al., *Effective Treatments for PTSD* (2008).

*Chapter 2*

# Jonathan Safran Foer's *Extremely Loud and Incredibly Close* (2005)

## Searching and Disinterring the Dead

### CRITICAL RECEPTION

Though separated by three decades of age, the psyches of nine-year-old protagonist Oskar Schell of Jonathan Safran Foer's *Extremely Loud and Incredibly Close* and thirty-nine-year-old WTC lawyer Keith Neudecker from DeLillo's *Falling Man* operate in similarly dismal Gothic mazes of injury, reenactment, dissociation, guilt, fear, self-contempt, and self-harm. In short, they both identify with the dead, enter a quest, experience rage that turns into either imagined or real violence, experience encounters with the uncanny, and pull away from the family that loves them and that could, conceivably, help them start living in the present instead of struggling in the past. The one difference is that in Foer's novel a second individual, the boy's grandfather, will eventually reveal the truth of what happened in his war-related trauma afflicting the Schell family decades before the 9/11 traumata commenced. But like *Falling Man*, burdens unbearable and traumas long untreated are the distinctive features of what, to date, is the bestselling of the American 9/11 novels surveyed here. *Extremely Loud and Incredibly Close* made the *New York Times* Bestseller List both on its release in 2005 (appearing as number fifteen in April 2005) and again in the year of its film release for two weeks in February 2012 ("Combined Print & E-Book Fiction"). The first 9/11 novel to be made into a film, it featured celebrity actors (Tom Hanks and Sandra Bullock) who brought large audiences to theaters.

The youngest of the writers considered here, Foer was twenty-eight at book release and a Princeton protégé of America's veteran Gothicist Joyce Carol Oates. He debuted his fiction and found an agent through a contest at *Zoetrope* magazine, a creation of director/writer Francis Ford Coppola whose Gothic mind also directed *Dementia 13*, *Bram Stoker's Dracula*, and *Twixt*.

Foer's creative writing thesis would become his first novel, *Everything Is Illuminated*, which contended with the trauma of Nazi extermination of a Jewish shtetl in Ukraine (his own grandfather was born within a Jewish shtetl in Poland). That a considerable portion of the reading and viewing public in America was engaged with both media forms of *Extremely Loud and Incredibly Close* at first suggests some mainstream tendencies in its character, thought, dialogue, and conflict that may be less visible in the other novels I address.

Despite its popularity with readers, reviewers habitually articulate five recurring complaints about the novel, the first being that it tends toward incoherence: "the novel as a whole feels simultaneously contrived and improvisatory, schematic and haphazard" (Kakutani 2005). Second, critics penalize the work for its narrator seeming too intelligent for a nine-year-old. Oskar, "the book's precocious, insufferable Montessori casualty of a narrator" (Beck 2005: 92), is "invested by Foer with little other than an intense desire for our attention" (Munson 2005: 80). Walter Kirn echoes the impatience, claiming that the boy is "a cross between J. D. Salinger's precocious, morbid, psychiatry-proof child philosophers and all those daunting city kids from children's books whose restless high spirits and social confidence get them into funny predicaments while their preoccupied but loving parents conduct their mysterious offstage grown-up business" (Kirn 2005). However, the fiction actually shows no adults saving Oskar. He will have to save himself, and perhaps them, too. Munson, for his part, rejects the book's supposed sentimentality at first, but then reveals what may underlie much negative commentary: the fact that Oskar, a high-operating child who nonetheless may have Asperger's syndrome, puts unusual demands on readers. As Munson reasons, "All this is Foer's way of showing us, or belaboring us with, Oskar's great pain, fear, and susceptibility. The trouble is that, despite the long stretches of time a reader spends listening to Oskar's hyperactive narration, his habitual and unstoppable overstatement prevents one from ever coming to know the inner character of his pain and fear and susceptibility" (Munson 2005: 83). Fellow 9/11 novelist John Updike concurs, prescribing that "a little more silence, a few fewer messages, [and] less graphic apparatus might let Foer's excellent empathy, imagination, and good will resonate all the louder" among this "family consist[ing] of a dog called Buckminster, an unusually permissive and remote working mother, [and] a loving grandmother who lives across the street and talks to him through a baby monitor" (Updike 2005). That describes the family to a degree, except that, to clarify the record, his Buckminster Fuller is actually a cat. The cat is one of Oskar's few friends, and a preternaturally patient one at that, who allows this budding scientist to execute gravity experiments on him, mostly by being dropped out of window to test his righting reflex to make himself into a parachute, recalling Oskar's understandable obsession with the bodies falling out of the WTC and what could have saved them. Beck takes his agitation one step further, monstrously wishing the narrator ill: "Had we a real Oskar, we'd shut him up, Kaspar Hauser-style, in some damp and cobwebbed oubliette—that is, if we couldn't just send him the way of Little Nell" (Beck 2005: 93). The fourth tendency is to judge the book as being overly obsessed with American rather than world's suffering: "But not only is Oskar's vision disturbingly regressive, the use of the first-person-plural pronoun in the final sentence of the book limits even these powers of textuality to the restoration of safety only for those who can be counted as victims of the World Trade Center Collapse" (Greenwald Smith 2011: 157–158). Mitigating Rachel Greenwald Smith's concern for narrowness, the portrayal of the Allied firebombing of Dresden and American atomic bombing of Hiroshima in this novel both well support Caruth's claim that "history, like trauma, is never simply one's own, that history is precisely the way we are implicated in each other's traumas" (Caruth 1996: 8).

I suggest that the foregoing faults and limitations cited regarding *Extremely Loud and Incredibly Close* are largely attributable to interpreters being attentive to one-third of the conversation. There are actually three narrators in this novel: Oskar's consciousness fills eight chapters, but his grandmother's mind directs four chapters, and his grandfather's thoughts rule the other four. Without initial reviewers and later scholars detecting weaknesses in the grandparents' half of the book, as well, they have not given sufficient reason to condemn the whole. The book opens to greater wonder, surprise, and traumatic commentary when we comprehend Oskar's thoughts, actions, and words as being in strange concert with those of his grandfather and grandmother (both paternal), as his grandfather exhibits many of the compulsive, artistic, and endearing habits of Oskar himself. Indeed, this novel's commercial success makes a bold exception to Elizabeth S. Anker's observation (which could nonetheless be applied to *Falling Man*) that "Almost unanimously rendering 9/11 as a crucible in middle-aged masculinity, [9/11] narratives" indict "American self-reference," and "American ineptitude, or the disavowed truth of late imperial impotence and failure . . . foreboding the waning of American fiscal, military, and geopolitical dominance" (Anker 2011: 464). In this case, however, the middle-aged Thomas Jr. is the missing presence altogether in *Extremely Loud and Incredibly Close*, as he dies at the novel's genesis before narrating a word.

The last common critical reservation is the narrative's post-postmodern inventiveness. Here, the presumed fault is that the novel's many photographs and typographical experiments are "by turns precious and poignant" (Frost 2008): that "Plenty of typographical gimmickry" becomes "heartbreaking folly, a staggering failure of imagination, punning on the title of Foer's first novel, apparently" (Beck 2005: 93, 94). Robert J. Hughes evaluated the ending as superficial and tasteless: it is "fairly offensive to see a novelist co-opt such an indelible image of desperation and death for such a trite purpose" (Hughes 2005). However, these experiments can also successfully mediate between the literary and photographic worlds in a way that few 9/11 novels have yet achieved, registering greater affect. For example, *Extremely Loud and Incredibly Close* meditates upon and shows a visual record of destruction and demise, with many scattered photographs, especially of objects connected with the sky and with falling, including birds in flight, upper windows and fire escapes, trestles from bridges, the Empire State Building, the twin blue beams eerily emitting from what American graphic novelist Art Spiegelman imagined as *The Shadow of No Towers*, and a controversial Associated Press photograph of falling man from the WTC (but this time falling in reverse, as rearranged by the narrator Oskar in his hidden *Book of Stuff That Happened to Me*). As Foer emphasizes, "To speak about what happened on September 11 requires a visual language" ("Interview with Hudson" 2005). If trauma is unwritable, this novel goes beyond merely pointing that out: it offers representations including photography to overcome the limits of language. John Updike was one of the very few to consider the power of the novel's flipbook: it is "one of the most curious happy endings ever contrived, and unexpectedly moving" (Updike 2005). The images project the boy's remaining fears and his attempt to remediate the past, all while he blames himself for his father's death, manifesting that by covered his body in thirty-eight self-administered blows. His speech detaches himself from his mother and makes her weep, as when in a wounding passage near the novel's midpoint, he remembers his scream at her: "As it came out of my mouth, I was ashamed that it was mixed with any of Dad's cells that I might have inhaled when we went to visit Ground Zero. 'If I could have chosen I would have chosen you [to die]!'" (Foer 2005b: 171). Outbursts like this one, accompanied by the self-bruising, victimhood at the hands of bullies, and an inability to make friends will tempt the boy's therapist to have him hospitalized, away from both the mother and grandmother who seem the most devoted figures in his life. It is an offer wisely rejected by the mother, because rather than medicating him into obedience she senses the worth of a risk, allowing Oskar to make some progress with an unknown stranger who reflects the idea of trauma as both the return of the repressed and the revisiting of unfinished business. The stranger is his grandfather, the so-called new secret "tenant" across the way. Within this chapter, we will examine how trauma sometimes makes its survivors unable to accept that others are truly dead and involves them in a quest to find the remains and to finally memorialize the dead with authentic mourning, releasing survivors from their ghosts.

## ESTABLISHING GOTHIC TENDENCIES INSIDE THE QUEST

> *It took me a week to finish the first sentence. . . . My mind wanted to wander, to invent, to use what I had seen as a canvas, rather than the paints. But, I wondered, is the Holocaust exactly that which cannot be imagined? What are one's responsibilities to "the truth" of a story, and what is "the truth"? Can historical accuracy be replaced with imaginative accuracy? The eye with the mind's eye?*
> —Jonathan Safran Foer, "Interview at BookBrowse" (2015)

*Extremely Loud and Incredibly Close* has none of the major Gothic paraphernalia that Anne Williams scrutinized in her influential *Art of Darkness: A Poetics of Gothic*, a critical study that helped show that Gothicism is more poetic than novelistic, that the Gothic and Romantic form one tradition, and that there are two congruent directions in the mode, male and female. Namely, *Extremely Loud and Incredibly Close* has no "fatal women, haunted castles, bleeding and mysterious warnings" (Williams 1995: 4). Nonetheless, that does not exclude this novel from the discourse on Gothic belongings. Buried in the novel are empty coffins, midnight disinterment, reburials, subtle hauntings, and reenactment for months (via a treasure hunt by a boy who remembers those searches his now-deceased father set him on before). And this novel has more stuff of Gothic dream and darkness as summoned by Eve Kosofsky Sedgwick (1980: 8–9), to wit: "an oppressive ruin" (which I identify as the fallen, smoldering WTC Towers 1 and 2); "sleep-like and deathlike states" (which the young Oskar and his Grandfather wander around in, as well as the grandmother to a degree); "live burial" (these worries Oskar has—he insists, for instance, that his mother save up for a "sarcophagus" to house his mortal remains); "doubles" (suggested by all those named "Black" that Oskar tracks and talks to); "the poisonous effects of guilt and shame" (Oskar's body is covered in welts self-administered: "I would have given myself the biggest bruise of my life"); "nocturnal landscapes" (Oskar and others dig up a grave under the cover of darkness); "apparitions from the past" (the grandfather, presumed lost or dead, comes back from oblivion; moreover, a mentor of the grandfather once sent off to a Westerbrook concentration camp materializes decades later thumbing through books in NYC though it is nearly impossible that he could have survived that death camp and that he should be alive so long); and "Faust-like and Wandering Jew-like figures" (Oskar's sojourning grandfather is an exemplar of unexpiated guilt—he has run a continent away from his pregnant wife and only come back when their child, grown to middle-age, is dead). *Extremely Loud and Incredibly Close* has what all the 9/11 novels of victimhood investigated here have: a focus on the body of those trapped by the burning towers, not a normal body but a Gothic one. Steven Bruhm's meditation on Gothic fiction's "gratuitous spectacle of the pained body" (Bruhm 1994: 146) from two centuries before 9/11 is apt as both literatures know themselves "only through acquaintance with physical agony" (Bruhm 1994: 147). For the son, his sensory take of body-destruction is primarily visual: how do these people about to die look in free-fall, how do they look on the ground, and which one of them—when he enlarges the photographs to the point of utter pixilation—is his father? The photographs are inconclusive, and this reinforces the vexing and haunting ambiguity over the identities of the dead suggested in the introduction, as well as in Bruhm's thesis of attraction and repulsion. What is more, the pictures engender a ghostliness of their own. As Fitzpatrick intuits, people "in these photographs [of the falling] are thus doubly condemned: first to the actual deaths to which these photographs are preludes; second to 'live' for eternity in the photographic emulsion" (Fitzpatrick 2007: 90). Interestingly, Avery F. Gordon extends this idea helpfully into the realm of hauntology when she finds that, "The ghost is not simply a dead or a missing person, but a social figure, and investigating it can lead to that dense site where history and subjectivity make social life. The ghost or the apparition is one form by which something lost, or barely visible . . . makes itself known or apparent to us. . . . [But] the way of the ghost is haunting, and haunting is a very particular way of knowing what has happened or is happening" (Gordon 1997: 8). Thus, the spirit draws us "affectively, sometimes against our will" into a past reality that becomes transformed by new knowledge (Gordon 1997: 8). Finally, this pictorial connection to ghosts, so inherent in the 9/11 novels and one which makes Oskar scrutinize the frozen frames of the WTC jumpers for weeks, also uncannily and poetically develops in a film that first released in the United States in September 2001, *The Devil's Backbone*. Guillermo del Toro begins the film with Dr. Casares' spiriti (Federico Luppi) reflecting on the ghostly nature of photographs and himself, "What is a ghost? A tragedy doomed to repeat itself time and time again? An instant of pain, perhaps. Something dead which still seems to be alive. An emotion suspended in time. Like a blurred photograph" (*The Devil's Backbone*). The question arcs over this whole novel, too: where is the blurred photograph that holds Thomas Schell Jr. falling in midair from the top of the tower?

When Jacques Derrida writes of terroristic "pervertability" of the media through photos of terroristic carnage, and the repetition of the tragedy *ad infinitum*, he anticipates Oskar's somber findings as the boy scours the Internet for images typically censored in mainstream print, but which he hopes will give him certainty about his father. Derrida calls coming across such images "the ineradicable root of terror and thus of a terrorism that announces itself even before organizing itself into terrorism. Implacably. Endlessly. . . .

[Here] is traumatism with no possible work of mourning" (Derrida 2003). Certainly when Oskar randomly performs his Google searches in unsafe mode, he finds all kinds of odd matter that he cannot process at the time, and which will return unbidden later, like a shark eating a girl, an actress receiving cunnilingus, and a man crossing the WTC on a wire stretched between their roofs. But one image is paramount in its terror, seen early and recast throughout the novel: that of a soldier getting his head cut off with a sword in Iraq. Even at the novel's end, the image of decapitation rolls back to him when he applies the possibility to himself. On his mission to the graveyard with his grandfather to finish a ritual for his father, Oskar stands through the sunroof of the limousine snapping pictures of the stars. It is then he realizes the danger: the driver yells at him every time they go under a bridge or into a tunnel to pull his head in or he'll get decapitated. Through his Google searching sans parental control, Oskar knows all about decapitated heads. Oskar applies the image to himself and tries to replace with any other thought he can: "In my brain, I made 'shoe' and 'inertia' and 'invincible'" (Foer 2005b: 317). However, the images of radical Jihadist beheadings of Westerners and Western-led foreign soldiers are not so easily sublimated: they will never leave his head. No matter what "blocking words" he throws at this headless Allied ghost-soldier, the image will continue to complicate Oskar's mourning. As David Carr convincingly argues, such still pictures and videos online "deliver in miniature the same message as the towers falling.... Everything has changed, no one is safe and the United States is impotent against true believers" (Carr 2014). Carr reasons persuasively that a video beheading from Al Qaeda or ISIS provides a "triple death": murder, defilement, and an electronic pike to put the head upon—YouTube. What must shock Oskar is the full sense of justice from the Other: that the victim deserves such an obscene killing; that the executioner is only, in Fehti Benslama's memorably dark phrase, "the instrument of God's *jouissance,*" and the one who makes day into endless night (Benslama 2014: 19).

When terrorists murder Oskar's father Thomas Schell Jr. on the morning of September 11, his only child loses not only his paternal guide, and the nurturing one who would tuck him in each night but also the one guide who launched intellectual adventures. The "suspended" emotion he thus feels for hundreds of pages would seem to be abandonment. Before the Al Qaeda attack, both father and son had an ongoing habit of scanning *The New York Times* for errors and, every Sunday, launching a "Reconnaissance Expedition." One ambitious mission from his father asked Oskar to retrieve an object from every decade of the twentieth century all in one day, and the son successfully did: he handed his dad a rock. Neither of Oskar's two antisocial "friends," Toothpaste and The Minch, seems to spend much time with him, outside of the three visiting a drugstore slyly to peek at pornography, and neither enjoys the intellectual pursuits that delight Oskar. Thus, as with Keith Neudecker's loss of Rumsey, the loss of Thomas Schell Jr. ushers in a depression as it also signals a vanishing of one's dearest friend.

Neither a body nor body part is ever retrieved of Thomas Schell Jr. after his visit for jewelry-business to the WTC, and an empty coffin is buried for him, a service straining with emptiness attended by Oskar's mother and paternal grandmother, a woman with whom Oskar's bond seems second only to his deceased father, yet a woman who is never given a name.[1] Everyone else has a name, including the doorman, the chauffeur, the cab driver, and almost everyone else Oskar stumbles into on his nearly year-long quest across Manhattan to find the mysterious owner of a lock of which his father had hidden a key. As central a figure as the grandmother in this novel is yet never named, perhaps to make her more easily fulfill the role of Anna, her dead sister. With a name not unlike Poe's Annabel Lee, this sister suffers the same fate as Poe's maiden, and shares three other resemblances. She and her lover are young ("I was a child and she was a child"), the love is intense and leads to a pregnancy on the first lovemaking ("we loved with a love that was more than love—/I and my Annabel Lee—"), she buys Thomas Sr. a typewriter to write her notes only when they are both in the room ("And this maiden she loved with no other thought / Than to love and be loved by me."), and she is killed by the rain of fire from the night sky out of the planes of the RAF and USAF ("the wind came out of the cloud by night, / . . . killing my Annabel Lee") (Poe 1849: lines 5–6, 9–10, 17–18). Thus, this unnamed woman assumes not only a reflection of Anna (as when she poses for Oskar Sr.'s sculptures only to find he has carved her dead sister), but actually stand-in status for Anna—she has married her sister's Intended and, breaking their agreement, has a child by him, forcing him to relive the trauma of begetting a child who could be killed by the night sky again, and prompting his escape from New York City to the city of his first trauma, Dresden. This is a novel of hurtful words and painful silences against loved ones, of hiding one's sorrow, and burying one's guilt, but what spans nearly the whole of the book is the conducting of a search. Oskar's mother searches for someone who can make her laugh and forget, the grandmother searches for peace and her husband (and thus memories of her sister, as her husband loved first her sister), and her husband searches for forgiveness and forgetfulness. Lastly, Oskar searches for an impossible reunion with his father.

Tellingly, Derrida makes the point in *The Specters of Marx* that mourning cannot commence without a body being visible, and here now mourning is thwarted by the absence of Oskar's father's corpse: "Nothing could be worse, for the work of mourning, than confusion or doubt: one *has* to know who is buried where—and it is necessary . . . that, in what remains of him, he remain there" (Derrida 1994: 9). Now through the uncertainty over missing bodies, the Gothic finds its aperture into terrorism fiction. With trademark ambiguity and despair, it is the Gothic that moves in 9/11 fiction's suddenly emptied, blown-asunder buildings and which fills the maws of graves otherwise holding only bodiless coffins. The Gothic takes possession of all the blood-stained stairs leading to open air after the commercial planes strike. This darkest mode appropriates as clues to an awful mystery all the torn sheets of writing blowing down Manhattan streets amid the unidentifiable scraps of burned skin and scalp left by the people who wrote them.

If full or "proper" mourning is blocked or repressed by an absent body, then, a Gothic search arises. By extending his dead father's usual "Reconnaissance Expeditions" from when he was still alive, Oskar seeks the owner of a key his father owned, tucked in a vase the son fortuitously tipped in a closet over a year after his father's death. Oskar probably hopes the person or persons named as only "Black" could tell Oskar what was on his father's mind on his last morning or give Oskar some missing essence of his father. All are on a quest, and all are doomed to find something darker than they thought they would.

A folly beyond hope may be Oskar's odyssey, as even he admits that there are 472 people named Black in New York, which would take him three years to interview. The mission, however quixotic, invests a purpose to his trauma. Bryan Reuther has noted how "surviving an event that places the individual's life or physical integrity in jeopardy propels individuals to realize the finitude of their own existence. When this occurs, an individual's orientation to the world changes, and previous ways of structuring the world no longer work" (Reuther 2012: 275). This insight elucidates this novel well, in the sense that with extreme distress, in this particular case, comes the need for a reorienting journey: to find what was lost, or process the meaning (literally, the lock and the owner) that the key holds. To accomplish this is in a sense to become his father, to go about his father's duties, allowing Oskar to take back the spirit of his father into this world for a time. The suggestion, then, is that this is a subtle ghost story—not only from a coming reference to *Hamlet* and the role that Oskar will play in that drama but also from the thoroughly off-script lines and actions that Oskar will give to the dead. Paradoxically, as with Neudecker, after Oskar loses his best friend/father, he only regains his will to live by becoming the dead.

One of the weirdest and most uncomfortable parts of *Extremely Loud and Incredibly Close* is the act of substitution. The grandfather Thomas marries his dead betrothed's sister only because she slightly resembles his lover, and, in that way, they can keep her alive, pretending that Anna is still with them. "Let your body house her ghost," seems to be the grandfather's wish. And as the little sister of Anna said, "I used to watch [him] kiss my sister. . . . I wanted to protect him, which I was sure I could do, even if I could not protect myself. . . . His attention filled the whole in the middle of me" (Foer 2005: 127). The grandfather Thomas has her pose nude and sculpts her. All the sculptures end up looking like Anna, a Poe-like search for bringing back the dead and once beautiful lover, and not letting her die again. "He was trying to make me be so he could fall in love with me." She asks him to marry her, he writes in a book that "YES and NO," and they marry the next day, with one condition that again he writes in his bland book's final page: "No Children" (Foer 2005: 85). It will be a rule that is broken, bringing into the world Thomas Jr. and eventually little Oscar. After a few sessions it became clear that he was sculpting the dead Anna. He was trying to remake the girl he knew seven years before. He was fifteen, and she was seventeen when they first met. At their first initial lovemaking, she becomes pregnant and will soon die in a Luftwaffe bombing of her home. I believe that Anna's loss entraps the grandfather Thomas. On the one hand, he wants to be part of this past; on the other hand, he is unable to fully keep himself there as after her death he has decided not to kill himself but to keep moving. Coincidentally, a relational-therapy scholar writes on this same problem in a case of a father dying in the WTC and leaving behind a three-year-old child and wife: the survivors want "to live bodily in the present but to remain psychically in the past and constantly relive the events that torment. . . . That inability [to resolve time and place] ensnares the trauma victim in an existence in which he is unable to love and attachment in new relationships" (Harris 2003: 145). This is precisely the trauma paradox that afflicts Thomas and shadows his marriage: he cannot love Anna's sister, yet, to stay with or to reach Anna, he felt he had to marry her sister.

## THE SHAKESPEAREAN GOTHIC CONNECTION

*There are more people alive now than have died in all of human history. In other words, if everyone wanted to play Hamlet at once, they couldn't, because there aren't enough skulls! . . . What about digging up Dad's empty coffin?*

—Oskar on the ride to his father's burial service in and later upon meeting his paternal grandfather in *Extremely Loud and Incredibly Close* (2005: 3, 259)

That the reference above to Shakespeare's Hamlet, Oskar's father, and whoever's bones are disturbed making room for the newly dead (whether the tossed skull of a Yorick—who Oskar will play—or a prior decedent in a New York City cemetery) appear at the novel's beginning and its end suggest the primary importance of all three to the narrator. Some of the most trenchant recent work of understanding Shakespeare gothically appears in *Shakespearean Gothic* (2009) and even more percipiently in *Gothic Shakespeares* (2008), where ghosts and their messages may ambiguously be either "of truth" or may be of "devilish purpose" (Hogle 2008: 207). Illuminating how "the Gothic can help us retroactively define some of Shakespeare's own dramatic and symbolic choices" (Hogle 2008: 201), the approaches in both studies cast light on *Extremely Loud and Incredibly Close*, as well. With a few references to *Hamlet*, Foer raises a multitude of Gothic associations and questions: how will Oskar avenge his father's death? Were his father's final dying thoughts of Oskar? Who is the man so soon courting Oskar's widowed mother? Where is the spirit of Oskar's father now? How will Oskar overcome his fears and find meaning without his father? Who or what whispered to his brain to cause him to disinter his father? And what does Oskar go to find, and what will he leave there? These are not rhetorical questions, but the ones that Oskar carries through the uncanny topography of Manhattan's streets and parks.

Freighted with perhaps too many dimensions (like the play *Hamlet* itself, infamous for being multifaceted and painfully delayed in its revenge), Oskar's trauma is a multiple complex of guilt, hiding, shame, searching, fear, and paralysis. To be bereft means to sustain a loss that no one can replace, and this seems certainly Oskar's condition as he is nearly friendless now, save for his odd trinity of pen pals—Jane Goodall, Ringo Starr, and Stephen Hawking. One of Oskar's first mailed letters and one of his last go to the celebrated Cambridge astrophysicist. No longer having a father as a mentor, Oskar asks in his first letter if he can be Hawking's scientific protégé, and in his fifth: "What if I never stop inventing?" (Foer 2005b: 305). It seems that creating clever machines—often ones that defy gravity—is Oskar's dominant mental process and joy. If he ceased inventing, he would seem to stop existing, but then he might be reunited with his father, as well. Curiously, out of his hundreds of inventions planned, Oskar dreams of no machine that could determine how exactly his father died and where exactly his remains went, the very concerns that plague him for hundreds of pages. Perhaps, and in this Oskar follows his Cambridge mentor's understanding, no machine Oskar imagines can overcome a rule of quantum physics. Hawking asserts, in his *The Grand Design*, that "Quantum physics tells us that no matter how thorough our observation of the present, the (unobserved) past, like the future, is indefinite and exists only as a spectrum of possibilities" (Hawking and Mlodinow 2010: 82). But perhaps, as Hawking argues further, "the fact that the past takes no definite form means that observations you make on a system in the present affect its past" (Hawking and Mlodinow 2010: 82). Never able to decide on one version of how his father makes his final "movement from point A to point B," as Hawking might put it, from life near the top of the

WTC to death in its plaza, Oskar entertains all the possible scenarios at once of his father in the burning tower, and this changes how Oskar appreciates his father. Moreover, the quest Oskar makes now—the search for who owns the lock, the investigation into what his father's relation was to the owner (helpful, giving, faithful, kind)—may tell something of Thomas Jr.'s end. If Oskar discovers now on his sojourn Thomas Jr.'s helpfulness and sacrifice of time for others at one stage in his life (with this key from his closet vase), then it raises the strong possibility that his father may also have helped people escape down floors the day planes crashed into the WTC, or perhaps comforted them by touch or word in their last breaths. His father, a steady partner in all of Oskar's adventures and Manhattan discoveries, was emotionally everything to him, and may have been everything to strangers in their final moments, too. He becomes through this imagining of his last moments, I suggest, a more giving man than Oskar had ever supposed.

The sought spirit of Oskar's father, however, is not represented by a ghost-like King Hamlet, who has voice and movement and some command over the living, but instead suggested by the skull without agency of the figure who Prince Hamlet in the graveyard scene supposes may be a politician, courtier, or lawyer, but turns out to be Yorick, moldering in the grave for twenty-three years. Though stilled now, how both Yorick and Thomas Schell Jr. once vitalized the space they were in. Yorick evokes the Oskar's father by representing his entertaining ways, his tricky questions and his ability to make the son "crack up" (Foer 2005b: 1). These are like the acts of the court jester who once put child Hamlet on his back, just as the Schell family remembers Thomas Jr. hefting and playing with Oskar. The skull may also be a *memento mori* to Oskar, intimating that he has not as much time as he thought he had. Last, as we shall see, the skull in *Extremely Loud and Incredibly Close* is used as a weapon by the defenseless and bullied, namely Oskar, in the middle of the school play. Oskar has no way to avenge his father as all the man's direct murderers were incinerated in the crash into the WTC, and terror mastermind Osama bin Laden at the time was still plotting from an ocean and a cave away. There is no ghost in *Extremely Loud and Incredibly Close* of the traditional kind that can be sighted, felt, or heard, giving instruction to a "sensitive," a warning to the unwary, or confession to the hoped-for avenger. However, Oskar, despite his atheism, does give some mild indication of supernatural thoughts coming from outside sources. The boy can summon the courage a skull gives to destroy—at least in his mind—all his tormentors, starting with Oskar's Enemy No. 1, a nerd-harasser named Jimmy Snyder.

Oskar is asked to play Yorick in an elementary school *Hamlet*, "actually an abbreviated modern version, because the real *Hamlet* is too long and confusing, and most of the kids in my class have ADD" (Foer 2005b: 142). Nemesis-bully Jimmy gets the prized Prince Hamlet role. This marks an unexpected reinvention of the revenge story, a way of aligning Oskar ever closer to the dead and to his father, all at a perilous time when Oskar, who meditates long on the "To be or not to be" speech "which I know about from the Collected Shakespeare set Grandma bought me," is considering suicide himself (Foer 2005b: 142). Oskar confesses his depression, "my boots were too heavy.... What exactly made it worth it? What's so horrible about being dead forever, and not feeling anything, and not even dreaming? What's so great about feeling and dreaming?" (Foer 2005b: 142, 145). Oskar is on to one of the great questions about trauma here that Freud faced and was not able to adequately answer: why are the dreams of some of the traumatized not disguised? Little wonder that Oskar does not wish to dream because his dreams are the nightmare of reality, of people jumping out of burning towers to a thousand feet below. As Caruth succinctly puts it: such dreams as Oskar's are, "purely and inexplicably, the literal return of the event against the will of the one it inhabits ... the flashback can only be understood as the absolute inability of the mind to avoid an unpleasurable event that has not been given psychic meaning in any way. In trauma, that is, the outside has gone inside without any mediation" (Caruth 1996: 59). We know a cornerstone of psychoanalysis to be that "Under the dominion of the pleasure principle, it is the function of dreams to make reality of wish-fulfillment, albeit on a hallucinatory basis" (Freud 1919a: 226). Yet the dreams of veterans of World War I contemporary to Freud's era had no masquerade. They were shattering, uncoded, unmediated dreams of foot rot and muddy trenches, the trenches, infection everywhere, men going "over the top," and rat-chewed human bodies. To the fact that none of the dreams of the traumatized veterans seem to be initially wish fulfilments because they are all of ghastly and unmediated suffering, Freud sheepishly concedes, that they are special dreamers. To the absence of the unconscious's masked symbols and protection of sleep for combat veterans' dream states, Freud admits to "the haziness of these deliberations of ours, which we term metapsychological" and that "this conception of drives sounds strange" (1919a: 238). The best he can do to get out of this bind of bald or realistic dreaming for the war-traumatized is to suppose, with some strain, that "these dreams seek to assert control over the stimuli retrospectively by generating fear—the absence of which was the cause of the traumatic neurosis in the first place," all of which is a function "more primal than the objective of gaining pleasure and avoiding unpleasure" (Freud 1919a: 226–227). Their initial absence of fear signals unpreparedness, wild surprise, or "fright" in combat: such undisguised or documentary-style dreams supply then past's missing fear.

Oskar's fright is certainly in the air during and before his school play. Eschewing the corpse role initially, he promises to play his tambourine as accompaniment to the school play instead. When the teacher Mrs. Rigley

**Figure 2.1 Oskar (Thomas Horn) Beneath Yorick's Papier-Mâché Skull in the Film Version of Foer's Novel.** A considerable part of Oskar's complexity of a character was lost in the movie by not showing him act out this part in his school's *Hamlet* (merely instead revealing this one-second image from his memory). A success of the novel is that he vividly imagines and expresses some of the violent urges occurring from being both the double victim of school bullying and international terrorism. Screenshot from *Extremely Loud and Incredibly Close*, Director Stephen Daldry, Warner Bros., 2001.

insists there will be "no orchestra," she flatters him and finagles his support, vowing: "It'll be terrific. You'll wear all black, and the makeup crew will paint your hands and neck black, [with] . . . some sort of papier-mâché skull for you to wear over your head. It'll really give the illusion that you don't have a body." The teacher adds one more promise that seems an outright lie: "If anything, I'm afraid you'll steal the show" (Foer 2005b: 142). We know from Shakespeare's play that Hamlet is unable to act. In the school production, removing Oskar from those roles that allow the possibility of action breeds the above bullied impotence and Gothic despair in him. There is a compulsion in him to move somehow through the play, but he has no script, no object of revenge, no Laertes, no obvious anger-target. However, when the school production aligns with Oskar's fantasy-designs, impotence gives way to dreaming. The costume department plays into Oskar's own plans for a prototype of an invisibility suit that could keep people safe,[2] so finally he accedes: "I was [now] excited to be Yorick" (2005: 142).

What Gothically and bloodily captivates in *Extremely Loud and Incredibly Close* is how Oskar becomes the dead in order to attack all the wrongs or brutality he sees living in his world. This not only sabotages the play of course but also lets Oskar construct his own vigilante tale, one where humor meets horror, and one that reddens the grave of this school stage. With the impossibility of playing the part of Hamlet in the production—despite the overwhelming intertextual presence of the play in his life—comes this substitute desire to become the dead. Ultimately to act dead is, for the son, to become the father for a time, to conjure the lost Thomas Schell Jr. Thus, rather than only attempting restoration of his father's damaged legacy as Hamlet does for his murdered father through "performance of dramatic roles" (Townshend 2008: 61), Oskar's ad-libbed and subversive dialogue as a skull identifies with his father's dead state. At the same time, Oskar's dead-one wreaks vengeance on all those who would terrify through threats or actual violence, such as the grand tormentor of the weak, Jimmy Snyder. But more than that, we see an anger erupt not only against the living who terrify others but also against *all* those alive, a kind of contempt and Gothic rage against the breathing for no longer being part of their world:

> ME. *I knew him, Horatio; a jerk of infinite stupidity, a most excellent masturbator in the second-floor boys' bathroom—I have proof. Also, he's dyslexic.*
> JIMMY SNYDER. *[Can't think of anything to say]*
> ME. *Where be your gibes now, your gambols, your songs?*
> JIMMY SNYDER. *What are you talking about?*
> ME. *Succotash my cocker spaniel, you fudging crevasse-hole dipshiitake!*
> JIMMY SNYDER. *Huh?*
> ME. *You are guilty of having abused those less strong than you: of making the lives of nerds like me and Toothpaste and The Minch almost impossible, of imitating mental retards, of prank-calling people who get almost no phone calls anyway, of terrorizing domesticated animals and old people—who, by the way, are smarter and more knowledgeable than you—of making fun of me just because I have a pussy [Oskar's cat]. . . .*
> JIMMY SNYDER. *I never prank-called any retards.* (Foer 2005b: 145–146)

Jimmy's amusing inability to remember the lines—comparable to Hamlet's amnesia—makes him produce a memorable counterscript. This is dialogue truer to his experience, and which subverts the canonical text. For Oskar's part, the combining of death remembrance and unmasking, along with "intolerable wrong," "thirst for revenge," and blood spilled "on hateful objects," as Coleridge conjured in "The Pains of Sleep" (Coleridge 1803: line 24), imbues the novel with Gothic bloodlust and madness. With this violent release comes a pairing with *Falling Man*, in the most explosive scene we will see of Oskar, where his mind, like that of another character from *Hamlet*, becomes "marvelously distempered" and pulls the prosthetic skull off his head: "I smash it against JIMMY SNYDER's head. . . . I keep smashing the skull against his skull, which is also RON's skull (for letting MOM get on with life) and MOM's skull (for getting on with life) and DAD'S skull (for dying) and GRANDMA's skull (for embarrassing me so much) and DR. FEIN's skull (for asking if any good could come out of DAD's death) and the skulls of everyone else I know" (Foer 2005b: 146).

Beyond reinventing a role for Yorick's bones, Oskar shows how violence against oneself and others is a predominant act among the traumatized, as the *DSM-5* reports, and so readers should not be shocked, despite Oskar's sensitivity throughout much of the novel and his angel-like preference for always wearing white. The triggering cue for the assault could be anything. The *DSM-5* reports that for the posttraumatic afflicted, the cue could be "high winds, tall buildings, a person who resembles the perpetrator, anything symbolic of the attack" (American Psychiatric Association 2013). Functioning for over a year with enormously high levels of stress hormones, Oskar detonates, and perhaps the cue was the bully saying and doing acts connected with Oskar's father, appropriating Thomas Jr.'s role and leaving the son violated. What is less understood are Oskar's self-administered bruises, which is not seen in the other 9/11 novels. Psychologist Jo Hemmings argues that self-harming is seated actually in a lack of inner self-esteem. Oskar knows himself to be a misfit, and if the bruises give pain, perhaps "the pain and pleasure access are quite close. Self-harming is quite similar to the high a drug will give you. It gives you pleasure while you're doing it. Again the self-harming leaves scars but at the time you're doing that self-harming the intensity of the pain is pleasurable and it is very hard for people to understand who have never considered doing something like that" (Hemmings 2013).

Outside of releasing pressure through self-bruising and tearing apart scripts, Oskar finds some solace in reversing natural laws throughout the novel via developing Dr. Seuss-like inventions. One invention makes a 9/11 jumper harmlessly bounce back to his or her office and not fall onto the WTC plaza, as seen in the book's final images to us, or the "flipbook" as John Updike calls it. Oskar becomes thus a tambourine-playing Orpheus of a boy obsessed with bringing back the dead and meeting his father. Hilary Mantel's understanding can reveal something of Oskar's mourning drive: "When we talk about ghosts, we are speaking in layers of metaphor. We are not usually speaking about wispy bodies in rotting shrouds, but about family secrets, buried impulses, unsolved mysteries, anything that lingers and clings. We are speaking of the sense of loss that sometimes overtakes us, a nostalgia for something that we can't name. We want to undo death; we love the idea of the soul, but we are incurably addicted to the body, and we want the dead back" (Mantel 2005: 4–5). Oskar despairs of the search for what is lost initially, but by meeting others who are wounded by divorce (Mrs. Abby Black), loneliness (her ex-husband, William Black), the death of a lover and the horrors of bombing (neighbor A.R. Black, Oskar's grandmother, and his newly found grandfather), he is spurred on, inquisitive of their trauma, entangled by their suffering and unhealed wounds. As Reuther notes, after a traumatic episode, "Individuals may question their self-concept and render themselves with a foreshortened sense of the future as well as a plethora of other psychosocial issues . . . [yet] experience a renewed sense of purpose" (Reuther 2012: 275). Thomas Jr. turns out to be the subtlest of ghosts in the cache of novels this book considers. He (through dying) invisibly brings both his son and his father physically closer. Oskar starts taking on the roles of the father in the family, and the grandfather begins accepting Oskar as a kind of son by skipped generation. The wisdom of the book is the realization of a communal trauma and attempt to help heal the others, as when Oskar repeatedly listens to and hugs other sufferers.

## BEHIND EVERY TRAUMA STANDS ANOTHER

A favored or repeated metaphor for the traumatized brain like Oskar's in much 1990s theory is the poem of the Crusader Tancred and his paradoxically twice-killed lover, one authored by Torquato Tasso in his epic *Jerusalem Liberated* and ruminated upon by Freud. Freud would deem the account exceptional in *Beyond the Pleasure Principle*, as possibly the "most moving poetic picture of a fate":

> Its hero, Tancred, unwittingly kills his beloved Clorinda in a duel while she is disguised in the armour of an enemy knight. After her burial he makes his way into a strange magic forest which strikes the Crusaders' army with terror. He slashes with his sword at a tall tree; but blood streams from the cut and the voice of Clorinda, whose soul is imprisoned in the tree, is heard complaining that he has wounded his beloved once again. (Freud 1919: 24)

As Caruth interprets it, "The actions of Tancred [are] . . . the way that the experience of a trauma repeats itself, exactly and unremittingly, through the unknowing acts of the survivor and against his very will. . . . [R]epetition [is] at the heart of catastrophe—the experience that Freud will call 'traumatic neurosis'" (Caruth 1996: 24). The seemingly impossible second death that the killing lover delivers (who is also a trauma victim from it) is worth contemplating in relation with *Extremely Loud and Incredibly Close*. An aspect that trauma scholars have not much inspected is that the second killing occurs in a "strange magic forest" that even seasoned crusaders who have traveled over Europe and Asia Minor fear. Tancred is not in a place that others can typically access when this second murder occurs, just as figures in *Extremely Loud and Incredibly Close* are consistently operating—during their frequent periods of traumatic dissociation—in a place not in the present but a strange forest of the past. Certainly, a portion of Oskar's trauma is repeated again and again. Part of his unhealed wound is that his father left five messages at the home, and Oskar was too fearful to pick up the phone on the last call: one assumes he did not know how to talk to a man about to die, and slid into denial, burying the message machine in the closet. He recites his father's messages throughout the novel down to the seconds between his father's pauses, has reinterpreted it into Morse code, and even fashioned a bracelet out of the messages for his mother. Consistently in the readings of Bessel van der Kolk in the 1990s (which influenced Caruth) to his memoir/trauma-meditation in 2014, *The Body Keeps the Score: Brain, Mind, and Body in the Healing of Trauma*, it would appear that the central problem of the trauma victim is the unexpected, unwanted return to the scene of the trauma and all this repetition, leading to a steady cancelling of the future for the victim.

Caruth via van der Kolk hints at the Gothic-possession dimension when she addresses how Freud wonders at the peculiar and sometimes uncanny way in which catastrophic events seem to repeat themselves for those who have passed through them. In some cases, Freud points out, these repetitions are particularly striking because they seem not to be initiated by the individual's own acts but rather appear as the possession of some people by a sort of fate, a series of painful events to which they are subjected, and which seem to be entirely outside their wish or control (Caruth 1996: 1). Strongly in *Extremely Loud and Incredibly Close*, this construct is borne out as the paternal grandfather comes back to New York City only because of a replay of an earlier trauma, the death of his child (the first time the child was embryonic; the second time the child is middle aged). However, one of the most emphatically argued claims of 1990s trauma theory is that the victim cannot remember much of the experience due to its "overflooding" nature; here, in particular, is where some of our novels under study issue the most stringent challenge.

## MEMORY DEBATES

*The ordinary response to atrocities is to banish them from consciousness.*
—Judith Herman, *Trauma and Recovery* (1997)
*It is hard to forget repulsive things.*
—Mark Twain, *The Innocents Abroad* (1869)

We can assuredly agree by now with Rachel Greenwald Smith that "representing 9/11 as narrative content is . . . a highly problematic endeavour" (Greenwald Smith 2011: 164). As I have developed, Butler, Herman, Caruth, Felman, Greenberg, Leys, Radstone, van der Kolk et al. contend that some violence is so obscene, towering, or injurious to one's integrity, self-concept, and worldview that its victims do not comprehend the import of what happens at the time or even later. Memory reduces to dysfunction because the degree of "violence has not yet been fully known" (Caruth 1999: 6), and the experiencer may entirely forget the event. Dissociation (from "the thousand-yard stare" to nightmares to night terrors to flashbacks), shame and destruction of self-image (Wirth 2005: 38), and ruptures to human relationships frequently follow. As Uytterschout and Versluys attest, the survivors may "externalise their emotions into physical or bodily symptoms," yet there is not conscious "access to the memories of the incidents that formed the basis of their condition" (Uytterschout and Versluys 2008: 218). Kacandes argues there is no hope for the victim ever recovering his or her pretraumatic identity (Kacandes 2003: 179–180). What Pierre Janet termed in 1925 of World War I soldiers in his work *Psychological Healing: A Historical and Clinical Study*, "le souvenir traumatique" is the result—a self-imposed amnesia. As Uytterschout and Versluys describe it, "The solution to overcome this dissociation consists of guiding the trauma victim from his disjointed traumatic memory to a coherent narrative memory. In other words, traumatized people have to learn to express themselves and try to fit their experiences into a larger, coherent whole" (Uytterschout and Versluys 2008: 218).

This model from the 1990s' first wave of trauma theorists is still widely accepted and vociferously defended. Prominently in 2000, Ruth Leys devoted her final chapter in *Trauma: A Genealogy* to describe Cathy Caruth's ideas, as much as she gave to Freud's concepts on trauma. The healing possibilities within Caruth's popular theory are well summarized by Joshua Pederson, "[I]maginative literature—or figural, rather than literal language—can 'speak' trauma when normal, discursive language cannot, and fiction helps give a voice to traumatized individuals and populations" (Pederson 2014: 334). Contemporary critical studies of trauma typically make reference to Caruth's concepts, while as recently as 2011 in London, Cambridge University's Centre for Research in the Arts, Social Sciences and Humanities (CRASSH) sponsored a colloquium on her work and its application to literature.

Indeed, Uytterschout and Versluys cite many of this 1990s model of trauma theory in a 2008 interpretation of who is melancholy (namely Oskar) in *Extremely Loud and Incredibly Close* and who is mourning (namely Thomas Sr.). They note the obvious sign of being overwhelmed by trauma—that Oskar's grandfather develops aphasia or the loss of speech after the firebombing of Dresden, and never regains his speech in the novel. They argue that "in a very literal sense, Thomas Schell Sr. is unable to share his traumatic experiences . . . and precludes every attempt at coming to terms with that past, . . . encompass[ing] the victim's urge to hide, to live bodily in the present but to remain psychically in the past and constantly relive the events that torment him" (Uytterschout and Versluys 2008: 222). While I accept that Thomas Sr. is in a constant state of reenactment (from watching his suffering as he approaches doors and buildings that he senses could blow off or fall at any time), the claim that he is unable to share the trauma should be reconsidered, just as Caruth's once nearly unquestioned theory should be open to critique.

While Uytterschout and Versluys and other critics consistently apply a Caruthian model to the traumas of *Extremely Loud and Incredibly Close*,[3] dissident opinions exist from psychology, and they should be considered. Trauma theory, as we shall see, is not monolithic. Although Caruth's model fits and explains *Falling Man* more than competently, the difference with *Extremely Loud and Incredibly Close* is that the narrator Oskar and his grandfather and grandmother have keen memories of the traumas they experienced and can express them—although in *writing* not in speech. The grandfather is an exemplar of this as he has not been able to speak since the firebombing of Dresden in waves from February 13 to 15, 1945, by the RAF (with over 750 Lancaster bombers) and the U.S. Air Force.[4] However, he has written over two suitcases overstuffed with letters to his son—which will be stuffed into Thomas Jr.'s coffin—giving reasons for the desertion of his wife and details of the grisly firebombing of Dresden.

Through the lens of the novel we see the cruelty of the attack, leaving civilians nowhere to run,[5] so pointlessly vicious and sweeping it would even be denounced by Prime Minister Winston Churchill.[6] The American and British efforts to put the art-city Dresden to ruin, the so-called Florence of the Elbe, were an attack so dreadful that we are still trying to measure it almost eighty years later. The photographs of the Dresden carnage are still labeled as too objectionable for viewing, and this could lead the way to meditations on the actual images of the WTC jumpers about to perish in *Extremely Loud and Incredibly Close*, much criticized for their publication in newspapers from the day after, which all the novels in this monograph muse upon.

My stance is that for some of the 9/11 terrorist novels (or *parts* of those novels), we should activate the Caruthian concepts for the way they dredge the submerged traumata, but for other texts we should be aware of this particular trauma theory's limits. For instance, in *Extremely Loud and Incredibly Close*, we could argue that the Caruthian model helps understand a character's aphasia (like the grandfather's) or some lacunae in the narrative, places where the victim leaves out something elemental that must be sleuthed. But rather than exclusively meditate on what is missing in a text and what those missing parts may mean, it is also beneficial to scrutinize what *is* said in the novel by the sufferers of trauma. It may be too reductive to imply or declare that trauma cannot be fully expressed, when a wealth of survivors' accounts of the Holocaust already exists, denoting horrors with explicit detail (witnessed vivisection, starvation, shooting of children, mass hangings). Spanning four decades, a sampler of Holocaust-oriented nonfiction and autobiographical fiction startles us in what it is able to express, from Tadeusz Borowski's harrowing *This Way to the Gas, Ladies and Gentleman* (1959), to Simon Wiesenthal's *The Sunflower* (1969), Elie Wiesel's *Night* (1972), and Primo Levi's *The Drowned and The Saved* (1987). These form a quartet of voices of the traumatized that nonetheless unflinchingly tell of the abyss, all remembered by the victims themselves instead of imagined by nonparticipant novelists. All of these memories strongly reinforce Richard McNally's important and well-supported challenge of van der Kolk and Caruth's paradigm, especially from his *Remembering Trauma* (2003) and *What is Mental Illness?* (2011).

Harvard experimental psychopathologist McNally finds a wealth of errors, supported by over twelve other studies, to show that van der Kolk's "theory is plagued by conceptual and empirical problems" and supporting that critique with reference to no fewer than a dozen other clinical studies (McNally 2003: 179). The neuroscience research and empirical studies that McNally cites do not support the idea of "traumatic amnesia." Moreover, he wisely points out that "one cannot conclude that a person who does not think about something for a long period of time—who has 'forgotten' it, in everyday parlance—is suffering from amnesia. Amnesia is an inability to recall information that has been encoded. We cannot assume that people have been unable to recall their abuse during the years when they did not think about it" (McNally 2003: 184). His opponents on trauma face their greatest challenge over representing the "unexpressible." As McNally points out, though, "Contrary to van der Kolk's theory, trauma does not block the formation of narrative memory. That memory for trauma can be expressed as physiologic reactivity to traumatic reminders does not preclude its being expressed in narrative as well" (McNally 2003: 183). Frequently, "[P]eople who have experienced harrowingly close brushes with death (such as falling off a mountain) often report extreme dissociative alterations of consciousness (time slowing down, everything seeming unreal), yet they remain fully capable of providing detailed accounts of their experiences" (McNally 2003: 182). Joshua Pederson sums up McNally's findings well by concluding that "After reading McNally, one recognizes that Caruth's theory of trauma is damaged by the material he gathers, as significant strains of contemporary psychological research suggest that trauma victims can both remember and describe their traumatic past in detail" (Pederson 2014: 338).

As literary evidence for McNally's view, I would like to raise ten places (in the block quotation below) where the grandfather can indeed recall his traumatic suffering at will on the night that his pregnant beloved is murdered by the Allied planes overhead (as noted in a letter to his son on March 11, 1978). Registered in greatest detail, it increases our understanding for his need to run away from his new baby in New York City, as he didn't want to bring life into the world a second time after losing the first baby along with the mother Anna during the firebombing of Dresden. These vivid memories of his also suggest weakness in the trauma theory that overstresses or oversimplifies how memory works for the traumatized. Key is to quote the grandfather at length to suggest how seemingly in control, detached, unflinching, and specific he is, without breakdown or interruption. On the same night his lover tells him: "Don't be a child. . . . I'm pregnant. . . . Please be over joyed [*sic*]" (Foer 2005b: 210), incendiary bombs fall over Dresden. Thomas Sr. "kissed her, I kissed her stomach, that was the last time I ever saw her. At 9:30 that night, the air-raid sirens sounded, everyone went to the shelters." Then, through the night, over one hundred Allied planes fly over and the bombs start falling. Thomas Sr. sees a mother on fire running with a quiet baby in her arms, witnesses humans melted into pools, and sees the doors to the zoo's carnivores ripped open. A zookeeper with his eyes burned closed insists to Thomas Sr. that he must find the carnivores and demands that he shoot every animal he sees. Thus, Thomas Sr. will kill a bear cub climbing atop its dead mother, a camel (though it takes twelve bullets), a rhinoceros, a giraffe, a zebra, sea lions, and an ape (in whose simian "eyes I was sure I saw some form of understanding, but I didn't see forgiveness" [203]). It is hard to imagine where Thomas Sr. has left out any of the horrors from his sensory-overloaded memory of Allied attack here, as his five-page account, of which the above is a small portion, is shattering. Notably, the grandfather's index of horrors is not partial, missing, fragmented, or unrecoverable. It has simply not been asked for by anyone. In fact, one discovers the same bitter sharpness to anguished memory elsewhere via Lawrence L. Langer's extensive interviews from *Holocaust Testimonies* (the 1991 National Book Critics Circle Award winner) with survivors detailing Axis horrors. There, survivors of the Shoah offer amply detailed memories of atrocities they suffered and witnessed in the concentration camps and in Nazi slave-worker factories.

## CONCLUSION

*In our postmodern era of terrorism, it is significant that postmodern literature has become possessed by a Gothic imagination.*

—Maria Beville, *Gothic-Postmodernism: Voicing the Terrors of Postmodernity* (2009)

The Gothic impulse in this novel is spotlighted by how characters attempt to live physically in the present, but psychically in the present. The ghost—or just an imagined voice of what the dead might be saying, as often in Oskar's case—becomes the uncanny mediator to the victim between these uncanny states and times, of when Dad was here, and when he is not, despite all the ghostly objects of the father surrounding Oskar. Negotiating the edge that represents the time before 9/11 and after it is poignantly described by another child whose father died on 9/11 in real life: "When there is noise in the hallway, . . . Daddy is coming back. [Yet] I know he isn't because he was in World Trade Two" (Harris 2015). Now, with some hope rising by book's end, Oskar imagines his father's voice saying he *is* proud of him, not that he *was* proud of him, a vital difference.

Oscillating then between the Caruthian model (of the mind overwhelmed and retaining little or no conscious recall of the event and being prey to intrusions of actual instances or scenes of violence) and the McNallian theory of complete or overmuch traumatic detail that can be summoned, this field of 9/11 novels supports two different, even oppositional readings of trauma. Keith Neudecker had only partial memory of the WTC fall and death of his office mate in *Falling Man*, Oskar and Thomas Sr. seem to recall past events (especially explosions and bombings) at will, and the next novel *The Writing on the Wall* features overwhelming shocks and sexual abuses buried decades ago that are exceptionally difficult to disinter, except in the face of a new disaster that weakens the crypt of memory where past traumata lay. The erupting theoretical differences between the two major trauma schools will

Figure 2.2  The Traumatic Loss of Innocence in the Young Face of Oskar at Left (Thomas Horn) Evokes the Lost Look in His Grandfather's Visage, One Having Lost a Father and the Other Having Lost a Son. For his mournful part as the grandfather at right, Max von Sydow was nominated for an Oscar, and the movie itself was an Academy Award nominee for Best Picture, losing to Director Thomas Langmann's *The Artist*. Screenshot from *Extremely Loud and Incredibly Close*, Director Stephen Daldry, Warner Bros., 2001.

advance an argument regarding the place of the Gothic in trauma that I will elaborate in the following chapter.

## NOTES

1. As central a figure as the grandmother in this novel is yet never named, perhaps to make her more easily fulfill the role of Anna, her dead sister. With a name not unlike Poe's Annabel Lee, this sister suffers the same fate as Poe's maiden, and shares three other resemblances. She and her lover are young ("I was a child and she was a child"), the love is intense and leads to a pregnancy on the first lovemaking ("we loved with a love that was more than love—/I and my Annabel Lee—"), she buys Thomas Sr. a typewriter to write her notes only when they are both in the room ("And this maiden she loved with no other thought / Than to love and be loved by me."), and she is killed by the rain of fire from the night sky out of the planes of the RAF and USAF ("the wind came out of the cloud by night, / . . . killing my Annabel Lee." Thus, this his unnamed woman assumes not only a reflection of Anna (as when she poses for Oskar Sr.'s sculptures only to find he has carved her dead sister), but actually stand-in status for Anna—she has married her sister's Intended and, breaking their agreement, has a child by him, forcing him to relive the trauma of begetting a child who could be killed by the night sky again, and prompting his escape from New York City to the city of his first trauma, Dresden.

2. Much of the novel is an inventive, sometimes exhausting display of 9/11post-traumatic stress and obsession, shown by Oskar driven to insomnia by imagining inventions that could save people from the disaster next time: "All I wanted was to fall asleep that night, but all I could do was invent. What about frozen planes, which could be safe from heat-seeking missiles? What about subway turnstiles that were also radiation detectors? What about incredibly long ambulances that connected every building to a hospital?" (Foer 2005b: 258–259).

3. Following Caruth's conceptual framework as they explore Foer's novel are Buráková (2011), Contos (2013), Gleich (2014), Greenwald Smith (2011), Saal (2011), Watkins (2012), and Codde (2007), who observe Oskar facing the Caruthian "Catch-22" of "the radical inaccessibility of the past, [and the] . . . impossibility of closure."

4. Even an actual British bomber crewmember Miles Tripp was, in trauma theory language, "overwhelmed" from his sky view of the Dresden destruction: "The streets of the city were a fantastic latticework of fire. It was as though one was looking down at the fiery outlines of a crossword puzzle. Blazing streets stretched from east to west, from north to south, in a gigantic saturation of flame. I was completely awed by the spectacle" (Taylor 2005: 322).

5. From Dresden resident Margret Freyer, witness to the carnage that night: "From some of the debris poked arms, heads, legs, and shattered skulls. The static water-tanks were filled up to the top with dead human beings, with large pieces of masonry lying on top of that again. Most people looked as if they had been inflated, with large yellow and brown stains on their bodies" (Taylor 2005: 339).

6. Winston Churchill in a "Memo to Chiefs of Staff, 28th March 1945": "It seems to me that the moment has come when the question of bombing of German cities simply for the sake of increasing the terror, though under other pretexts, should be reviewed. Otherwise we shall come into control of an utterly ruined land. The destruction of Dresden remains a serious query against the conduct of Allied bombing" (Taylor 2005: 430).

*Chapter 3*

# Lynne Sharon Schwartz's *The Writing on the Wall* (2005)

## Avenging and Resurrecting the Dead

### CRITICAL RECEPTION

Covered far less in media than *Falling Man* and *Extremely Loud and Incredibly Close*, yet more consistently lauded than them, Brooklyn-born Lynne Sharon Schwartz's *The Writing on the Wall* (2005) garnered praise by book reviewers, novelists, and literary critics for its affecting meditations on how past losses direct characters facing a new trauma of disaster. *The New York Times* sounded perhaps the sourest notes of any media surveyed on the novel, though. The pattern of *The New York Times*' complaint undoubtedly is familiar now: the tragedy of 9/11 seems beyond words for this novel. The reviewer Cowles complains that after the protagonist Renata's "past marked by incest, a stolen child, a possible suicide or two and, centrally, the death of her twin sister at 16," the 9/11 passages seem "strangely remote" (Cowles 2005). However, *The New York Times* does concede that Schwartz's novel reveals how a latter trauma can at least reveal more of an earlier cataclysm: "the novel's most provocative aspect is its questioning of the ways public tragedy can inform and amplify private grief" (Cowles 2005).

*New York Magazine*, on the other hand, gives Schwartz's novel inordinate praise, ranking it as one of the three "best literary fiction" works to come out of America in the year of its release (Leonard 2005). John Leonard observes a rich psychological portrait "superior to the 9/11 fictions of both Ian McEwan and Jonathan Safran Foer" in Schwartz's protagonist. Renata is traumatized by the WTC fall, yet willing to handle domestic disasters at the same time: "a crazy mother, an importunate lover, a teenage mute, a dead twin, and the child she thinks she lost on a merry-go-round" (Leonard 2005). Countering his praise of style and content, however, Andi Diehn finds weakness in the novel's arrangement of the events, noting that the "plot seems to slide into a too-convenient pattern: Schwartz takes advantage of the aftereffect of a national tragedy and brings together people who would otherwise have remained ignorant of each other's proximity" (Diehn 2005). To Diehn, these collisions with others' traumas indicate a fascination with alternate histories, twins, and doppelgängers. Schwartz's characters—a teenage girl on the 9/11 streets resembling the niece the protagonist lost, an aunt who disappeared twenty years ago, and her husband long suspected of pederasty and now dying in a Houston hospital—all convincingly "tug [the protagonist] toward both an act of selfishness and one of self-destruction" (Diehn 2005). Renata's facing of the suspect uncle leads us to the matrix of trauma, memory, terrorism, and Gothic in which dread grows most fiercely in the novel. David Cockley approaches a much-meditated-upon aspect of trauma studies freshly when he notes how "Renata cannot change her own history of the facts of the past," but that she can change what parts of them she emphasizes, and this might make her a different person, either perhaps less of a wrongdoer or less of a victim (Cockley 2009: 18). Struck by the process of the traumatized victim gaining perspective on disaster, using private languages, and sometimes moving out of a "delusionary state," Bimbisar Irom stresses how Schwartz employs characters to use other characters as empty slates to "reclaim [their] lost family" (Irom 2012: 539, 535). The keenest of the novel's observations, he finds, pertain to the "quest for domestic fulfillment" and outsiders' pressure to "relinquish [traumatic] memory" (Irom 2012: 533), two yearnings expressed through all the novels I survey. At *Harper's*, John Leonard acknowledges the tendency I have addressed earlier—critics' unjustified marginalization and neglect of 9/11 novels, which always leaves the novelists' insights on trauma unprobed and untested. His notable idea is that New York City critics who were in Gotham on 9/11 tend to "project our own uneasiness, hysteria, or relief on the writer: he or she hasn't described the way we feel, or has softened and sanitized it up. . . . Thus Jonathan Safran Foer gets kicked about like an Aztec skull" (Leonard 2005: 85). Schwartz's truth-seeking through the dust and debris, Leonard contends, should be favorably compared to how trauma reveals itself in the essays of Joan Didion and novels of Norman Mailer (Leonard 2005: 85–86).

One of the untraced yet most striking patterns throughout the body of 9/11 novels delineated here is how a new trauma develops the obscurest aspects, unacceptable thoughts, emotional tangles, repercussions, and repressions from a previous trauma, for a reawakening of suppressed terrors. Caruth demonstrated this tendency, as we explored earlier, with the example of Freud's discussion of Tancred's accidental double-slaying of his lover. Indeed, Gothic writers frequently fashion a skeleton key to their own works of Gothic terrorism when they conclude, as Patrick McGrath has done, that "one trauma always hides another, and can therefore function to uncover it" (McGrath 2016: "Afterword"). Of all the novels surveyed here, *The Writing on the Wall* (2005) most potently portrays the dangerous but necessary resummoning of sunken memory and unprocessed horrors and unmemorialized losses that a new trauma entails. In exploring this, and in structuring her protagonist's path through a labyrinth of Gothic obsessions, Schwartz is framing the 9/11 terrorism/trauma text as a Gothic one. In what follows, I seek to illuminate the Gothic tensions prevalent in *The Writing on the Wall*, revealing the extent to which they can be decrypted through a range of trauma theories. In turn, these trauma frameworks help us to understand characters' mournful, furtive, self-destructive, and quizzical behaviors and expressions.

After categorizing these texts as a strain of the Gothic, the more consuming question that remains is what does the Gothic presence allow these books to achieve? How does the Gothic function in this trauma text, and what functions does it undertake that could not conceivably be fulfilled by another literary genre, mode, or impulse? I propose that the Gothic mode forms a ghostly trace or ghostly template, even if both reviewers and scholars often deem the texts surveyed here as realist novels. Post-9/11 fictions, I argue, make frequent recourse to a 250-year-old "carnivalesque mode," thus serving as a "discursive site" for "representations of the fragmented subject," as Robert Miles attests of the Gothic (Miles 1993: 28). It is a locus for excess, vanishing, ruin, death, and even the supernatural return for a dead twin, which we see represented in *The Writing on the Wall*. Coursing through its pages, the Gothic mode (fashioning secrets, dissembling, and family ruptures through taboo) permits this text to encrypt at the same time as it decrypts, offering a vision and vocabulary for the return of the lost, dead, and the presumed-dead. The Gothic functions in Schwartz's novel, in particular, to give its personages the fantasy that they will see their dead or their lost ones again, or the sense that their identical twin is indeed *at home* or actually *inside* of them. Beyond giving hope of the supernatural return of those from another realm, the Gothic strain in *The Writing on the Wall* suggests a revenge fantasy for the finding, control, and destruction of those for wrongdoing long ago in the past. The Gothic presence thus satisfies a Poesque need for retribution in some of these characters, namely the protagonist. At times, the Gothic works as a self-imposed punishment for one's own mistakes in love; at other times, it is sentencing without jury for others' neglectful behaviors, including sex crimes and murder.

*The Writing on the Wall* begins with a lost chance at love and will continue to structure itself with points of lost opportunities and unheralded moments of final goodbye, often producing grave survivor-guilt for its cast. On the dawn of 9/11 and before the cataclysm, social-worker lover Jack is in a hurry to get to work. Declining to make love to his girlfriend (the protagonist Renata) despite her overture, this could easily have been the last chance for him to ever touch her. For her turn, thirty-four-year-old Renata joins the morning Gotham crowds trudging to their employment. She works at the New York Public Library, and within that place, a center for languishing languages. One of her tasks is to attempt to explain in English those foreign-language concepts for which there is no one-word equivalent. With admirable brevity, Schwartz makes us cognizant of the limits of language, and focuses readers' minds on those acts and emotions that are seemingly unrepresentable by words, a constant and contested interest of trauma theorists such as Caruth, Felman, Laub, van der Kolk, and Lifton. Traversing Brooklyn Bridge, one of the most celebrated bridges in American poetry, inspiring verse from Walt Whitman to Hart Crane, she is a close witness to a vision more apocalyptic than either poet would dream. The first hijacked jet slams into the WTC North Tower, and she watches as the second strikes deeply into the South Tower, too. Then, what had been a sleepy and languorous longing for sex in her moments before turns to a wide-awake disbelief at mass murder on the scale never seen inside the USA. The language of the sublime and the spectacular summarily ensues: "Adrift in her erotic fantasies, she didn't see it happen, although she's seen it so many times since that it feels like she saw it. People around her screamed, so she looked where they were looking, at a huge marigold bursting open in the sky, across the river, flinging petals into the blue" (Schwartz 2005: 45). This first direct vision of terror amidst the screams (unmediated yet by the TV broadcasts of the attack that will intrude relentlessly upon the rest of the novel) is directly marked in the text as "nothing comprehensible." It must be filled instead with metaphors for Renata to express it, curiously mixed with attraction, eroticism, bursting, and release. The violent and horrible are made beautiful, to a degree, with the blooming marigold reference. Unexpected gorgeousness is, as in the groves of orange and lemon before the Alps in Ann Radcliffe's *The Mysteries of Udolpho*, "sleeping in the lap of horror" (Radcliffe 2008: 55). This "wondrous horror," as Renata describes it later (Schwartz 2005: 229), brings to mind the Gothic's intensely "pleasing terror," as Samuel Johnson called it in *The History of Rasselas, Prince of Abissinia* (1759). A heightened awareness of the simultaneous pull of sex and death, a Gothic staple from *The Castle of Otranto* onward, comes at the same fateful skyfall for Renata, along with a transformed vision of her world. Renata, whose Latin name literally means "Rebirth," will start seeing the world freshly now. She begins digging up the past she has buried, and what she has not disinterred will claw itself out on its own through mere chance and coincidence. The fall of these buildings is a structural echo of the collapse of the walls restraining her— her guilt, her recklessness with her three-year-old niece, her own repressed memories of her sister's loathsome seduction—and it figuratively scorches then consumes her. Such memories include the disappearance and death of her twin sister, Claudia (by either accident or foul play); the discovery that her uncle was molesting her sister (making Claudia pregnant); and personally losing Claudia's little daughter Gianna to an abduction in broad daylight ten years after she lost Claudia. When the planes cut into the WTC Towers, with their resulting grotesqueries, new anguish fills the vault housing Renata's repressed memories, threatening to take her on to her twin sister's own deathward drive.

The explosions themselves are an intriguing example of the process of the Gothic in general wherein, as Vijay Mishra observes, "the sublime threatens our very capacities of cognitive judgment" (Mishra 1994: 16): Witnesses describe what they see, but cannot understand the horrors or explain why they happened. Extending the Gothic framework higher and wider are the coming strange impulses and fateful meetings and identifications and misidentifications, fateful unions and reunions, as the order in the narrative moves toward what Mishra calls the Gothic mode's "extravagant, colorful, complicated plot[ting]" (Mishra 1994: 27).

Despite the panic-driven impulse to "walk as fast as she can" homeward to Brooklyn on the morning of the terror, Renata pauses as the flames and poisonous smoke climb higher, a gesture that recalls Keith Neudecker's refusal to run in *Falling Man* as the human stampede rushes past him. However, she is not stunned into paralysis. Rather, her stopping is to recover something long lost, though the object found would seem to readers a substitute and not the lost thing itself. Her pause in the midst of the largest attack on American soil confirms Derrida's observation in "Autoimmunity" about 9/11, namely, that on that day we would all "deny the irresistible foreboding that the worst has not taken place, not yet" (Derrida 2003: note 10, 189). The novel's third-person narrator tells us:

> An impulse she would never fathom [comes], to riffle through the papers gathered at the edge of a grilled sewer lid coated with ash. Among the paper, as if she'd been hunting for it, she found the twenty-dollar bill. . . . She had the absurd notion that it might be the same twenty dollars that went missing when she was eleven years old, causing the estrangement from her now-dead twin sister and lasting grief. Changing the course of her life. (Schwartz 2005: 47)

What is striking here is how the tower attack and this reaching for twenty dollars will explode the lies and silence which Renata has kept for eighteen years. Peculiar things happen during catastrophe, but this one concerning cash is not motivated by greed; instead, it is highly steeped in Gothic reference, revealing, as it does, ghostly traces of traumata to be decoded later. In this chapter, we will track how trauma breeds new reflections on past crimes and disappearances, giving birth to righteous rage, finally finding and holding those responsible for earlier violations.

Figure 3.1  As New Yorkers Run for Their Lives on the Streets Surrounding the WTC, Renata Weirdly Holds Back to Fetch a Twenty-Dollar Bill Tied to Traumatic Memory. Screenshot from *Inside 9/11: Zero Hour*, Supervising Producer Nicole Rittenmeyer, *National Geographic*, 2011.

## GOTHIC SCRIPTS

*Cinema is the art of ghosts. And I believe that the cinema, when it's not boring, is the art of allowing ghosts to come back.*

—Jacques Derrida, *Ghost Dance* (1983)

Before discussing the text's correspondences with the tradition of Gothic romance, and how these correspondences change our perception of the disaster, it is useful to look at other creators who have fused one genre or subgenre with the Gothic (as we examine the fusion of terrorism tale and the Gothic impulse), and how they describe and facilitate this act of genre-merging. Accepting Linda S. Kauffman's belief that "since cinema and psychoanalysis were born, like conjoined twins, near the end of the nineteenth century, cinema provides a useful lens for examining the workings of [traumatic] memory, displacement, condensation, and melodrama," I assert that we may include Guillermo del Toro as one of the foremost Gothic-oriented moviemakers in our time. Kauffman rightly cites del Toro, along with Hitchcock, Marguerite Duras, Sarah Kofman, Maya Deren, and

Tracey Moffatt, as one of cinema's key Gothic filmmakers and screenwriters (Kauffman 2009: 650). Del Toro shows a similar Gothic modality at work in many of his films, blossoming perhaps most darkly in the 2015 film of roofless mansions and incestuous, murderous twins, *Crimson Peak*, where the murderess Lucille Sharpe admits one of love "makes monsters of us all."

The day before 9/11, a war film[1] showed in North America that was also a Gothic romance and ghost story (of a dead boy and old doctor), to wit, *The Devil's Backbone*. Its director Guillermo del Toro admits to me that he now recalls nothing of the Toronto Film Festival where it premiered because the Manhattan blasts of the next day obliterated memory. The film soon engendered discourse in media related to traumas in its depiction of innocent deaths from an orphanage explosion; the forming of a proto-fascist (in the character of Jacinto); summary executions of Republican soldiers and International Brigade volunteers; and the covered-up murder of a boy long before. Because of concerns about the depiction of deaths of civilians (especially children) in the month of its release, the distribution company scaled back the release to only an art-house premiere of twelve screens in America during that September. What is especially interesting and applicable to *The Writing on the Wall*, a text which also deals with sudden death and the disappearance of children, is del Toro's appraisal that even in our terrorism-ravaged time, "the elements of a Gothic Romance have not changed that much":

> Generally, most of the action is linked to a place, to a building. In the case of *The Devil's Backbone*, it's clearly the orphanage that lies in the middle of nowhere. Within this building there is always a dark secret that is buried in the past and that affects the lives of the people living in it. It is mostly shrouded in silence. In the case of *The Devil's Backbone* it is both the murder of this child and the existence of a stash of gold hidden within the orphanage. . . . There is always a link to a treasure in a Gothic Romance, it is either gold, or a family treasure, fortune, inheritance. Finally, the element that is very important is the Romance, the passion, and absolutely carnal desires and the sexuality that brews and broods. . . . The arrival of another element in the Gothic Romance—in the center of all this darkness, all this plotting, secret hideaways, secret passages, cellars— . . . stands a pure heroin or hero. In *The Castle of Otranto* it is a pure boy and girl who are in love, and in *The Devil's Backbone* it is the arrival of Carlos the orphan, who brings a new set of eyes which explores the secret, and through the purity of his heart, unravels the mystery. . . . The Gothic Romance, and the predecessor the horror tale of [eighteenth-century] Germany, always required this virginal presence, or an innocent pair of eyes. And in that I think you have a third evolution, which is the modern horror tale, and that innocence is abandoned slowly. But to make the Gothic romance, you have to have those

almost fairy tale elements here and there. (del Toro 2013: *The Devil's Backbone* Voiceover, minutes 5.13–7.06)

If we follow del Toro's helpful description and taxonomy, we recognize that from early to late, *The Writing on the Wall* is a terrorism novel with startling plot similarities to all of the qualities of the most traditional Gothic romances that the director describes in the film and in an interview with me. However, the absence of a much-earlier trauma also sets these two Gothic works apart, and partially explains how the young hero of the film avoids the paralysis detectable in the older heroine of the novel.

In both the book and film, an adult pushes someone much younger against a pillar: the victim stumbles, falls into water, and drowns with a massive head injury. The recovery of the victim's corpse is a fraught process. The dead one then returns to the living at night.[2] In the del Toro's war film's case, ghost boy/manslaughter victim Santi (an abbreviation for the decapitated Santiago, the patron saint of Spain, and suggestive of Spain itself facing its international eclipse during and after its the Civil War) communicates with the hero/new orphan who takes his bed and desk place. Santi communicates his wish to the fearfully intrigued Carlos, but not his murderous backstory—only the words: "Bring [my killer] Jacinto to me." Carlos for a very long time has no idea why; nor could he know that little Santi looks the same as he did when he died, as there are no photographs of him about. Like many visitants

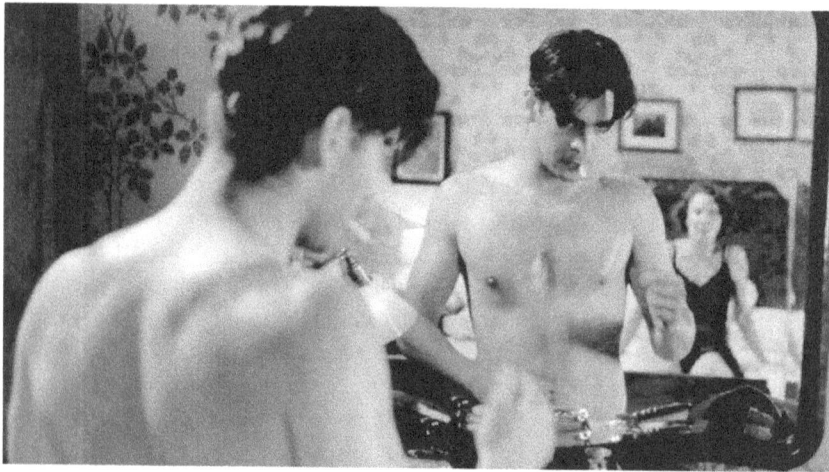

Figure 3.2 A Doomed Gothic Romance of Secrets and Ulterior Motives between the Headmistress Carmen (Marisa Paredes) and Her Former Orphan Student and Current Orphanage Caretaker Jacinto (Eduardo Noriega). Screenshot from *The Devil's Backbone*, Director Guillermo del Toro, Canal+ España/Tequila Gang/Sogepaq/Anhelo Producciones/El Deseo, 2001.

in Gothic stories, Santi wants to express his nearly unutterable story to an empathetic or sensitive listener and to hold his murderer in a death embrace. As it transpires, Santi will kill Jacinto and express his story through the help of the living orphans. Though he explodes the Santa Lucia Orphanage, the former orphan Jacinto will never achieve his base wish—to steal the orphanage's gold reserved for the Republican war effort. The gold bars only weigh him down and he drowns in a cellar pool, still a "prince without a kingdom." Though explosions also thunder over Renata's head, and though a thousand tons of gold and silver sit not far away (beneath the WTC plaza in a vault of the Bank of Nova Scotia), it is the splitting of her psychic vault that is of primary interest. The buried storehouse of traumatic memory and secrets fractures for Renata. Her subterranean life-story frees itself after the shattering of the WTC above, and the Gothic mode, as in del Toro's film, becomes its interpreter.

Just as Carlos in *The Devil's Backbone* becomes what Geoffrey Hartman terms an "intellectual witness" (Hartman 1998: 37) to another's trauma (the murder of Santi), so too, then, other 9/11 survivors would become the witnesses to Renata's multiple traumas. Their hearing of her shocks will move unprocessed "traumatic events" in others into what Caruth calls "narrative memory" (Caruth 1995: 153). As Richard Gray observes, with an attuned and therapeutic audience, one's narrative memory can be "verbalized and communicated but also . . . assimilated; the dispersed, and in most cases repressed, pieces of the event can be disinterred and delivered into some kind

**Figure 3.3 The First Sighting of the Struck and Drowned Santi's Ghost (Íñigo Garcés) by the Newest Orphan Arrival Carlos (Fernando Tielve At Right).** Screenshot from *The Devil's Backbone*, Director Guillermo del Toro, Canal+ España/Tequila Gang/Sogepaq/ Anhelo Producciones/El Deseo, 2001.

of sequence . . . with the text [becoming] both symptom and diagnosis" (Gray 2008: 130). Finally, the victim can, as Judith Herman perceives it, "see more than a few fragments of the picture at one time, . . . retain all the pieces and . . . fit them together" in a full account (Herman 1992: 2). Just such a process helps Renata move beyond blaming the victim for the violence.

Mediating the gap between cinematic example and literature, we observe a similar pattern of seeking punishment from *The Devil's Backbone* to *The Writing on the Wall*. To begin the Gothic Romance parallel in *The Writing on the Wall*, we keep in mind Derrida's observation that "modern technology of images like cinematography, instead of diminishing the realm of ghosts (as does any scientific or technical thought [leave] behind the age of ghosts as part of the feudal age with its somewhat primitive technology as a certain perinatal age), [actually] enhances the power of ghosts and their ability to haunt us" (Derrida 1983: *Ghost Dance*). One could buttress Derrida's insight with the fact that electric illumination replacing candles and gaslight did not, despite Edmund Wilson's famed prediction in "A Treatise on Tales of Horror" in 1944, kill the ghost story, and neither has any other technology so far. As Derrida intuits, such inventions—particularly when they inexplicably fail—only give ghosts one more surface to play upon, as suggested in the cinema of fright with every inexplicable light flicker and eventual stormy blackout. Though they stood as gleaming towers of postmodern 1970s design and not ancient castles, the WTC Towers still may have, in the midst of their rubble, a Gothic surface to build upon possessing taboo secrets and spectral presences.

I posit that the texts previously discussed in this volume hover between two different theoretical possibilities about trauma: that overwhelming situations cannot be adequately inscribed, remembered, and expressed, on the one hand, and the conviction that their terror is expressible, on the other.[3] This place of indecision between two perspectives on trauma is useful for showing how the Gothic functions in relation to trauma, and where the Gothic resides, as the text of *The Writing on the Wall* oscillates between these two poles. Where repressed memory will not provide details, and when a victim cannot articulate them and never expand and reconfigure the disabling flashes of violent disruption into a full account, Gothic elements emerge to ghost the margins of characters' smoky recollections. Ruined towers, the diminished skyline, ash-filled streets, and the silhouettes of body parts thrown upon the avenues act to fill the "empty coffins" of fictional trauma narratives. But beyond a Gothic *mise-en-scène*, protagonists and antagonists themselves employ metaphors of the Gothic, consciously or not, because they supply a template that intimates the horrors of the individual trauma. Very soon into this novel, we already have a skeleton of a Gothic story in its tropes. A plethora of Gothic identifications rises: doubling, unexplained disappearance, splintering of identities, grotesque violence, furtive incestuous sex, predatory males who stalk women half their age and hide their crimes well, doppelgängers, the sublime, abysses of madness, disrupted time, the uncanny, compulsions to repeat actions, hungers for revenge, paranoia, xenophobia, muteness, paralysis, and "mutilation beyond recognition" (Kauffman 2009: 649, 653, 654, 656). A sense of disintegration weighs over all, and what is worse, a lack of commemoration for what vanished. For the days to come, there is only DeLillo's forecast: terrorism's menace to kill hope for generations and make "ruins of the future" (DeLillo 2002). When trauma *does* "speak" here, it articulates in the language of the Gothic.

Gothic dread in *The Writing on the Wall* escalates by concentrating on the perils of vulnerable heroines first. Renata's twin Claudia seems always unprotected. Like the Gothic heroines stretching back to *The Castle of Otranto*, and continuing through *The Monk, The Mysteries of Udolpho, The Italian, Dracula*, and beyond, we perceive in Claudia a young woman who is "at the mercy of a . . . wicked older man. . . . She is a potential victim of his desire" (Horner 2009: 180). Her uncle Peter preys upon Claudia (the novel keeps a black veil over the details of the whole violation), but he is mentally so benighted that sometimes he confuses one twin for the other, starting shameful romantic play before he discovers the misidentification and retreats from predation. When Peter assumes that it is Claudia's whose back he erotically rubs while in the garage, when it is actually Renata's bending over to tend her bicycle, he ushers a budding shame and confusion in Renata. She feels instantly a partial victim: through the mistaken identity, Renata feels a fraction of soul-sickness and self-disgust that Claudia must face daily, and in a sense Renata becomes Claudia for a moment, long before she houses Claudia's ghost and longings in her own body. Shy at the time and caught in a liminal state between girlhood and womanhood, Renata will not fully understand or confess what was happening at this moment of intolerable intrusion until years later, when 9/11 will refocus her mind on imagining this early sexual trauma of her sister. For her part, Claudia's silence to Renata (and others) about the extent of Peter's attraction and possible molestation may not be mere passivity. It could be Claudia's sharing of the desire her father has to protect his younger brother/the twins' uncle. Gianna, the child of Peter and Claudia's taboo sexual intercourse, is born when her mother is only seventeen years old and promptly given to another family without a chance for Claudia's input or a chance for her to mourn the relinquishing of her own blood. Ten days following the birth, Claudia suffers a head injury in the early hours of the morning from falling against a pillar, and drowns in the Hudson River not far from the family home. The police never conclusively solve the case, and ambiguity reigns over all unto the novel's final pages. The remaining family will have to watch on shore later as Claudia's bloated body, looking like some rotted and unspeakable human/animal hybrid, is dredged from the river.

Ruled accidental by the authorities, the death of Claudia causes implosion in the family. Renata's father turns to alcoholism, drives into a tree, and dies—again it is unclear if it is intended or not, but enough doubt remains for his daughter to consider it suicide. The molester, Uncle Peter, goes missing, and his wife disappears soon thereafter. Renata's mother Grace, giving quixotic answers to unasked questions and making Renata feel uninterrupted survivor-guilt, finds herself institutionalized and a victim to electroshock therapy. Grace's worldview changes to that of a defeated, traumatized victim marooned by her nostalgia: "There's nothing for me out there. Nothing. You can't make things the way they were before. Don't bother trying" (Schwartz 2005: 251). Renata's guilt alloys with some real wrongdoing, however, or at least strong negligence. While Peter and Claudia's child of incest is given up for adoption initially, Gianna eventually returns to Renata's family, and Renata at eighteen years old assumes mothering duties for the niece. On one otherwise cheerful outing to Central Park, with weather much like the crystalline skies that open this novel on 9/11, the niece vanishes. Renata leaves her spinning on the horse carousel, goes away for two minutes to fetch ice cream, and the child is gone, forever to haunt the protagonist and to make the grandmother repeatedly, almost ritualistically whisper: "Where is she now? . . . Where is she?" (Schwartz 2005: 119). Ironically, when on the streets of blown-apart Manhattan years later, Renata finds a dumbstruck teenager whom she thinks resembles Gianna, and later insists she *is* Gianna, despite the inestimable odds. Renata takes her to the distraught grandmother and senses her quest has finally come to a good end. Grace, in the only moment of lucidity in the entire book and speaking as one traumatized woman to another, levels with her daughter: "Listen Renata, you need to get this child to a doctor. . . . She can't keep hiding out with you. . . . And listen, don't bring me any more children. I can't take it" (Schwartz 2005: 251). A rare and wintry smile comes to Renata, and she quips: "You're seeing things so rationally, all of a sudden. Did they change your medication or what?" (Schwartz 2005: 251). Perhaps this remark hints that Renata realizes that the "miraculous rescue" of Gianna is false, yet she has nothing with which to replace this fantasy of restoration, so she lets her dream abide.

## A CLAMOR OF GHOSTS

*What is the ghost, after all, that it should frighten us so, but our own face? When we observe it we become like Narcissus. . . . [W]e need ghost stories because we, in fact, are the ghosts.*

—Stephen King, *Danse Macabre* (1981)

As mentioned earlier and recorded in the psychiatric reports of Adler and Lindemann following the Cocoanut Grove nightclub fire in 1941, revenants of trauma victims sometimes "creep" into survivors. Indeed, the ghosts in 9/11 fictions internalize so successfully into the living that we often do not recognize them except through a trauma disorder manifesting in a protagonist's perceptions, words, and actions, mimicking those traits of the deceased. Bringing in an identical twin to the trauma equation, as *The Writing on the Wall* does, introduces more variables that we will explore later. The Gothic concentrates on the presence of ghosts as a sign of something that is unsettled and unsaid. Schwartz's fiction, like the other novels presented here, communicates the unfinished business left by terrorism, mass murder and thousands of missing bodies. Something terrible happened in the past that haunts characters and which seeks some form of resolution. Being a severe trauma, though, it is still happening. The violation so overwhelming is not over; yet characters feel they must bear witness to it and mourn it even they cannot articulate it. They cannot capture its immensity and sublime sorrow; still they heroically try, and through such a mere, imperfect medium as words.

The mimicking of the lost one, as observable in *Falling Man*, begins extremely early in *The Writing on the Wall*. It is unclear whether Renata knows that and will not admit it or whether she does not know the correspondence at all. As Irom succinctly diagnoses it, "The 9/11 attacks set in motion a series of events through which Renata tries to compensate for the past by finding substitutes for her lost family" (Irom 2012: 60). I would go further and suggest she *herself* becomes the substitute for dead family, especially her dead sister (whether killed by Claudia's own suicidal impulses or by Peter arranging a meeting by the river, dashing her against the pier, and impassively watching her fall under the waves). Within months of her sister's unsolved death, Renata withdraws from college, and in a move of identification with her sister, moves to New York City, for "that was where Claudia used to sneak off, to escape" (Schwartz 2005: 123). This is a detail that we do not learn until at almost the halfway point of the book. Like all of the 9/11 novels analyzed here, this split-time narrative format allows characters' memory to discharge at readers like shards from an explosion, fragments and splinters that are not all gathered orderly, or in a typically linear fashion but that explode in a circular blast, glimpsed at but not fully realized. What is more, this fractured narrative allows us to understand how the ghost is operating, and what characters in the novel become witnesses for the traumatized to confess to (like her first long-term boyfriend/social worker Jack), slowly pulling out some of the darker truths. Ghastly and gruesome details are exposed, reaffirming that in the Gothic, "deception, conjecture and mystery that surrounds the dead must, in the course of the narrative, eventually be submitted to the rigours of empirical proof, even if this amounts to the rendering of death and the dead, decaying body as a horrid spectacle" (Townshend 2008: 74). We will need to see how "each of Renata's corpses had . . . a distinct way of being dead" (Schwartz 2005: 122).

At this point, a concept of Derrida's dilates the portals toward the haunted world of this novel, and we see clearly, as Virginia Woolf once wrote in discussion of Walpole and others, "the ghosts within us" (Woolf 1945: 51). In *Ghost Dance*, we remember that "To be haunted by a ghost is to remember something you've never lived through. For memory is the past that has never taken the form of the present" (Derrida 1983). Caruth describes that same paradox through trauma theory, by defining a flashback as a "history that literally *has no place*, neither in the past, in which it was not fully experienced, nor in the present, in which its precise images and enactments are not fully understood" (Caruth 1995: 153). Therefore, a catastrophe like 9/11 has an impossible "history that is constituted by the very incomprehensibility of its occurrence" (Caruth 1995: 153). Likewise, time-boundaries between discrete events vanish in *The Writing of the Wall*. In one paragraph, the WTC trauma forces together the disparate past into one agony. Renata flashes back to her sister leaving the house on the fateful night of her death, believing that she should have followed her; she has a similar strobe-like memory of the police delivering the news of Claudia's death days later, and then Renata casts ten years forward placing her sister's daughter Gianna on a carousel in Central Park before someone abducts the little girl. The young Renata who was witness to both vanishings is not the protagonist that we have in the story now, older, with different reactions to pain, with nuanced understandings of love and sacrifice and longing and desire for forgetting, though she remains just as psychically blocked as when she lost Gianna. In one other critical respect, the Renata providing this story is different. She is haunted not only from the outside. Like other living victims of 9/11, in particular, DeLillo's Keith Neudecker, there is someone else inside of her. Though others will peer at her and swear they had "seen a ghost," she protests halfheartedly "I'm not a ghost. I'm Renata" (Schwartz 2005: 197).

We recall how Maria Torok and Nicolas Abraham developed their theory on the arrival of ghosts through a rereading of Freud's *Mourning and Melancholia*, an endeavor which Derrida discusses at considerable length in a forward to their *The Wolf Man's Magic Word* (1976). In that volume and in other media (from strikingly unconventional films of interview and action like *Ghost Dance* that in 1983 that explored living traces of the dead, to volumes investigating the vulnerability a friend's death opens in us like *Memoires: for Paul de Man* in 1986, to anthologies of essays on a number of dead colleagues like *The Work of Mourning* in 2001), Derrida keeps revisiting ideas of the presence and the absence of the dead. As the years go by, Derrida's philosophical remembrances of his dead friends grow more affecting. The cry of the heart in them and the utter loneliness from missing these intellectual friends can often be summed in the idea of missed chances, that is, how would these fellow thinkers be challenging me, changing me, and completing me if they were still alive now? This longing for what we are missing pairs well with what one widowed survivor of 9/11 Abigail Carter says, exactly fifteen years later on September 11, 2016, of her husband forever lost in the burning towers: "I think the hardest thing is just not knowing what you're missing. And at the same time, knowing how much you're missing" (Laura King 2016). Beyond exploring the impossible query of what we are missing, Derrida also keeps revisiting ideas of introjection/ idealization versus incorporation/interiorization in these meditations. In Freud's idea of "normal" mourning, Derrida contends, "one internalizes the dead. One takes the dead into oneself and assimilates them. This internalization is an idealization. It accepts the dead. Whereas in mourning which doesn't develop naturally, . . . part of us. They just occupy a particular place in our bodies" (Derrida 1983: *Ghost Dance*). Later, with a careful skepticism, Derrida notes *both* types of mourning have flaws: the mourning that supposedly introjects (that assimilates; the one where we even imitate the dead for a time, as he admits he did with some of his friends) and the melancholia that incorporates. Both rather narcissistically "betray the [deceased] other's otherness" (Derrida 1989: 95). As he raises the aporias, lists the incompatibilities, and explores the contradictions of mourning and melancholia in the aforementioned works, he ends arguing compellingly in *Memoires: for Paul de Man* that "impossible mourning" would be preferable. Such a mourning is the kind where the loss can never be comprehended or "closed" as it would be in introjection, and yet it is ethically preferable to incorporation as well, since it leaves "the other his alterity, . . . [and] refuses or is incapable of taking the other within oneself" (Derrida 1989: 95). Impossible mourning, his theory goes, would be precipitated by "a movement of renunciation which leaves the other alone, outside, over there, in his death, outside of us" (Derrida 1989: 35). A "kind" renunciation of the dead becomes the necessary betrayal: it would, paradoxically, signal the greatest respect for the dead.

For years, Renata and her parents' melancholia for the dead Claudia (and their grief for the missing and possibly dead Gianna later) seem to follow the "tomb-creating" incorporation which does not signal respect, which does not ethically acknowledge Claudia's "infinite remove" (Derrida 1989: 6). They take the two dead females "inside them" and do not let them be spoken of on "the outside." But it may be that after 9/11—which is the great tribulator for characters, the great vault-breaker of once securely sealed past traumas—that Renata's incorporation of the dead fails, and she starts to move to this impossible mourning. What makes her incorporation "successfully fail" and move her to a more ethical relationship toward the dead is, ironically, her "tender rejection" of the dead, as Derrida would put it. The rejection comes in the form of breaking a vow once given to her twin: ending the silence over Claudia's incest and her murder at the hands of a family member, and dissolving the incorporation of her sister by finally divulging all to her boyfriend Jack, confessing and releasing all this decades after the Gothic events transpired. It is a draining and torturous process, summoning self-hatred and restless ghosts, but it ensures that the twins will no longer *both* be dead to this world.

As evidence that Claudia was not properly mourned at her death, but simply "taken inside" the survivors, we could remember that there was no mention of commemoration for her, no rites, and not even a basic funeral. Instead, we see what the family calls a "something" recovered, which receives neither ritual nor recognition, nor any full investigation of "its" death. With Gothic ominousness, Renata detects a noticeable wince as her parents look at her when police hook and pull her twin's swollen body—just ten days after delivering her baby—out from the river mud and muck. The human looks inhuman and sinister here, and family cannot say to each other that this corpse is either their daughter or sister. There is retrieval, but there is not an accompanying ceremony and celebration of what she gave her family and others in her short lifespan. They are authentically overcome by her death and cannot stop thinking of it; yet they cannot ask too much about it because to enquire means they have to ask more questions of who the father of the baby is, and their suspicion must be for the worst as they never saw Claudia with a boy—only her perversely attentive uncle. The incest-shame surfaces when, even dredged from the waters, the twin's cadaver betrays a monstrous, obscene, and impossible fertility: "Claudia's stomach was puffed up, as it had been when she was pregnant" (Schwartz 2005: 100). The parents cannot admit much to others of the loss of their daughter, which must only add to their unbearable suffering and keep the grief constant, because this taboo strikes them dumb.

Three moments arise in *The Writing on the Wall* revealing how Renata's grief for his sister is changing. The three moments each give a deeper clue about her twin's suffering, and each is occasioned by a 9/11 discovery. The first flashback to Claudia's movement from missing person to recovered body comes immediately after Renata spies signs plastered everywhere after 9/11 showing faces of those yet missing from the WTC. Significantly, Claudia sees an image and caption of a lost young woman—"Stefania Pignarelli, worked on 87th floor of South Tower, wearing striped miniskirt and black top, mole on right cheek, yin-yang tattoo on lower back" (Schwartz 2005: 94)—and the sign ushers reflection on her own loss. The "writing on the wall" here is allusive,[4] but it is literal for Renata: a search for what she still loves and what she has no more.[5] Renata muses on "Signs, what a good idea. It never occurred to her to put up signs for her missing. Claudia: age sixteen, 5'7,' slim, long black ponytail held in a wide chrome barrette, dark eyes, olive complexion, wearing jeans and Nike sneakers, striped tank top" (Schwartz 2005: 94). Looking at this mirror-like sign of a lost young woman, Renata sees herself, and sees her dead sister as herself. It makes her recall when the Hudson River dredgers "dragged in something big and dark and caked with mud, hauled it onto the boat and headed to shore.... A terrible smell drifted to shore; soon they could see Claudia's face, green and bloated, her hair tangled with mud and reeds, her clothes shredded, her leg bent back at a crazy angle" (Schwartz 2005: 100). Now, after 9/11, Renata remembers that moment as if "it was like seeing herself, the way she might look, dead" (Schwartz 2005: 100). A ghostly possession follows.[6]

Claudia becomes the shade that lives in Renata, as well as a ghostly burden of guilt, failure, and separation. Indeed, such traumas and their neurosis-fueling power became an interest of Abraham and Torok, so much so that their English translator and foreword-writer Nicholas T. Rand describes their meditations in perfectly Gothic terms: psychic obstacles "include the phantom, an undisclosed family secret handed down to an unwitting descendant; the illness of mourning, which the authors define as bereavement complicated by an untoward sexual outburst in the mourner at the time of loss; incorporation, or the secret and vital embrace of an alien identity; and the secret, or crypt, which 'entombs' an unspeakable but consummated desire" (Rand 1994: 16). Rand's recourse to Gothic vocabulary and tropes to explain trauma matches Renata's metaphors of anger, miscommunication, and disease as well, a pattern observable in all the fictions that this book researches.

Into this vacuum of mourning, as if to occupy the space where ritual and commemoration often exists elsewhere, ghosts stealthily move, a characteristic dread that locates the novel firmly within the Gothic tradition. Claudia is dead but not gone, not contained. Encrypted onto or entombed inside her sister, in times of disaster, Claudia returns in force, for "a ghost never dies, it remains always to come and to come-back" (Derrida 1993: 123). Just as werewolves may "wear their fur on the inside" according to Stephen King, so some ghosts dispense with winding sheets, instead becoming the visitants within us: "They can haunt our body and ventriloquise our speech. So the ghost is enclosed in a crypt, which is our body. We become a sort of graveyard for ghosts.... The other's unconscious speaks in our place ... plays tricks on us. It can be terrifying. That's when things start to happen" (Derrida 1983: *Ghost Dance*). The ghost Claudia "ventriloquises" Renata's speech, and adds her own rashness, contempt, disdain, and wounded distrust. Indeed, "things start to happen" when Renata becomes Claudia in her behaviors, in both her sexual abandon to many men and in her search for her sister's daughter. Renata, who had shown no interest in promiscuity and saving lost girls before her sister's death, becomes obsessed with both of these drives: she brings home male patrons twice her age for indiscriminate sex and simultaneously scans the lonely streets for waifs who need rescue. This is not merely an identification with the dead, but a traumagothic reaction, as we previously explored with survivors of the Cocoanut Grove nightclub fire where the living hosted the dead inside them. After that fire, the living soon dressed like the deceased, and began reflecting their tastes, personality, motivations, and even careers. We remember this syndrome in fictional terms, as well, when Neudecker "becomes" his dead best friend Rumsey, pursuing the identical women to those of his friend's tastes, pursuing the same fetishes with them and leaving his job to play poker, these three forming the games that Rumsey most loved. We observe, again, how young Oskar "becomes" his father when he objects to what he perceives are the new suitor Ron's intentions on his mother. Similarly, addicted to death yet unable to mourn Claudia openly, Renata *is* Claudia enfleshed. Significantly—as one disaster often makes room for another—she can confess this conduct to no one in the novel until after 9/11. The information of her new mores comes only from a third-person limited omniscient narrator: "She started letting [bar patrons] come to her apartment after work. In this way she learned all about sex, and sometimes the sensation of Peter running his finger down her spine in the garage came to mind. . . . She slept with them to keep her body quiet. It was loud, her body; it set up a clamor only she could hear" (Schwartz 2005: 124). Read the first time without the benefit of combining Gothic and Trauma theories, Renata's later alarmingly frank language perplexes: "Don't leave me alone with the words I dredged up. Drown them out. . . . Fuck me like you fucked her. Ram me into oblivion!" (Schwartz 2005: 228). Such outbursts could evoke a nymphomaniacal nun from a Ken Russell film of phallic-frenzy, or the fully possessed Regan McNeil with a crucifix in one lewd hand beckoning to the priests inside her bedroom from William Friedkin's *The Exorcist* (1973). But a key difference is the tight joining of sex to death. If we sense that a substitution has been made, and remember that the only reference to dredging earlier in this novel is that of victim-recovery, we could easily replace her cry "Don't leave me alone with the words I dredged up" with "Don't leave me alone with *that body* you dredged up." The sexual phantom that screams inside Renata seems a cipher for unrepresentable fears and the horrid until we accept that could also be the response of her dead-yet-active sibling.

A fictional case that illuminates Schwartz's ghost brightly is Sarah Waters' novel *The Little Stranger* (2009), where spooks, ghouls, goblins, and poltergeists are names necessary for representing a much greater dread inside crumbling Hundreds Hall in rural Warwickshire, perhaps an ineffable, unnamable one. On the one hand, the Gothic gives trauma a voice, it inscribes trauma but it also points to that which exceeds a Gothic register. Both operate at the same time through the Gothic: this modality of anxiety allows some inscription and recording, but also lets that which must always slip away, exceed, and go unmemorialized to have a place (things that characters cannot or will not admit, but which we determine despite their reluctance to share them). The Gothic inscribes at the same moment it encrypts, puts the truth into another code, and also tucks it into a crypt. Time stays and defeats old orders and a cast of characters in Gothic and trauma novels—and for the Ayreses from *The Little Stranger*, the time is fixed at twenty minutes to nine. But the Gothic mode itself is unfixed and shuttling, flitting, peeking through the keyholes, recording, signaling its dark knowledge all the time. Between tightly held secrets and brazen confession from traumatic times, there the Gothic exists. Its ghosts are representatives for what we cannot talk about or show without destroying ourselves or bonds with others. Like the boy analyzed by Abraham and Torok, who carried his older dead sister "alive" within him by stealing garments she would have needed if she had still been growing, Renata carries her sister within her, who was, after all, the first person Claudia shared her guilty, fateful news with: "I'm pregnant" (Schwartz 2005: 58). Renata is not fully authorized to decode the encryption yet, and the ghost grants no passkey. The loss of her twin keeps Renata lost and engaged in "cryptophoria" (Abraham and Torok 1972: 131), having become, as Timothy Murray gracefully posits, "a carrier of melancholic phobia" in which "a phantasmic world sustains a separate and occult life" (Murray 1993: 89).

Carrying a sexually hyperactive phantom in her body, Renata propositions men of all kinds. Renata will not admit this, but the dependably intrusive narrator confesses it: She "wanted to think as little as possible. . . . When the men were inside her she was stopped up, less liable to spill out, leaving a crumpled skin. The man inside her was like a cork holding her together. She did it because Claudia had done it, to keep something of Claudia close by" (Schwartz 2005: 125). A dybbuk resides, clings to, and sickens her body and her longings. Renata is, in effect, reborn as her twin sister. The horrors of lost identity, amidst all the other suffering post-9/11, ensue. No more potentially debilitating or "comprehensive haunting," to use a phrase of Geoffrey Hartman, could be imagined than to house the ghost inside oneself of another (Hartman 1981: xviii), but that is what happens now.

## THE TWINS' TOYS AND GOTHICIZED PLAY THERAPY

*Surely there must be a possibility of observing in children at first hand and in all the freshness of life the sexual impulses and wishes which we dig out so laboriously in adults from among their own debris.*

—Freud, "Analysis of a Phobia in a Five-Year-Old Boy" (1909)

So far we have explored five ways in which the Gothic expresses traumatic truth in this novel: ghostliness; corporeality (the shuddering horrors of exposing the human as a rotting animal in the Hudson River or food for rats on the WTC plaza); versions of the sublime (with language of the towers' fall); the uncanny; and mourning. But more remain, in particular, aspects of the uncanny (doubles, toys that tell allegories, and coded messages). Resisting the supposed power of twins to communicate their pain telepathically is the sexual trauma experienced by Claudia. With such identical twins, there are boundaries called into question and demarcations blurred: where does the dead Claudia end and the marginally living Renata begin? One of the most prominent messages never told by the deceased sister is that her uncle made her pregnant. When as a sixteen-year-old, Renata asks who the father of her sister's baby is, she hears only from Claudia about being attacked. Claudia says she was raped, "well, sort of—and spun out a story about going in to the city with two girlfriends a couple of months ago. They met some guys in a bar, ended up in a dorm room, drank too much. . . . She didn't want it to happen but it happened anyway" (Schwartz 2005: 59).

In twins of myth (Gilgamesh and Enkidu, Hercules and Iphicles, Apollo and Artemes, Castor and Pollux, Freyer and Freyja), tragedy often befalls the one who is a shadow self, the one who is a force of wildness opposed to any civilizing influence, and to some degree Claudia may be that. If twins have suggested duality since antiquity, as Freud suggests, then we could find resemblance here, as Claudia is the twin who cannot be controlled: "She had always been the restless and impetuous one" (Schwartz 2005: 13). However, we could not say so reductively that one twin absolutely embodies light and the other darkness, one good and the other evil, one resistant to disorder and the other opening the barriers to chaos. There is something more here: Schwartz's twins are both victims, though not entirely passive ones, and Claudia's victimhood simply comes earlier than Renata's. Thus, to some degree, the pattern with myth is broken and the narrative is in a closer dialogic relationship with twin behaviors and abilities in Gothic literature, especially Claudia and Renata's telepathy. In the twins of Gothic novels and stories, there exists a bond more intense than in nontwin siblings: there are far better ways of communicating than by words and greater defenses to shield their past from intruding outsiders. Examples could include Sophia Lee's narrating twin daughters of Mary, Queen of Scots in *The Recess* (1783–1785), William Child Green's Alphonsine and Victoria in *The Algerines, or, The Twins of Naples* (1832), Poe's Madeleine and Roderick[7] in "The Fall of the House of Usher" (1839), Daphne du Maurier's unnamed psychic twins of "Don't Look Now," Anne Rice's redhead twins Maheret and Mekare in *The Queen of the Damned* (1988), Diane Setterfield's Adeline and Emmeline Angelfield in *The Thirteenth Tale* (2006), or David Mitchell's nearly immortal Jonah and Norah

Grayer in *Slade House* (2015). Yet with all the powers they may have, trauma is still the destroyer of their bonds. Following Hartman's delineated pattern of trauma theory, Claudia cannot express her violation or give "testimony" to an "intellectual witness" through any twin-telepathy, nor can she through other means, including a darkly improvised Play Therapy.

The first documented analysis of play and games to help express a patient's fear dates to Freud's case of Little Hans (1909), who would grow up to be the successful Viennese opera composer and conductor Herbert Graff (Wakefield 2007). Largely through letters sent by Han's father (but also by rare visits), Freud examined the boy's play wishes for undercurrents of anxiety. Any creative substitutions the child would make Freud would mine with care: "[I] know that the game which Hans intended to play with the loaded carts must have stood in the relation of a symbolic substitute to some other wish as to which he had so far uttered no word. But, if it did not seem too daring, this wish might already, even at this stage, be constructed" (Freud 1909: 47–48). Charles E. Schaefer holds that throughout Freud's works, he considered play to serve three functions: "Promotion of freer self-expression (especially of those instincts considered taboo), wish fulfillment, and mastery of traumatic events" (Schaefer 2011: 4). Controlling the situation of the drawing or the toy, a child abreacts, bringing "repressed memories to consciousness and reliv[ing] them while appropriately releasing affect" (Schaefer 2011: 4–5). Through repeated play again and again, dangerously "negative emotions are brought out and released slowly as a child gradually assimilates the experience," a process that Freud's daughter Anna would bring larger attention to in her work with children (Schaefer 2011: 4–5).

Likewise thus far, key characters in the 9/11 novels have tended to invest themselves, often unknowingly, in games, play, or drama: in *Falling Man*, Keith Neudecker retrieved memories and a "presence" of his card playing best friend by leaving his job to play poker full time; in *Extremely Loud and Incredibly Close*, Oskar Schell expressed his loss and his rage through acting as the skull in *Hamlet*. In *The Writing on the Wall*, Claudia invests what cannot be expressed—what the days of incest were like, when they begin, what her pedophile uncle would say to her in the "wooing"—in play. Close textual analysis reveals how Claudia is articulating terror, its psychological impact, and its tie to trauma theory, by encoding her play farm with her rape. As there is no professional therapist the girls see who can meditate on the revealing patterns of psychic violence and physical violation from the shadow story of the girls and their play-farm, we become a therapist by default.

We know as very young children Renata and Claudia receive a colorful handmade toy farm with little wooden people one Christmas from Peter, their faraway uncle in Montana, who will not substantially enter their lives until a few years later. The children decide to name the homesteaders Farmer

Blue, Mrs. Blue, and their children Sky Blue, Powder Blue, and Pastel Blue. There is also one more little man: they make him deaf and mute and call him "Hired Hand," as someone must tend their horses. A guilty pleasure, a "lulling routine," they keep playing with the toy farm in secret for years, well into junior high. Much of Renata's memories of the farm could seem a desire to return to childhood, except for one incident whose significance needs tilling. At age eleven, Claudia's engagement toward the entrancing "little house on the prairie" abruptly and darkly changes:

> Claudia had been pressing for something truly terrible to happen. She lusted for mayhem. She wanted strangers to ride in from the plains and steal the horses or kidnap the children. She got the notion that Hired Hand, who had served the family faithfully and mutely from time immemorial, was actually an ex-convict who was planning to destroy the farm and run away with the savings Mrs. Blue kept in a cookie jar. (Schwartz 2005: 12–13)

This is seemingly a shadow story connected to the secret abuse (never exactly shown) at the hands of her uncle—one who is traumatized himself after his parents die in a hotel fire, and who is in constant need for his elder brother (the girls' father) to fund him. Encoding the farm in shocking ways, Claudia's sudden script-changing from idyllic pastoral to *In Cold Bold* merges farm play with her own nightmare and survivor fantasy/revenge saga, for "maybe Farmer Blue would catch and kill him in revenge" (Schwartz 2005: 13), a murder dream that ironically Renata will nearly act out near novel's end. The "savings Mrs. Blue kept in a cookie jar" are possible substitutions for Grace's own imperiled children, Renata and Claudia, which the Hired Hand wants to steal. What rises in the farm play is an expression of the unutterable. The Gothic keeps chipping at the cheerful bright blue paint of these farm characters to reveal their ugly underside. Hauntingly timed, her soured play dates to the same moments of the predation on her body, since Renata discovers much later that her sister and uncle started the incest while she was in junior high school. Nonetheless, Renata is not a therapist and cannot then interpret the destructive impulses in the play as a message of inner turmoil, shame, and death wish. Unknowing of it all, Renata only gives up her attachment to her farm after Claudia tosses Farmer Blue over her shoulder and he lands in a patch behind the house.

> *Renata:* "But the farm is ruined.... Why did you want to kill them all? What's the matter?"
> *Claudia:* "They've gone on long enough." (Schwartz 2005: 15)

This memory of the stoic, laconic execution of her toyfarm family comes back years later at 9/11, finally reacting darkly with the memory of Uncle

Peter's licentious stroke of Renata's back in the old garage, mistaking her for the twin he molested. The difference between Claudia's tossing Farmer Blue into a garden versus months and months of supervised therapeutic play by a psychiatric professional following sexual predation is immense. For professionals treating children who have suffered sexual abuse and who afflict other children (often younger and even more defenseless) the point is for them to "act out in *dramatic* play [only] . . . their traumas" (Moffatt 2013). For instance, through Tinker Toys, one therapist of thirty-years' experience treated a little boy named Mateo who had been sexually abused by his male babysitter. The therapist witnessed how with "His eyes wide and his face full of rage, [Mateo] took a Tinker Toy, an apparent phallic symbol, and repeatedly jammed it into the doll's mouth. 'He doesn't want it in his mouth,' Mateo said into the air, 'but he's going to get it in there anyway!'" (Moffatt 2013). When the boy forced the Tinker Toy into the small therapy doll's mouth, he was abreacting safely in a therapist's office. At unsafe moments, he was also reenacting sexual abuse "when he fondled children on his school bus, and his masturbation was also a form of abreaction" (Moffatt 2013). When the same therapist arranged ten months of play therapy for another child, the boy abreacted toward a perpetrator by "burying a little toy man in play dough" instantly. As sessions went by, he more confidently uncovered the dough, telling the therapist that, "OK, I can handle him," and working through, the therapist suggests, "his abduction and abuse" (Moffatt 2013). A vital distinction from *The Writing on the Wall* is that this counseled child still holds the man in the dough and shows that he is watchful and in control, not loosening the threat, but monitoring it. Claudia's action is the opposite. By throwing all the farm family into the garden, she shows that she relinquishes control, that both victims and perpetrators are still "out there," tossed far but not far enough, hardly buried at all and sure to surface again at unpredictable times.

Upon confessing to Renata her pregnancy six years later, Claudia, without the aid of the farm as a shadow story, laconically declares: "it happened anyway." She reaches for what Renata calls "Plain English" to explain her trauma and its aftereffects: it is what they also both term the language their parents can understand (opposed to their rapid-fire, vowel-sliced and syllable-sacrificed "Twin Language," a special argot developed since their earliest lisps and warblings, forbidden by their spooked parents, and only spoken in secret to "conspiratorial glee"). But our protagonist again understands none of it. Claudia to her closest friend and sibling can only plead: "Why don't you believe me? Because I didn't come home bleeding with my clothes ripped off? It's not always like that" (Schwartz 2005: 59). "Plain English," unfortunately, will not permit the asking of more questions that Renata needs to answer in order to settle her doubts. Normative language, like a dark screen hanging between them, cannot transfer the overwhelming details of the incest trauma, but their "Twin Language" can express something—that Claudia has been lying for years. Claudia has nullified the long explanation in normative language with two words of code that translate to "Not true." Thus, the reader is left in a mixed state: we sense some man has made her pregnant who is still a hidden threat, an unknown identity. On the other side, we are left feeling Claudia is not utterly helpless because she has not left us with a lie: she has only made an omission. She is not powerless, and this leads to more conjecture about her death. A murder or an accident could underscore her haplessness or passivity, but a suicide could suggest she made the fateful decision herself. Only one witness saw the death and his testimony is unreliable, but following this textual analysis, there seems more evidence to believe she had the strength to take her own life.

## ART, LOVERS, AND GOTHIC CONTAMINATION

*The lessons in death that the Gothic extracts from Shakespeare's play are two-fold. First, death, however resistant, must be drawn into an intimate and enduring relation with truth. That is, the situations that led up to any particular death—its origins and its causes—as well as the physical embodiment of that death—in the form of a corpse, or, more frequently in Gothic, a mere skeletal remainder—must be disclosed in their full immediacy.*

—Dale Townshend, "Gothic and the Ghost of *Hamlet*" (2008)

Borne fully by Schwartz's narrative, the lessons above maintain that before mourning can be achieved, there must be full discovering of the cadaver in all its shuddering horror and also a clear reporting of the stages leading to death. Seeing body parts strewn about Manhattan streets raises what has been repressed in Renata: the very detailed memory of her sister's body rising from the river. We have reviewed the first memory, but the second and third memories of body retrieval have different details. It is as if the whole memory can never be testified to at one time, but its parts seep out over many moments. The family "stood on the banks of the river and watched Claudia being dredged up, her face pale green like some kind of sea monster, her leg twisted and her body puffy—from languishing underwater, from childbirth. . . . Did Renata imagine it, or did her parents really wince when they looked at *her* face [Renata's face], the image of Claudia's before it underwent its sea change?" (Schwartz 2005: 120–121). Here exists a dreadful ambiguity: the parents look at Claudia's face but at the same time they somehow see Renata's face. Simultaneously, they see a face in blooming adolescent life and a bruised face of decomposition, sexual victimhood, and fearful isolation.

Kristeva's formulation on abjection is especially useful for a reading of Renata's own confrontation with the abject:

> The corpse (or cadaver: *cadere*, to fall), that which has irremediably come a cropper, is cesspool, and death; it upsets even more violently the one who confronts it as fragile and fallacious chance. . . . [R]efuse and corpses show me what I permanently thrust aside in order to live. These body fluids, this defilement, this shit are what life withstands, hardly and with difficulty, on the part of death. There, I am at the border of my condition as a living being. My body extricates itself, as being alive, from that border. Such wastes drop so that I might live, until, from loss to loss, nothing remains in me and my entire body falls beyond the limit—*cadere*, cadaver. (Kristeva 1982: 3)

Seeing her twin dragged lifeless out of a river is a barely disguised version of seeing how Renata would appear as a Kristevian cadaver. Claudia is a kind of corpse-doppelgänger at its most gruesome for Renata. And as Freud has it, observing a dead body is the fundamental uncanny experience.

Before her meditations on the dark gifting from the river of her sister's body, and all the physical and psychical taboo and contamination that entails, Renata muses on another defilement. This contemplation brings her to a significant painting and to her mate and seems a thinly guised version of an actual legal battle in 1999 between the Brooklyn Museum and Mayor Rudolph Giuliani, who Jess Walter dubs "Little Mussolini" from his time ghostwriting for the Mayor's Police Commissioner (Walter 2006: Interview). In the novel, Renata attends a New York City art exhibition called "Sensation" under threat of fundcutting by the Mayor. The painting there causing a furor with City Hall is of an African Madonna with "dollops of elephant dung plastered here and there" (Schwartz 2005: 87). While looking at the painting, Renata meets her significant other, Jack.

In real life, Mayor Giuliani viewed this same painting only in a Christie's auction catalog, but from that insisted it was sacrilegious, calling it "disgusting": "The idea of having so-called "works of art" in which people are throwing elephant dung at a picture of the Virgin Mary is sick" (Abrams 2005: 195). He vowed that a museum receiving city funds could not show it, threatening to cut the $7 million municipal support headed to the Brooklyn Museum and force its eviction. The Brooklyn Museum director Arnold L. Lehman challenged the Mayor's office with a First Amendment free-speech trial in federal court, and "The Holy Virgin Mary" would remain on view during the entire trial, which the complainant eventually won (Abrams 2005). For his part, artist Christopher Ofili noted that the painting registered his understandable confusion as former Roman Catholic altar boy that a virgin could give birth (Vogel 1999; BBC Staff 1999): "I really think it's a very beautiful painting to look at, full of contradiction which is perhaps why it's been misunderstood" (*Christie's Exhibition Catalog 2015*). Its seller, Christie's auction house, argued that "Applying elephant dung directly to the canvas was, for him, a way in which to bring the environment directly into his painting. . . . Dung is a symbol of growth and motherhood. In this way, Ofili's Madonna is at once of heaven and earth. Gilded with sparkling beads, it becomes a metaphor for transformation: the humble material elevated in the same way the Virgin becomes sacred with the birth of her son" (*Christie's Sale Catalog, #10381*). Its previous seller, South African professional gambler David Walsh, admitted that "Chris Ofili's wondrous painting was a bit of controversy at the Brooklyn Museum. I just don't see the controversy in it. You have a few cut-out portraits of vulvas and some elephant shit, but these are profoundly integrated into what is an incredibly aesthetically pleasing, beautiful painting" (*Christie's 2015 Special Features: The Man from Mona*). What connects deeply between Ofili's art and 9/11-themed novels and photography is the inability of some viewers to stand gazing at the body and what it produces—or what can be done to it. Indeed, despite its selling for £2,882,500 in 2015 at Christie's, the painting still gathers complaints of its odor, even from otherwise sympathetic museums. Just as American politicians (especially the late Republican Senator Jesse Helms) assaulted American-artist Andre Serrano's alarmingly beautiful photographs of blood, semen, milk, urine, and pus in the late 1980s and early 1990s, starting with his painting "Piss Christ," and threatened to cut off funding to the National Endowment for the Arts for underwriting him, so too, politicians would attack 9/11 sculpture, photographs and paintings that showed too much of the body, in particular bodies coming into contact with the ground, or photographs that showed a disturbing contradiction or a lack of mourning. Discussed below are several paintings, sculptures, and photographs alluded to in this study's novels. These artworks produced uncommon fury and condemnation among observers.

From photographer Thomas Hoepker on 9/11 came a composition of a group of people in a Brooklyn park, talking in the sun and looking at each other instead of the WTC Towers as the flames climbed higher, causing outrage among viewers for its detachment and a condemnation as "shocking" photography by *New York Times* reporter and regular columnist Frank Rich. Eclipsing the blast against Hoepker's photography, the Associated Press would receive more criticism from readers and fellow media outlets for Richard Drew's photograph of the jumper than any other photograph in recent memory, as noted by Drew himself. Similar assaults came at Erick Fischel's "Tumbling Woman," modeled on images of the 9/11 jumpers that DeLillo described in *Falling Man*, after its display in Rockefeller Center's lower concourse. A barrage of critics attacked it as a mere "naked woman with her arms and legs flailing above her head, as if in a backward somersault" (Staff for Associated Press 2002). Abruptly covered in a cloth and surrounded by a wall of curtains, a Rockefeller Center spokesperson apologized for the installation: "The sculpture was not meant to hurt anybody. It was a sincere expression of deepest sympathy for the vulnerability of the human condition" (John Gregory Brown). Last, Todd Maisel, who described the fires at the WTC as "like Hell coming towards you," photographed a blown-off hand on a street ("The Hand, 9/11") for *The New York Daily News,* and more critics rebuked the newspaper the next day (*Behind the Lens* 2008).

Ofili's painting, meanwhile, would be assaulted by eggs, ink, and white paint in Brooklyn, while Staten Island-artist Scott LoBaido would hurl horse manure at the Brooklyn Museum walls (Dubin 1998; Plate 2006). The painting represented an invasion of something foul, unutterable, base, and contaminating to some viewers. Yet it is at this same moment that Renata looks on Ofili's "The Madonna" with wonder that Jack walks into her life, a man she will have the longest relationship within her life, sleeping with him for eight months and telling him in stages about the traumata of her past. The narrator notes with a mixture of mockery and admiration that Jack would "step right into it" while looking at the Madonna and at Renata, "even though he didn't know the early chapters. That took nerve. And he was patient. He could wait for the story. He would wait a long time" (Schwartz 2005: 6).

A parallel exists between defilement and invasion by the Other—and the threat to her borders that Jack represents. Their coequal timing suggests such an uncanny relationship. As Kristeva asserts,

> In the first place, filth is not a quality in itself, but it applies only to what relates to a boundary and, more particularly, represents the object jettisoned out of that boundary, its other side, a margin. . . . The mistake is to treat bodily margins in isolation from all other the danger of filth represents for the subject the risk to which the very symbolic order is permanently exposed, . . . the frailty of the symbolic order itself. A threat issued from the prohibitions that found the inner and outer borders in which and through which the speaking subject is constituted. (Kristeva 1982: 6–7)

So, too, through a painting accused of violation, intrusion, and filth, Renata is moved and impelled to absorb what she has before rejected, a man who will stay will cross a boundary into her most personal space, and become a presence that seeks out her secrets, those hidden dirty facts which make her feel debased, subhuman, isolated in grief, forever unlovable, and unacceptable to the living world: "the shit . . . [that] life withstands," in the words of Kristeva.

It is Jack's questions and observations that help precipitate each of Renata's searches into memory, too. He shares 9/11's sublimity when he notes, "You can't grasp it [all the wreckage] from what they show [on TV].

It's huge. Thousands of tons of steel tied up in huge knots. Crushed cars and fire engines all over the place" (Schwartz 2005: 88). Then he shares its gruesome violations and contamination: "And the smell. It's all still burning. It'll burn for months. . . . Shoes strewn all over. That was the worst, the shoes. . . . No bodies. Parts. I saw a foot."[8] She has had concern that this one man who mourns with dedication and passion, and who works with a socialworker's instincts and curiosity about human motivation, will tease out her past. Before a reader assumes so, she already knows Jack is more committed and a better listener than any of her previous one-night stands. For our investigation on trauma, as well, Jack's live-witness reporting differs from the standard media reporting of 9/11 where, as critiqued by Žižek in *Welcome to the Desert of the Real*,

> [T]he same "derealization" of the horror went on after the WTC collapse: while the number of victims—3,000—is repeated all the time, it is surprising how little of the actual carnage we see—no dismembered bodies, no blood, no desperate faces of dying people . . . in clear contrast to reporting on Third World catastrophes, where the whole point is to produce a scoop of some gruesome detail: Somalis dying of hunger, raped Bosnian women, men with their throat cut. (Žižek 2013a: 15)

Žižek elaborates that Western media posits that the most viewable grotesque and suffering must occur "over there" rather than "over here" in the West. He builds the case that Western citizens live in some "numbness," an "immersion in our everyday ideological universe," existence in a continual, "hypnotic consumerist state" (Žižek 2013a: 10). In short, Western ideology through layers of deception attempts to blunt or even lock out "the Real in its extreme violence" (Žižek 2013a: 5). Technically, his thesis could be challenged as there were very few remains—except for parts of twelve bodies that could be identified on the WTC plaza—that were recognizably human in the debris out of the nearly 3,000 dead. As I have described in the Introduction, the combination of jet fuel, extreme heat and flame and explosive shock wave quickly turned innocent lives into ash. In short, except for a few cases, and perhaps some of the two hundred jumpers, there was very little for a camera to show as a cadaver; Žižek's argument about Western media resisting showing our own cadavers seems initially questionable. However, the few photos of torn-apart bodies that were shown on the first and second days were so heavily censured, that his contention of a double standard toward showing the exploded Westerners seems valid. What is more, the French filmmakers Gedeon and Jules Naudet do admit on the voiceover of their that they saw burning bodies at the WTC but decided not to film them—that "nobody needed to see that"—so again Žižek's argument holds to a limited degree

*(9/11: The Filmmakers' Commemorative DVD Edition (2001)*. However, the Brothers Naudet's film does record in painful loudness the noisy thud of bodies falling onto the concrete around them and captures the distressed firefighting crews' heads swiveling back and forth as they hear the last sound from those that they can no longer rescue.

## ON THE TERRORS OF THE FUTURE

An inner debate soon consumes Renata, raising the question of whether she will be reborn as her name suggests, or stay born only to William Blake's "endless night." As evidence of this internal discussion, she wonders: "If she cedes herself to the future and gives up clinging to the past, would it be a betrayal? What about her dead father and sister, the lost Gianna, her anger, her remorse?" (Schwartz 2005: 294). While not living in one of the fantastically described "melodramatic dungeons" described by Ann Radcliffe, Renata does inhabit an abode decorated with newspaper cutouts of murders by malice aforethought and manslaughter by neglect, and she sleeps under clippings on the wall of child abductions and unexplained disappearances. Her one steady boyfriend Jack is so mortified by these gloomy rooms of cold cases that he has trouble concentrating on sex at her apartment, and typically makes a case for them wander over to his place to make love. A parallel exists between her psychic struggle within her dismal apartment and Derrida's reflections both on the terrors of the future (the sense the terror act is actually unfinished), as well as on the missing ghostly elements of her "archive," for no matter how she searches for completion, she fails. The news clippings of lives transformed by other people for the worse that she hoards on her walls helps explain Renata's fear of long-term involvement, or how since all the years since her sister's unsolved death, she has never considering starting a life with one partner, never wanted anyone to move in with her, and never considering having children. It would at first seem counterintuitive, then, to insist that what Renata dreads most now is not the horrid past but the awful and unknown future. However, it is difficult to mourn or build memorials or return to normalcy when the greatest evils (e.g., biological threats including anthrax poisonings, chemical bombs, and dirty nuclear weapons) still seem immanent. After an act of major terrorism (and repeated television coverage of it), the trepidation over plots still secret generates a chain reaction of more fear and greater terror in the public—and increases the chance of state attacks and even war. In short, as Derrida astutely summarizes: "Traumatism is produced by the *future*, by the *to come*, by the threat of the *worst to come*, rather than by an aggression that is 'over and done with'" (Derrida 2003). Rather like the case of Oskar's grandfather who ran from his American family back to Germany, Renata may wish to hold back from loving and staying with others now because the trauma of past losses makes the prospect of future losses impossible to withstand. Yet, equal amounts of loneliness and bravery in her seem to overcome such dread, and she does not abandon her lover, Jack.

Only after the violence of 9/11 does she admit to anyone (in this case, Jack) that she had a twin who met a violent end, and that she has never stopped feeling pain over Claudia's incest and murder, and that she is in ceaseless bereavement for her (of the Derridean kind). It is to Jack (and to no other person outside her family) that she utters the four words made more haunting by what they leave out: "There was a baby." This confession could be seen as the betrayal of secret information that has held them together beyond death itself, but it also ethically functions as the announcement that Claudia is the "other," not just the incorporated twin. Renata's expression of grief is a constant pining (for her sister's living, nonghostly company), a regret (that she cannot talk with her sister about their lives and discoveries now), and a pain (like Derrida's for Paul de Man, that they can no longer be with each other and thus transform each other). And now, by facing her own mortality in such an honest, graphic way after the fall of the towers, Renata becomes even more like Claudia was: utterly susceptible, endangered, and frightened. The novel becomes a study in how seeing effects from one disaster (along with a fateful visit to a museum's exhibit on tombs and killers) disinter memories long suppressed, just at the same moment crews are digging out human remains from the WTC disaster site. The terrorist attack comes as Renata's attempted incorporation or internal entombment of Claudia within herself is failing: the "psychic mummification" unravels. Renata can still long for her sister yet see her as separate—a ghost elsewhere. Whatever its defects this "living" grieving may be, it is still, as Derrida would have it, a "gesture of faithful friendship, its immeasurable grief, but also its life: the sublimity of a mourning without sublimation and without the obsessive triumph of which Freud speaks" (Derrida 1989: 39). Indeed, there grows a sense in the novel that such "an aborted interiorisation is at the same time a respect for the other as other" (Derrida 1989: 35). Confessing the traumatic past to Jack untwines the twins.

Declaring it removes the shroud over the Gothic mysteries of victimhood and starts to dissolve the incorporation of Claudia within Renata, fostering a Derridean ethical/impossible mourning to take effect. Renata and Claudia are no longer the closed human unit that developed and then spoke their own argot which could hold sensitive facts away from their parents and others for years. And they are no longer the twins that literally spoke as one, like the slaughtered Grady twins from Stanley Kubrick's film *The Shining*.[9]

## DOPPELGÄNGERS AND PERPETRATORS

One of the most pondered-over Gothic tendencies within 9/11 and its aftermath is how New Yorkers suddenly saw their city as familiar, estranging, vulnerable, and forbidding all at the same time. Renata frequently experiences the uncanny, shuddering at a corpse (her sister's) who is like a double in death. But following 9/11 she has more frequent uncanny encounters, seeing her missing niece, who was thought to be dead. Intriguingly, even the limited omniscient narrator slips three times into calling this stranger from the streets "Gianna," who the reader might reasonably instead assume from her description is an underage Jodi Foster-looking prostitute out of *Taxi Driver* (1976).

The uncanny first emerges in the novel after an unexpected cell call from her long-lost sister-in-law, Cindy, ex-wife of the pedophile Peter. Unable to find her new boyfriend in the days after 9/11, Cindy reconnects with Renata, and they agree to meet at New York's St. Vincent's Hospital to search for the missing man. It is still September 2001, and even before going into the hospital, the matrix of ambiguous loss and chance encounters starts expanding. Facing a "Missing Wall" where survivors place images of their vanished beloved, Renata sees at the periphery a little stranger scanning faces of the missing:

> She wears small, thin gold hoops in her ears, the kind Renata got for Gianna when she was seven. . . . The olive skin, the earrings, the lithe body and that elegant Botticelli profile are so eerily familiar that Renata shudders, the way they say you shudder when someone walks over your grave, still empty. . . . There's something else odd. She doesn't carry any purse or backpack, nothing at all. She must be homeless, a street kid, yes, with that look of no place to go, all the time in the world to do nothing. When their paths cross, her glance falls on Renata and becomes a bland stare. She looks like she's about to speak but she doesn't. Renata acknowledges her with the tiny nod she's given the others at the wall, the sign of communal sorrow. . . . When the girl reaches the end of the row of photos she starts drifting back in the other direction. As she does so, Renata feels she's watching her through the wavy glass of Jack's window; the molecules that make up the girl shiver and reassemble, again and again, so that she never quite keeps her firm shape. She's about the age Gianna would be now, and come to think of it—but truly, the thought has been there from the first instant—it's uncanny how much she resembles Claudia at that age (and me, too, Renata thinks). (Schwartz 2005: 148–149)

This use of the Gothic Uncanny moments before the meeting with Cindy, ex-wife of the pederast uncle, is extraordinary and heightened to an unbearable degree for the protagonist. Within this passage, we see recognition clash with doubt over the waif's identity, leading to seemingly absurd conclusions: that Gianna has not died, that disaster has somehow flushed her from bondage (from abduction? from prostitution?), and that she walks toward her aunt now. It is magical thinking, all at a wholly understandable instant when 1,157 other families were still hoping their missing loved ones would knock on the door, as happens in DeLillo's *Falling Man* (and happens in dark fiction elsewhere occasionally, perhaps most famously in W. W. Jacobs' 1902 story, "The Monkey's Paw"). Somehow survivors still in shock find their way home from makeshift triage centers or hospitals after the most unprecedented crisis in New York history. On September 12, 2001, researchers at Berkeley developed a website that allowed people (or hospital administrators overseeing them) to post that they were alive. By the last days of September 2001, when at least 1,157 individuals did not include a report or confirmation they were alive, "many [surviving] families began to lose hope" and concluded their significant others, relatives, friends, or fellow employees had perished. Some of the most devastating search boards are still available to view.[10] That said, many families were split in their rulings of disappearance equaling death:

> Therapists encountered tensions between couples and among siblings in cases where family members disagreed whether their relatives were lost. Some family members 'were incredibly hopeful beyond all logic,' while others wanted to start notifying friends and arranging memorial services. . . . Some held funeral services where they buried empty coffins; others buried coffins holding the possessions of the deceased, including photographs, musical instruments, and bowling balls. (Seeley 2008: 76–77)

Likewise, Oskar in *Extremely Loud and Incredibly Close* observes an empty casket stand for his father and suffers the psychological distress of an obscene ritual he finds empty as well. As a result, he is not able to begin a grief process "that encourage[s] psychological resolution" (Seeley 2008: 75). Instead, he physically attacks himself and repeatedly distances himself from his mother.

Out of the thousands declared missing, only eighteen people surface as alive following 9/11, all discovered within two days of the catastrophe (Langeweische 2002). However, Schwartz's fiction does posit miraculous thinking. Near novel's end, Renata clips a newspaper article about a mother in La Paz, Bolivia. Ms. Ortega assumed that Al Qaeda had killed her four undocumented immigrant children working near or inside the WTC on 9/11, because no word had come from them. Finally, the Bolivian Embassy ruled their missing cases as deaths, and she was invited to a memorial ceremony in New York City a month and a half later. Touching down to New York City, she discovered that all her children were actually alive. In the novel, one clearly traumatized son explained his cryptic decision not to contact his distraught mother: "I didn't want to do anything. I didn't want to speak with anybody. I was left with nothing" (Schwartz 2005: 283). In Renata's mind, the miraculous can happen, and thus we track the uncanny. Cindy, after all these years, looks unlike herself but still sounds exactly like Cindy from decades ago; a boy in St. Vincent's who has no apparent physical problem makes Renata's "heart flip" when she discovers his leg is a prosthetic, "a blue and white sock, which lies absolutely smooth on the plastic leg. The sock almost undoes her. She quickly turns away." Cindy's boyfriend appears in the hospital, but so swathed in bandages his girlfriend can only mutter disbelief that it is he: "Hal? Baby?" Further, Renata looks out a hospital window and cannot believe that "there's empty space where the towers should be. . . . It resembles a scene from a movie about interplanetary travel, . . . yellow machines move slowly, like enormous, menacing bugs . . . where they mine for bodies." Then she finds from Cindy that her niece was sold to people initially—"Renata can't speak. She will have to let it all spool out, then sort it through later" (Schwartz 2005: 155). Last, Cindy admits that her husband was in fact the father and was with Claudia the night she drowned.

Upon delivering missing pieces of Renata's past, Cindy speaks in the language of psychotherapy: "Confront what you [now] know. It's no good living in denial" (Schwartz 2005: 160). This advice leads her to travel to Houston to face the perpetrator on his deathbed. Before leaving New York for the first time since 9/11, she finds the strange waif girl floating about in a couple of other places in the city in the days following, disappearing, then reappearing: "With the world turned surreal, notions of the supernatural were tempting, notions of transformation. Had the girl metamorphosed into a tree, perhaps? A parking meter?" (Schwartz 2005: 172). When Renata asks the mysterious girl if she needs help, the lost child says nothing but only nods. It is no surprise that readers would think her not real—possibly an apparition, more likely a traumatic hallucination—and odder still, this character has no "money, no bag, no shoes, no bra" (Schwartz 2005: 163). Later, however, other characters will see her too and suggest that she has a verifiable, physical presence. Less a ghost than a cipher, she silently eats, brushes teeth, buys makeup, reads romances, and watches *Nickelodeon*. In a sudden move that surprises the reader, Renata invites the girl to stay at her apartment, and the girl accepts—without a word, but again a nod and a mouthed "thank you." Renata then tells the girl to make herself at home, take her apartment keys (which she has not even given before to her boyfriend of eight months, Jack), and promise to still be there when Renata returns after a trip away to Houston for a few days. This creates a useful tension between reader and protagonist, as well as a dramatic irony, because while the waif is perhaps not a convincing Gianna-doppelgänger for the reader, the strange girl *is* such a one for Renata and for even the unknown narrator, who three times embeds the identity of the missing Gianna into this living lost girl. Discovering the stray girl is weirdly synchronous with Cindy's confession that her ex-husband Peter sold drugs and possibly children. The more Renata interrogates her fellow female sufferer Cindy, the more wrongdoing she suspects of the Gothic villain Peter, not only of impregnating her sister and pushing her off a rotting pier to her death but also of actually taking his own daughter little Gianna off the carousel years ago for criminal ends. At this juncture, Renata without much proof becomes convinced that Peter may be involved in "kiddy porn," too. Perhaps deeper suspicions also engulf Renata now because the world seems more inherently predatory in the wake of the towers' fall. I would extend Deborah Willis's convincing analysis that argues

> When trauma is caused by human agents (rapists, for example, or war criminals), it can do more lasting damage than trauma caused by accident or natural disaster. One's assumptions about human relationships, one's basic trust in others, may be profoundly tested or undermined by such experiences, making it difficult to reconnect to the human community, to form new attachments or sustain old ones, to reach out to or feel empathy for others. (Willis 2002: 27)

Anyone's trust in others is obviously damaged after a major terror attack (though, to be sure, one can also be surprised by the valor and sacrifice of those who rushed to save the trapped of the towers). The addition I make to Willis's conception is that terrorism could cause an inventory of past intense suffering and a reevaluation of its cause: barely understood trauma from years before could be seen then as less by accident and more by malicious design. One burden of trauma is the testing of our previous interpretations, an assault on our history and our relationships with others and the "truth." All along, Renata's interpretation of how and why her twin died could have been a myth, perhaps a self-protective one.

## PURSUING REVENGE

The influence of Elizabethan and Jacobean revenge tragedies on Gothic novels is well defined in recent criticism, with Douglass Thomson constructively adding that "the most Gothic version of revenge in Gothic Literature is the idea that it can be a guiding force in the revenance of the dead" (Thomson n.d.: 23). I would like to adjust that idea to note that the sighting of a doppelgänger can be tied, or even become a "guiding force," to a woman exacting vengeance on an older male figure. Gothically driven vengeance by women against men—a tossing off the "gentle garb of a female," as Mary Ann

Radcliffe would capture it in *The Female Advocate* (1799)—arises in many places. As Hoeveler has it, "The gothic feminist heroine ... co-opts the father, she survives and creates a ... world in which men exist as chastened versions of themselves" (Hoeveler 1998: 101–102). This "urge for vengeance," as Snodgrass sums it, "is often the outgrowth of misogyny, repression, threats, and violence against women. ... [It is] the wreaking of havoc against oppressors, torturers, and rapists provid[ing] the satisfying comeuppance in such vengeance lore" (Snodgrass 2004: 291). As Tóth describes it, revenge gives the chance and the change to "step out of the role of the objectified, victimised woman" (Tóth 2010: 30). While all of the beliefs are accurate, none of this yet fully registers the impotence behind *The Writing on the Wall*'s gestures of vengeance.

Suturing the Gothic uncanny with the unfinished mourning, unresolved questions, and unreleased rage, Schwartz has Renata take a killing journey to Houston. She finds the hospital where her sister's violator sleeps, emaciated, hanging on to life from the ravages of lymphoma cancer, and she struggles to overcome the sympathy for the dying that washes over her. Readers may well sense he resembles in condition too closely Cindy's new lover, seen just days before, bandaged in a New York's St. Vincent Hospital, to fully ignite Renata's hate and revulsion into violence. During her dilemma over murdering him, the uncanny rises again along with a succession of grotesquely Gothic images: "Peter's hair, once so black, was a steely gray, matted from sleep, his face a sickly ivory, the skin blotched with grayish spots. The stubble on his chin was white. His lips, greenish gray. . . . [H]ands the color and texture of used waxed paper" (Schwartz 2005: 196). She can barely recognize this yellow-toothed specter as Peter. So slight he is that the bed appears concave, as if the maw of a grave is widening beneath him. Adding to the uncanny, her reflection from his pupils shows her as an avenger in pause, deliberating on her kill-target: Peter's eyes "opened straight onto her, and the look in them, gathering terror, was worth years of grief. The same look as in her father's eyes when they dragged the river. In her own [eyes, too], in the mirror, when she entered their [her and Claudia's] bedroom and knew she would sleep there alone from then on" (Schwartz 2005: 197). Throughout this novel, she insists that "I am not a ghost"; she vows that she is "not destroyed, like a twin star slipped out of orbit. [Claudia] is lost but I will not be destroyed." But Peter's surprised, deathbed eyes (with apparently no guile) indicate that she is a punishing spirit. Indeed, the narrator claims of the pederast: "He'd seen a ghost" (Schwartz 2005: 197). One of the most unexpected and disturbing acts in the book then occurs. An unusual deal is proposed, namely, that she will leave the room without killing him if he fully and truthfully confesses what happened the night of her sister's death. He says he will, but only if she kills him, as well, for "You'll be righteous. You always liked being righteous" (Schwartz 2005: 201). He continues his odd plea, as we sense the real motive is that he would rather die than spend one more minute with this woman: "You hate me. So do it. Now. Hold your hand over my mouth. . . . You won't get caught. They expect it any minute. Pull out the tubes. Do something. You know you want to. You'll be satisfied and I'll be done with everything" (Schwartz 2005: 201). Finally, he confesses: he went to the river to meet Claudia, she demanded her baby back, he refused, and she ran off onto a rotting jetty and fell in. After scanning the river for her for a time, he assumed she was simply hiding and not drowned, as the water was rather shallow, and she was in the mood to punish him. Then he sidled off home. Not all of this account seems particularly believable, but there are no other living witnesses and no possible corroboration. His story does stay consistent under Renata's rapid questioning, so she takes what admission she hears and leaves. In a motion reflected by women in some very recent and similar Gothic accounts (Olson 2011b), she chooses not to suffocate him, perversely I would argue, because he wishes to die. Killing would make her resemble him more than she could withstand. In a line that stays faithful to this novel's constant ambiguity, she vows, "I'll think it over. Maybe I'll come back and do it tomorrow" (Schwartz 2005: 201). Reinforcing a crueler fate upon him in the style of one of the most-famed Gothic revenge accounts, Poe's "The Cask of Amontillado," his life will be an extended death while held in a hospital of no visitors save for her. Unlike the vengeance fantasies that sustained victims through their suffering hours in many Gothic accounts, though, Renata's "revenge didn't feel sweet. If felt like more to add to the past" (Schwartz 2005: 201).

Recalling how the Gothic situates itself in the space between representation and nonrepresentation of trauma (and oscillates between them), Renata's compromised revenge is one where she neither smothers the dying man, as was her earlier fantasy, nor offers forgiveness, and a promise of no harm. She moves toward one pole and then reverses course to the other. Hers is an in-between state, pledging she "may" come back tomorrow to be his angel of death. This power play reflects trauma theorist Judith Herman's observation that "The revenge fantasy is often a mirror image of the traumatic memory, in which the roles of perpetrator and victim are reversed" (Herman 1997: 189). Renata may long have nursed this fantasy of torturing Peter, but exercising it is a failure. Everything in her dream of vengeance has hinged on violence achieving something meaningful or revealing important secrets. But such fantasies, just as George Orwell discovered upon visiting a concentration camp where the former inmates took control, frequently reveal "there is no such thing as [true] revenge. Revenge is an act which you want to commit when you are powerless and because you are powerless: as soon as the sense of impotence is removed, the desire evaporates also" (Orwell 1945: 5). Monsters no longer seem the same vicious monsters as time goes by or when we have leverage over them: "indeed, once under lock and key, they almost cease to be monsters" (Orwell 1945: 5). Derrida exposes the fallacy of revenge against those declared as monsters further: "Monsters cannot be announced. One cannot say: 'Here are our monsters,' without immediately turning the monsters into pets" (Derrida 1989: 80). I perceive the last victim of the monster is the monster itself—once we begin early acts of domesticating it with a name and a history.

The observation of the "merely pathetic and disgusting" actions of "impossible revenge" follows observations in trauma theory elsewhere on other concentration camp inmates upon liberation. The prominent Romanian trauma theorist and Holocaust survivor Dori Laub describes a young woman whom he knew and whose "relatives had been put into a boarded-up wooden shack that was set afire" (Laub 1995: 64). Following Allied liberation, the woman took part in partisan hunts of local collaborators. Giving free hand to avenge herself against a seventeen-year-old Axis soldier, she "bandaged the German's wounds and turned him over to the POW group instead" (Laub 1995: 64–65). When asked why, she said, "How could I kill him—he looked into my face and I looked into his" (Laub 1995: 65). Similarly, with Renata's face just inches from Peter's, smelling his breath of "rot," she could pounce on and hold the nurse's buzzer-cord before he could call the staff for rescue. She does initially feel that "predator's thrill, a flutter behind her ribs, a low whir in her head" that called out to murder (Schwartz 2005: 196). The possessing spirit inside Renata could try to reenact a trauma scene, this time with her as the victimizer, but it is all too obviously false (for Renata and her possession ghost, Claudia). Renata looks into the dissipated face of Uncle Peter and recognizes her own gaze of terror and her father's. It is this recognition that I judge saves Peter from asphyxiation, and perhaps saves her from future trauma visited upon those who kill the helpless. She does not deny him his life, but she denies him forgiveness when he asks for it, which seems an honest and authentic act on her part. (Neither will she give Peter reconciliation or amnesty.) We could offer Derrida's insight as her defense as "by its own internal logic, genuine forgiving must involve the impossible: that is, the forgiving of an 'unforgivable' transgression" (Derrida 2001: 32). In this way forgiveness links with trauma. Both suggest the pain is not ever over, and that there is a "permanent rupture, or a wound that refuses to heal" (Reynolds 2004).

After this encounter in Houston (especially in her greater trust of Jack and her release of the waif to her proper parents upon return to New York City), it strongly appears that this confrontation sets free *some* trapped and paralyzing conflicts and emotions in Renata. She neither exhibits as much self-hatred, self-blame, and excessive holding on to the past, nor the multidirected anger and distrust at those people in her life who had no part in her sister's death or niece's long-ago disappearance. It is illuminating that the only dream Renata has in the novel follows the Houston hospital encounter. It comes after she and Jack have just made love, despite the fact that he admitted returning to his old lover (just once) on some kind of sexual "healing mission" during her absence. I would argue the dream is restorative for her. It looks at but reconfigures her past, brings back objects of the dead, just in the way that Freud found that "Dreaming is another kind of remembering" (Freud 1899: 302). The dreaming here could represent a mode of honest or conditional mourning, free from the cant and political posturing she detects in official memorials involving President George W. Bush on television. She dreams of being part of a great crowd on a lawn with Ferris wheels, parachutes, and carousels. A slender large, dark rectangle made of mist materializes: couples race toward it, and both they and the tower gently ascend into invisible heights, leaving witnesses with a "wondrous horror." Her night dream may seem a wish fulfillment (as if the jumpers that held hands as they threw themselves out of the tower on 9/11 were reunited and now ascend), a phantasy, a record of her unconscious's masqueraded statements (the carousel suggesting the one from which an unknown person or persons snatched Gianna), and a reordering of history (the tower suggesting both WTC Towers' disappearance). As Lacan would say of the importance of Freud's work, so too in Renata's dream, "the real supports the phantasy, the phantasy protects the real" (Lacan 1981: 41). But there is also something beyond reciprocity in the dream: a kind of ceremony in her "dream work" where she attempts to say goodbye to the dead of her far past and recent past. Here in dream, she is not alone in her suffering or grief anymore (a crowd "waited" with her, "witnessed," "grasped" what happened). What is striking is that after her encounter with the perpetrator and this communal dream, her earliest action on returning to New York City is to search for and reunite the parents with the stray girl in her apartment. Before going to Houston, she had no interest in contacting New York City Child Welfare Services to find whose child this is. The child functioned largely for Renata as a living image of what was inside her, as an avatar for both her sister and her niece. But now Renata moves to respecting the girl's independent personhood and humanity. The girl exists as more than an uncanny substitution for what is lost.

## CONCLUSION

When Renata cries to her lover Jack, "Don't leave me alone with the words I dredged up," we could reasonably make a substitution as "Don't leave me alone with the body you dredged up," because it is the traumatized body that haunts here. Jack signals risk to her, and to her mournful incorporation of Claudia, more than anyone else in the novel. For Jack "was curious; some time soon he'd be asking about her past, her family. She'd have to be evasive, and everything would turn sour. Sometimes there is comfort to be found in lies. She would keep silent as long as she could, to make this feeling last" (Schwartz 2005: 53). Nonetheless, Renata is brave enough to break the vault of incorporation within her through a Derridean "tender rejection of the dead," remembering and confessing the secrets and loss of her sister and niece in full detail, letting her memory express through words what has been heretofore unrepresentable. Just as courageously, she recognizes what Torok terms the "hallucinatory wish-fulfillment" in herself as a phantasy, after she returns the waif she found on the post-9/11 streets to the rightful parents, rather than keeping her in her home as a replacement and a receptacle for the missing Gianna who disappeared ten years before 9/11. She thus understands and empathizes with the anxious horror that the missing girl's adoptive parents are feeling, valuing that sympathy over her own narcissistic desire for a substitute. Renata—the twin who avoided involvement so long ("Ever since she'd lost Claudia, she hadn't wanted to be close to anyone else")—is now aware that she is part of a community hurled together by two planes destroying twin buildings on a sunny Tuesday in September.

The trauma is of course not magically "over," and indeed what Derrida calls full and "true forgiveness"[11] is not obtained. Still, there are conditional advances. While Renata was too naïve, obtuse, or denial-prone as a teenager to help her sister, she now has the confidence and knowledge to at least interrogate the male figure who cursed her family's life, even if she cannot yet share that conversation with the other male in her new life, Jack. Her guilty uncle may not give answers that are satisfactory or provable, but he at least responds. From such responses, her perceptions of herself change somewhat. She begins to recognize the limits of her young self, and of her ability to solve all of the family's problems or recognize every sign of abuse. As the novel heads to its end and a dream vision, Renata no longer seems so strangled by guilt, passivity, and negligence. She begins to forgive herself even if there is no way she can (or should) grant Peter "true forgiveness."

Certainly, the two most successful individuals to deal with traumata in the novels we surveyed so far are Oskar and Renata. Their commonality is that though they are self-serving for a time, they finally accept a greater community of fellow sufferers into their lives and take a more objective view of their trauma. That objective view is a catalyst for compassion: Oskar finally cries, admits the secrets that destroyed him with guilt and caused him to bruise himself nightly, hugs and enfolds his mother, and allows her to love a man again whom, significantly, she met in a trauma-support group. He is a man "who makes [her] laugh again." All of this change and empathy only come about after a quest taken with others who have likewise lost much. It appears here that for Oskar, he must empathize with another's trauma before he can start to positively manage his own life and enframe or limit the devouring powers of his own trauma. One can see a similar development in the case of Renata. Both protagonists appear to follow the sociologist Kai Erikson's claim on devastated groups that

> [T]rauma can create community. In some ways that is a very odd thing to claim. To describe people as traumatized is to say that they have withdrawn into a kind of protective envelope, a place of mute, aching loneliness, in which the traumatic experience is treated like a solitary burden that needs to be expunged by acts of denial and resistance. What could be less "social" than that? But traumatic conditions are like no other troubles to which flesh is heir. They move to the centre of one's own being and, in doing so, give [a band of] victims the feeling that they have been set apart and made special. (Erikson 1995: 187)

Following Erikson's observations to a degree, once Renata becomes enmeshed in the trauma of the whole of Gotham itself on 9/11, she can face more clearly and start to remember her own earlier private family trauma. Not remaining silenced, Renata takes actions to still seem alive in the dead man's zone of trauma, including her face-to-face meeting with Peter as he lies dying. Meanwhile, she is moving out of her private morass to actually helping others. The people in her apartment building need help on 9/11 and in the days after, and so she shares with people she barely acknowledged or spoke to before such useful things as towels, aspirin, milk, bread, Valium, and Bourbon. She finds herself taking care of an infant named Julio because his mother died in a WTC Tower. Neighbors who had seldom knocked on each other's door before now beg to help her: a woman brings Renata an outgrown stroller and a used bassinet; a gentleman with a resonant tenor offers to coo the baby to sleep when it cries. In the days following disaster, a secret nature blooms and Renata observes she cannot "go down the street without stopping every half block to talk" (Schwartz 2005: 92).

Along with all the horrors, there is doubtless a candle in the darkness after 9/11. Renata discovers "these are her neighbors, and though she's usually reserved, just a nod and a smile [before], she's as transformed as all the rest, . . . and the hot-dog man is giving away pretzels out of gratitude [of being alive]. Renata takes one to share with [baby] Julio . . . [whom] everyone fusses over, . . . and he gives his brightest smiles as people murmur their sympathy for his loss" (Schwartz 2005: 92). One can search but cannot find in our lifetimes a moment in Manhattan's history when people cared more for each other and less for themselves, save perhaps during our Coronavirus outbreak. And this moment enters Renata's being, permeating her. As she strolls the motherless baby, she seems to realize the utter fragility of everyone—and how they are suffering an unending trauma and facing mourning just as or more disabling than her own. Perhaps, as Roger Luckhurst argues, such a community may be a temporary "transcendence from torturous times" (Luckhurst, "Torturous Times" 2010: 18). For a time, at least, Renata is not wholly alienated from others, not giving sex away to anyone only for forgetfulness, not wanting to die the suicide of a melancholic, not merely existing in a quietly larval form of death, but alive in the united states of grief.

## NOTES

1. To add to the correspondence and secret language between disaster and cinema, Claire Kahane wisely considers how 9/11 is understood and contextualized through earlier films in "Uncanny Sights": "Even as this historical event unfolded, it was quickly recognised, placed in a familiar category, and given a local habitation and name: 'it's just like a movie,' the newscasters blurted out, a remark echoed repeatedly that morning. . . . Thus the actual reality before our eyes was almost immediately transformed into and by the virtual reality of Hollywood and made familiar, déjà vu. In this assimilation, as we turned to the movies to orient us to the real disaster, the historical was confused with the fictional, and the event of 9/11 itself—familiar and unfamiliar, real and unreal—took on an uncanny ambiguity. . . . Our response to 9/11 made disturbingly clear how much our perceptual experience as well as our psychic life is filtered and managed through films we have seen, even experienced as films we have seen" (Kahane 2003: 107).

2. Derrida simultaneously shares etymology and tracks ghosts in one sentence: "You know, ghosts don't just appear, they come back. In French, they are the 'ones who returned' [or les revenants from 'revenir']" (Derrida 1983: *Ghost Dance*).

3. This ambivalence evokes Renata's own movement between the extremes of loving her dead sister and resenting her. The melancholia she suffers (and self-blame, denigration, and self-punishment) also evokes much of Freud's thinking on melancholia, and its vast difference from mourning. For advancing my own idea on her possession ghost, I trace Freud's intriguing exposition of the loss of the beloved becoming part of the ego, and in a sense possessing one, directing action: "There is no difficulty in reconstructing this process. An object-choice, an attachment of the libido to a particular person, had at one time existed; then, owing to a real slight or disappointment coming from this loved person, the object-relationship was shattered. The result was not the normal one of a withdrawal of the libido from this object and a displacement of it on to a new one, but something different, for whose coming-about various conditions seem to be necessary. The object-cathexis proved to have little power of resistance and was brought to an end. But the free libido was not displaced on to another object; it was withdrawn into the ego. There, however, it was not employed in any unspecified way, but served to establish an identification of the ego with the abandoned object. Thus, the shadow of the object fell upon the ego, and the latter could henceforth be judged by a special agency, as though it were an object, the

forsaken object" (Freud 1917: "Mourning and Melancholia" 3–4). Lukacher's pithy sharpening of the above describes Renata's psychic plight precisely and partially explains why she bonds to no one after Claudia: "The patient's feeling of guilt at he death of the loved one, as the result perhaps of a deep-seated satisfaction or relief at the other's death, creates an impasse that blocks the normal process of mourning as introjection" (Lukacher 1988: 89).

4. The eponymous "writing on the wall" may suggest a mighty power's vulnerability, or even stand for the decline of the American Empire or the end of President Bush's reign, as could be obviously inferred by the use of the phrase from the Book of Daniel, in which Nebuchadnezzar's son and enslaver of the Jews, King Belshazzar, has the end of his reign announced in the midst of feasting through a disembodied hand writing on a palace wall, "Mene Mene, Tekel, Parsin" [Translation: God has numbered the days of your kingdom and brought it to an end; you have been weighed on the scales and found wanting; your kingdom is divided and given to the Medes and Persians] (Seow 2003: 75).

5. Commemorating searches for the missing exactly one year after 9/11, *Lamentation: 9/11* is a coffee-table-sized book of photographs of the actual signs that appeared on streets at such "Missing Walls" with the disappeared often smiling, often on vacation and hugging their families. With text by E. L. Doctorow and a foreword by past Secretary-General Kofi A. Annan, the book remembers the chaotic and surreal days afterward with David Finn's large pictures snapped at "those places where outpourings of grief—and shattered shreds of hope—blanketed walls, sidewalks, trees" (New York: Ruder Finn Press, 2002).

6. As developed convincingly in *Gothic Shakespeares*, the works of Richard Wilson (especially his "Monstrous to Our Human Reason: The Empty Grave of *The Winter's Tale*"), and *Shakespearan Gothic*, the Gothic mode gets its repeated notion of the rising of ghosts from incomplete memorialization through Shakespeare's plays, and mourning (through proper burial and/or continuous recollection of the dead) becomes "the fundamental obligation in Gothic writing" (Townshend 2008: 75).

7. Bizarrely, despite the fact that "Roderick Usher had been one of my boon companions in boyhood," the narrator does not realize, or at least announce to us, that Roderick has a twin until the twenty-third paragraph and by that time she (Madeleine) is dead, or *so she appears to be:* "A striking similitude between the brother and sister now first arrested my attention; and Usher, divining, perhaps, my thoughts, murmured out some few words from which I learned that the deceased and himself had been twins, and that sympathies of a scarcely intelligible nature had always existed between them" (Poe 1839: 399).

8. Jack illustrates what Derrida saw as missing from 9/11 reportage. Derrida, who arrived in Manhattan two weeks after the attack and stayed for a month more, critiques news agencies for repetitively playing the crash but not showing the human devastation on the ground. But where Jack has an intuition, Derrida has a concept: "We thus deny the irresistible foreboding that the worst has not taken place, not yet. Thus to the [limited yet recycling] visual archive there have recently been added the recordings made by an amateur radio operator in San Francisco of all the messages exchanged by police and firemen during the collapse of the Twin Towers. The only

testimonies that escape archivization are those of the victims, not of the dead or of the cadavers (there were so few) but of the missing. By definition, the missing resist the work of mourning, like the future, just like the most recalcitrant of ghosts. The missing of the archive, the ghost, the phantom—that's the future—." (Derrida 2003a: note 9).

9. Curiously, the penchant of the young twins Louise and Lisa Burns to speak new thoughts in harmony (along with their resemblance to two strange, dark twins in a Diane Arbus photograph) convinced Stanley Kubrick to choose them for this iconic haunted hotel film, according to the twins themselves and the casting director/acting coach Leon Vitali. As Lisa Burns put it: it was "funny weird, funny peculiar" for Kubrick as "he might not have met many people that talked at the same time." Louise Burns added that what is weirdness to the rest of the world is normality to twins: "We hadn't noticed it was anything special because we spent so much of our lives" doing it (McAvoy in Olson 2015: 405).

10. A heartbreaking reality about such life-report boards is that some people in their hurry read the instructions wrongly and reported names that were actually dead as those who were alive, causing yet more ambiguity and trauma, making ghosts of the living and vice versa. Many life-report boards were taken down as a result. Their names and old URLs, however, still appear at the Library of Congress. One entry speaks for many of the desperate urgency of the disaster and the sense of community formed between the strangers of New York City. From Rina Rabinowitz on Friday, September 14, 2001: "I am looking for anyone that [has] heard from or seen Denise L. Benedetto. She is my one and only sister. Mother of 2 daughters and a devoted Catholic. She was last seen on the 78th floor in Building 2. She works for AON corp. Any, I mean any, information is a help. I was on the phone with her when the first plane hit. I heard the crash and the screams. I know that I am scarred for life, but I still need to know any whereabouts of my big sister. . . . I heard that she was on the elevator w/ a lot of people and a man saw her and left down the stairway. Please, please help me! We all need each others' help right now. I'll help you and you help me" (Library of Congress 2001).

11. Derrida explores the paradoxes of conditional and unconditional forgiveness further (alluding to crimes from Japan, South Africa, France, and beyond) in remarkable essays within *On Cosmopolitanism and Forgiveness* (Paris: Éditions Galilée 1997; London: Routledge, 2001).

*Chapter 4*

# Griffin Hansbury's *The Nostalgist* (2012)

## Conjuring and Romancing the Dead

### CRITICAL RECEPTION

We are wary of talking about healing in most 9/11 novels, as the definition of trauma itself is of an unhealing wound. Too many sufferers never find "closure" in these narratives, if such a state ever exists. And yet it is equally true that some victims do start embracing life more near the end of the novels, including Renata and Oskar. Surviving trauma victims also start increasingly reaching out to others in the works of our final two authors who have adopted New York City as home, Griffin Hansbury and Patrick McGrath, who both meditate on healing in their works. One of the most schizoid and disastrously nostalgic characters in all of the fictions here, Jonah Soloway in Hansbury's *The Nostalgist*, also provides one of the more astonishing stories of a victim opening again to the living world. But at first its protagonist has a kind of dreadful, magical, dark fairytale thinking where he supposes that he killed the people inside the WTC, and inadvertently kills his lover, as well as his mother. He thinks this because, while riding the Staten Island ferry in August 2001, he blotted out the styleless WTC by squinted an eye and raising a thumb to cover over it—and made a wish to for the towers to ever disappear, to remove "gigantism architecture" forever from the NYC skyline. Two weeks later, on the same day, the Twin Towers are burning, and his fantasy girlfriend is atomized by their fall, while his mother dies in an automobile accident by a distracted driver within view of the fiery WTC. This chapter will test the relationships between fantasies and realities inside this irrationally guilty character, analyze his dead girlfriend as well as the living one, scour for meanings in his night dreams and waking visions, and expose the significance within the novel's transference and countertransference. New insights about trauma and healing in this novel may be discovered by sinking our probes into the depths of its (a) nostalgia and ghostworld, (b) strange sexuality and the terror of a Gothicized vagina dentata, and (c) mourning and melancholia. Then we will examine some of the same concepts in a well-paired novella to Hansbury's from McGrath, *Ground Zero*.

*The Nostalgist* is perhaps the most surprising of the novels investigated herein: it is very lightly covered in media, existing almost a ghost itself. It is composed by a poet (of *Night for Day, 2000*), who is also an essayist (writing as "cranky," "cantankerous," and "exasperated" Jeremiah Moss his well-received *Vanishing New York*, 2017, which is favorably compared to Jane Jacob's sociology classic *The Death and Life of Great American Cities*), a scholar on transgender issues who dated controversy on *This American Life* for speaking out on how transitioning from female to male has changed his perception of and approach to women, and a New York City professional psychotherapist and licensed clinical social worker practicing since the towers fell. His troubled protagonist is one who hated the Twin Towers, and their skyline-marring silhouette, before they imploded. Indeed, most of the disorders and problems Hansbury treats are those that his protagonist (the eponymous Nostalgist) exhibits, and he could profitably consult Hansbury for listening, interpretation, and treatment. The psychopathologies Hansbury mediates are clearly listed on his own business page where he offers to work

Figure 4.1 Through Trauma and Magical Thinking, Protagonist Jonah Soloway (A Staunch Architectural Conservative and Nostalgist) Vividly Believes That His Distaste for 1970s Buildings and His Blotting Out of the WTC with His Thumb during a Ferry Ride (While Leaving Traditional Buildings Alone, Like the Foregrounded Church in the Screengrab) Has Somehow Led to Their Explosion and Falling Two Weeks Afterward. Screenshot from *Inside 9/11: Zero Hour*, Supervising Producer Nicole Rittenmeyer, *National Geographic*, 2011.

well with a spectrum of issues including "Anxiety, Depression, Grief and Loss, Trauma, Shame and Guilt, Self-esteem, Body Image and Mind-Body pain, Life Transition, Family Dynamics, Couples & Relationship Difficulties, Dissatisfaction with Work, [and] Feeling 'Stuck' in Life" (Hansbury 2020). Jonah has all the aforementioned problems and would keep a psychotherapist's appointment book scheduled for years, if he were only willing to see one.

Despite *The Nostalgist*'s rich psychopathologies, intimate details of New York City traumata, and search for love revealed during its character development, dialogue, and plot, only two reviews at press evaluate this book and no scholarly journal articles on it appear yet. Still, the two short reviews capture some of its distinct nature and raise thoughtful questions. Doug Childers understands the central debate for timid Jonah—should he stay with the ghost lover, or give himself to the lover whose blood is still circulating? Childers argues that weird internal struggle spans the narrative and keeps our interest all the way:

> Should he leave his insular, possibly haunted world of nostalgia and loneliness for a shot at real happiness? And if he does, what should he do about Rose and her mother? [This] exceptionally engaging debut, succeeds in part because Hansbury has built it around a small, tightly controlled set of recurring images and themes. Among them are the Starbucks logo, Freudian psychology and the dizzying interconnectedness of all things. . . . But Hansbury's greatest accomplishment might be making the internal life of a seemingly unappealing protagonist intriguing enough to make us sympathize with his plight. (Childers 2012)

Childers correctly intuits that Hansbury's higher skill is making us engaged with both the humanity and stubborn oddness of his antihero, and we have to ask how and why. The other reviewer, Michelle Anne Schingler, finds Hansbury's narrative mostly a meditation on "mortality and melancholia," with "a stunning addition to the budding canon of 9/11-literature . . . [with] quirky and appealing characters and beautifully disquieting prose" (Schingler 2012). It is true that select quotations from any chapter of the book can easily affirm that Hansbury's prose is achingly eloquent, possibly more so than any 9/11 novels covered in this book. Schingler goes further to argue *The Nostalgist*'s focus is on who owns a tragedy:

> Is [Jonah's living girlfriend] Jane right when she says that forgetting is an important evolutionary tool, or is Jonah's insistence on remembering the faces of all he's seen and now lost a more humane endeavor? Is life best lived somewhere in between? Jonah struggles to situate himself in a post-9/11 landscape,

all the while desperate to keep the [dead girlfriend's family, the] Oliveris[,] from comprehending the truth. (Schingler 2012)

How far would you go to craft and maintain a false past becomes another tension within the novel, and no matter what faults Jonah has, we will see that he does possess quite an imagination to keep all this island of untruths floating. In this chapter, we ask where a dream becomes pathological and investigate trauma's link to emboldening sexual fantasies, or the power of sudden mass death to jolt a survivor out of his old and hardened fears of intimacy.

## THE NECESSARY GHOST

That Hansbury's debut novel will probe mourning, as Schingler claims, will seem unlikely at first. *The Nostalgist* appears initially more to be a long and boring catalog of a collector's fusty, retro tastes. But then things get interesting, and it suddenly takes a dark turn that I believe few readers could have predicted toward Jonah's fantasies of necrophilia. It begins six months after the 9/11 attack. As he claims he's thirty years old, he must then be a child of the 1970s instead of his coveted 1930s and 1940s that he glorifies. Those Depression and World War II decades and their art and cultural artifacts are those he is spiritually at home with, as the old Bakelite phones and pinup art of his apartment attest. Alluded to earlier, he prefers his New York to be that of the one from Fay Wray and King Kong's heyday. Admiring the limestone and granite, chrome-nickel steel and aluminum of the Chrysler Building and Empire State Building, he despairs over the dreary and artless "monolithic, static monuments to commerce" of blockish glass and steel beams that were 1970s architecture, which the Twin Towers exemplified" (Hansbury 2012) before he curses them and supposedly causes them to collapse. His engagement with Golden Age thinking keeps him preferring what is long gone and that starts him creeping toward a love for someone from the past who fancied vintage fashions and pop art and hair styles, too. It is, in fact, a passion for a petit woman has been assumed dead for six months.

Once spoken, a terrible lie of Jonah's will be ingeniously likened by the third-person narrator to an in-utero embryo and then a birthed baby. What unites this book with our earlier 9/11 novels, however, is not just that it has characters that fulsomely lie. The bond with 9/11 literature is that searing space from which the lie comes: that sense of an unending and unscabbed wound, all the loss, and the search for love, for replacement of the lost ones, as impossible as that act would be. The novel has some directions we might predict by now—an antihero either will stumble toward the spiritual light out of all his emotional darkness or refuse it; he or she will move to some rescuing love or move away from it. The quintessential fragile and forgotten man in the big city, our Gotham loner and loser Jonah, is a blend of characters that are part of the American scene. He has the pretensions and absurdity and comedic slips of Ignatius J. Riley from John Kennedy Toole's *A Confederacy of Dunces* (1980), the solitary bumbling and clumsy dating moves of Allan Felix in Woody Allen's *Play It Again, Sam* (1972), and the skinny, balding, sex-obsessed, slouching, porkpie hatted figure Robert Crumb in his forays (out of David Lynch's unforgettable documentary *Crumb*, 1994). Like Crumb, Jonah likes to sketch people in cafes, subways, and parks, but this artistic side (as with Crumb) was fought by a strong father, who was also hostile to Jonah's obsessive comics reading, which was Crumb's childhood reality, as well. There is much perverted about him, and like Crumb, he seems a pathetic man at times, carried on the strapping shoulders of a much stronger woman. Nevertheless, something vulnerable and artistic and original is in him to keep us digging into his character and influences. There is an awakening in the reader that if Jonah found the right (living) person, he might be able to have some relative joy and avoid the kind of perversion to get him arrested, and to give another some healing love, as well. There would be someone to distract him from the smell of death that he still imagines emanating from Ground Zero, whenever he walks southward in Manhattan. More depressing to note, Jonah is in his third decade of life but still has never kissed a boy or a girl. His catalog of sexual experiences is one-sided, to say the least, and often with people who treated Jonah as just one more "teenage horndog" to be indulged at first and despised later. Noteworthy is that breasts weight heavily in all these unsatisfactory encounters for him, which we will analyze later in connection to the prototypical breast, that yearned for one, his Mother's, at one time possessed by his rival in love the stern father, and now possessed by death itself.

Jonah's sexual activity, I suggest, is largely voyeuristic, and wedded with the forbidden, the guilt-inducing, and the punishment-promising kind. Apparently, the first time he lets his eyes feast on developed breasts (outside of his Mother's) is upon another mother whose son is his best friend in sixth grade, a boy named The Biscuit in some cruel but inexplicable reference to his harelip. Going over to The Biscuit's house, the perverted true spring and motivation of the friendship is revealed: "The Biscuit's mother was a tired, joyless woman, but her breasts, Jonah was surprised to find from behind her bedroom door, were buoyant, youthful things, pink and fresh as just-scrubbed cheeks. He tried to explain this to his friend, but The Biscuit did not understand" (Hansbury 2010). The moment her son discovers Jonah's Gothically weird penchant, some guilt, self-deprecation, and shame comes to the protagonist that will shadow him for the first two parts of this three-part novel. The punishment for this irresistible thirst, this fondness and fixation for a substitute Mother Love is a lost friendship with a pariah like himself, The Biscuit. So a loss of community (however small) and friendship might be associated at the nascent level in Jonah's mind for his breast-lust. It will continue—this adult-breastfeeding wish and activity—for all his years that we are able to witness. Many Gothic novels from *The Monk* onward fixate on the breast, and so much of it delves into Sado-Masochistic activities concerning women's mammaries. Perhaps the most popular nineteenth-century Gothic to handle breasts is Bram Stoker's *Dracula*, which Nancy Armstrong finds new angles on. In *Dracula*'s "figure of the breast-feeding male[, the Count] cancels out the categorical distinctions between man, woman and child maintained by the family, a cancellation represented in and produced by the vampire's needy, all-consuming, and yet inseminating mouth" (Armstrong 150). Certainly, Jonah's hunger for breastfeeding starts blurring the lines between adulthood and childhood, and ushers some more neurotic fears we need to touch on. The blue Gothic vein pulses here with secrets, fantasy, and necrophiliac desire rolled into one once Jonah dares to wonder, "what were Rose's breasts like? . . . There was the thought anyway, with no one to around to punish him for it. Did he dare to imagine the body of a dead woman? . . . to imagine breasts turned to dust, two sorry puffs of smoke. But how good it would feel to be held close to the real flesh, before fire rendered them into something regrettably forgettable. . . . *I am a man to pity*" (Hansbury 2012). With the ghosts, Oedipal longings, disastrous fathers, and even "castrating bitches" Jonah is trailed by, his self-diagnosis of a pitiful nature seems accurate.

Jonah actually has all kinds of mental complaints besides his compulsive breast-addiction, actually. His constant fear of going out and his turning off of switches suggest both agoraphobia and an obsessive-compulsive disorder; his dislike of company along with his obsession with creating his own nostalgic private world suggests a schizoid personality; he can suffer panic attacks as well. His love of lies and challenge with the truth may border on or even fall into a factitious disorder like Munchausen syndrome. In the interview, the author suggests even more mental conditions, including that Jonah is "internal, introverted, passive, avoidant, [and] autoerotically organized, . . . [suffering] a retraction of self" (Hansbury 2013). When we add PTSD to the above, just as other New Yorkers are experiencing, we have a man in ruins. However, Jonah Soloway has no patience for what he suspiciously dismisses as "head-shrinkers." Perhaps he fears what shame they would bring to light that he cannot abide. This is the classic New York story of a man suffering an ever-increasing mental ailment, seen in the films of Gotham from *Taxi Driver* (1976) to *Joker* (2019), with seemingly no assistance in sight. Indeed, the final riddle from Oscar-winning Joaquin Phoenix's portrayal of Arthur Fleck (and host Murray Franklin's last guest ever) mentioned earlier in this book unsettles our minds when we apply it to Jonah. Correspondingly, if we want to understand terrorist trauma's effects on a traumatized sexuality, Jonah Soloway is the subject that our intellect might ask for.

Weighing all his psychopathologies, it may well be Soloway's unfinished Oedipal relationship with his mother and haunting fears of castration that cause him the most neurotic behaviors and distress, or at least they seem to in his dreams, utterances, and jittery and failed visits to brothels. Of course, R. J. Stoller has wisely noted that in most cases castration anxiety may be too limited a fear if we think purely of a loss of testicles. In treating many patients, he found "Identity stands behind anatomy. Men, that is, do not fear loss of genitals per se (castration anxiety) as much as they fear to lose their masculinity and—still more fundamental—their sense of maleness" (35). I would argue that in the special case of Jonah, however, both a literal fear of being emasculated and an emotional one, are at stake, and neither is less than the other. His loss of a sense of maleness seems compounded after 9/11. Even the author in interview, as a psychoanalyst, might justly feel obliged to do over his character, weighs in with an analysis that I have to agree with: "But I do like to think of *The Nostalgist* as a psychoanalytic novel. Freud said that 'hysterics suffer mainly from reminiscences,' which is the case for neurotics, in general. The main characters in the novel all suffer from reminiscences, from the haunting of memory, melancholy, their unwillingness—or unreadiness—to mourn" (Hansbury 2013). Accompanying what the author observes of Jonah's blocked mourning and the inability to let his Mother go, there is an oppressive blame and burning shame that he cannot relieve, and it affects all his sexual relations with women. His one-eyed monster becomes, which the novel refers to, becomes now in Gothic-horror terms a bisected worm.

Camille Paglia in her bestselling first book *Sexual Personae* (1990), based on her PhD dissertation written many years before, discussed at length the "tormented fragility of male sexual identity—which most feminist theory, with its bitterly anti-male premises, seems incapable of recognizing" (Paglia 2018: xi). She probed into this supposed vulnerability, suggesting that "too often, women fail to realize how much power they have over men, whose ambition and achievement in the public realm are often wedded to remorseless anxiety and insecurity" (Paglia 2018: xi). Even more revealing to *The Nostalgist*, we could apply her idea that "The toothed vagina is no sexist hallucination: every penis is made less in every vagina, just as mankind, male and female, is devoured by mother nature" (Paglia 1990: 41). I would say that Jonah's sexual behavior is tied to two words: rejection and abjection. He is confused, frightened, embarrassed, full of failure, and unable to keep boundaries between order and the abject. One mocking look at him by any man or woman destroys his sexual presence and brings back all the intimidation and disdain from his father. He would like to dismiss his oppressors and detractors, but he is too attracted to them and wonders what he would have to do to take them home for the night: he embodies ambivalence itself.

Even before 9/11, carrying guilt and shame from his uncontrollable fetish for lactating-breasts, sagging him with the feeling that he is unlovable, we see him slouching toward the subway as his attractive female neighbor approaches walking her dog. Much of the action of the novel takes place in this locus of the Lower East Side of the borough of Manhattan, especially East 6th Street, the place with traditions of a large number of German immigrants, then eventually Southern European and Italian immigrants. Indeed, the protagonist is the son of an Italian mother from Calabria and an assimilated Jewish father. The woman that leisurely approaches is the daughter of Calabrians, too. The Lower East streets where they walk has a resonant place in the American mind as the one-time center of squalid and crowded tenements, of rough slums of disease and addiction and crime, and indeed was one of the neighborhoods that Jacob Riis made unforgettable in his expose *How the Other Half Lives* (1890), a book of photojournalism of the dim, dingy dwellings and alleys, by a Danish immigrant who himself once lived in those Lower East Side slums. Riis's book helped to finally foster reforms like the New York Tenement House Act (which increased basic space and light coming into such apartment buildings, as well as ushering safety and fire codes). This old, unsafe past of this place is an analog for Jonah's mind—full of darkness, crowded, sleazy, seedy, and diseased. Moreover, this is the historic working-class New York City, though gentrified in our time as the author has written of in his highly regarded *Vanishing New York* (under the synonym Jeremiah Moss). It is a place of physical strain and broken dreams and very few fantasies coming true: this is the perfect place to set a sad dreamer like Jonah, because dreams here seldom flowered, and yet what sustains a soul like fantasy? Every day as the small, shapely, youthful dark-haired woman walks her pug, and looks at Jonah only for a nanosecond as they pass every day, Jonah gazes for longer and longer. One day, the woman drops her mitten in the snow. Jonah reaches for it, and this woman—who has been becoming his secret artistic muse as the months go by—says (without even looking at him), "I got it." He only managed to utter something once in her company—three unpromising words "Uh," "Ahem," "Oh" (Hansbury 2012). And at that point of mitten pick up his thumb may have grazed her index finger, or not. From that slightest meeting, pathetic Jonah is inspired. But months go by, Fall comes again, and Jonah learns from walking past Missing Persons poster, that the lady with the pet pug is named Rose, one of those who were in a high floor of the North Tower on 9/11. Never is a last call made from the towers, and not a trace of her DNA is found at the towers, we later will learn from the victim's Mother, Vivian Oliveri.

*Griffin Hansbury's* The Nostalgist *(2012)* 131

Figure 4.2 In Buildings and Streets, Jonah Soloway Studies Hand-Made Sheets Like These in New York City of Missing Persons (and Animals) from 9/11. Screenshot from *World Trade Center*, Director Oliver Stone, Paramount, 2006.

Soon after, Jonah absconds with a Missing Persons poster of Rose and adds it to a file of clippings of Google searches he does on her. Every night, after his boring and unlikely work editing a cheery crafts site for parents and their school-age children at www.pinwheelkids.com, he goes home to worship beautiful Rose, hauling out her picture and talking to her, as if she were his soulmate. But a reader's quiet gasp may give way to horror and weird wonder when Jonah call's Rose's mother on the six-month memorial of 9/11, while the blue "Tribute in Light" on March 11, 2002, is about to pierce the sky in a memorial ceremony lit from Ground Zero and visible from space. In that call, he says he knew and admired Rose from work. That lie begets another: that he was a friend of Rose's. Later, in a meeting with Rose's mother Vivian, he gives a lie that goes beyond the beyonds—that he and Rose were engaged to be married. Thus, the book is a chronicle of Jonah Soloway's lies, and his overwhelming guilt at delivering them, and the begetting of a ghost by them. The worshipped Rose starts to become a real phantom for him that talks with him for much of the novel. The irony is that someone so alone and who knew her so little will become so close, in a fashion: he becomes astonishingly intimate with her ghost and objects and passions from her life. He will lift her first paintings stashed in her bedroom, gaze upon her hairbrushes and even the stuffed animals of her girlhood, and touch her panties and bras (almost do more to them until he hears her father Frank—always a male figure to disrupt his bond with the replacement of his mother—in the house). All that subtle awareness of her is in Jonah's consciousness now, and yet he could barely utter a hello to her when she walked by him every day. That desperate encounter with the fallen mitten will be remembered and replayed in dozens of variations throughout the novel, and her ghost will keep asking him (in a Freudian fashion as if decoding a dream): what does my glove symbolize to you? From reading *The Interpretation of Dreams*, which Jonah apparently never does, readers might in Freudian style imagine the glove to be the vagina that Jonah never had the bravery to approach. But with strobe-like flashes of dramatic irony and frustration coming at readers throughout the novel, Jonah seems to have no conscious understanding of the glimmering symbolic seams running through the sexualized framework of his dreams.

As a boy Jonah had night dreams of hope and sensuality: dreaming of the hems of schoolgirls' clothes, of kissing girls whose mouths tasted of plums, and now as an adult he has dreams of death and what comes after, of actually being dead, looking vaguely like a Jesus in a Lower East Side Catholic church, in a glass coffin, hovered over by hooded figures. Truly, his fear from engaging women in flirting, play, talk, or sex symbolically keeps him locked in both a glass coffin and a bell jar, though he has no idea of this symbolic import, never bothering to unpack his dreaming life. Sometimes there is an intellectual laziness in him, though other interpreters may see it as a fright that keeps him mentally passive, deliberately not investigating signs because of what more disabling darkness and freakishness that they may reveal and that his consciousness could barely withstand. At any rate, this dream vaguely suggests that Jonah's unconscious, and the accidental memories and connections floating though his dream state, are forming a story of sacrifice and a dream girl. He also dreams in his sleep of being at Ground Zero at night. When our antihero takes a walk on the night of the six-month memorial anniversary of 9/11, New York City plans to shine its memorial spotlights (an image featured on several covers of 9/11 fiction studies) far up into the night sky, and there is a sense that past is surely with the present as Jonah can still smell the faint but certain scent of the dead as he walks to his workplace that painfully bores him, but for which he has not the courage to aim higher. We know that this is a novel with a Gothic stain and strain when Jonah later comes back from work, goes to his bedroom, retrieves a folder underneath his T-shirts of a presumed-dead victim, including a Missing Person poster, from the North Tower of his Rose. She is smiling in the photo; he lines up clippings up her on the bed; and he proceeds to do something on the bed that we are not quite shown: Mere masturbation? A memorial? a ritual and summoning of the dead? We are never told precisely, but after a time he brings her photo to the kitchen, grabs a beer, props it on his Jack & Jackie Kennedy salt and pepper shakers, and gazes at Rose. She seems to rebuke him; he decides to go outside: "The sky over Manhattan had cleared of clouds and now, as Jonah rounded the corner onto the avenue, there shone before him the twin beams of the Tribute in Light, like a pair of blue comet tails themselves—plunging to Earth or rocketing away?" (Hansbury 2012). As he steps away with his shoes slipping on the sidewalk, an old rhyme of guilt comes to him "Don't step on the cracks or you'll break your mother's back." (Hansbury 2012). There is both hope and despair in this passage. The city, momentarily, has the ghost form of one of its famed landmark backs, the blue lights streaming upward and representing the WTC, from which Jonah may navigate. However, Jonah's muddled direction is still back to the image of his Mother, and that childhood rhyme evokes the true fact that she flew out of a windshield and was found in broken pieces on 9/11—all because she was en route to bring him dishes and silverware for his new apartment, when an SUV crashed into her small automobile. So haunting is the detail from Jonah that she was not mourned as were the victims of the Twin Towers, and yet she would still be living if another driver had not been distractedly gazing at the towers at moment of impact. But though his mother's ghost is never to rise to meet him, Rose's ghost starts to follow him and take on agency, not merely an apparition that listens or groans, but one who disagrees and questions.

But this night offers both a ghost-girlfriend's company and the briefest company of a "totally live girl," as Time's Square signs used to tout before Mayor Giuliani ordered it cleansed of its seedy demi-monde life.[1] At a party he is forced to attend by a coworker, while Jonah is hiding in a bedroom and avoiding all contact, an alluring woman named Jane enters, and finds all of his usually geeky trademarks somehow attractive, from his motheaten, aged porkpie hat to an egg he carries to check whether he can stand it on its end that very night, the Spring Equinox. These may not normally be fetching details, but the deep love of quirkiness in Jane is aroused (who, like the author Hansbury at time of writing this book, had just completed her psychoanalytic training). However, Jane is like a vision too radiant to behold, for her strong, athletic, commercial, unartistic boyfriend comes into the bedroom and carries her away. Soon after, Jonah is lonelier than before. Upon a chance meeting at a dog park some days later, he sees Jane looking at him, and even taking a seat beside him. His passivity starts to abate, and he speaks more, and eventually they come about to the tragedy they share of 9/11. But as Jane sits beside him, almost flirting, the first moment for the ghost of Rose to utter a sound comes: she has followed him to the dog park. Her first word articulated that only Jonah and not Jane hears is "Go" (Hansbury 2012). We may interpret this as the ghost encouraging him to enter into life and relationships: to say, "Go to her, go talk, go live, go chance something." Or we may understand the one word to mean, "Run away from her. She won't understand you. She is going to hurt you." Just as Rose is declared as both imagined and real by the author himself in interview, I would also venture that the "Go" is not only an ambiguous term but an ambivalent one. Rose's elusive ghost, as divided in her soul as the rest of us or as any lover can be, is perhaps both saying, "I don't want to see her because I am jealous of the possible love and of what it is to be alive. However, I do want her here because all I have is reminiscence. She reminds me of what passion is, she tells me what you should reach for." This is in part based on what her parents say of her.

Rose is a necessary ghost. Because Jonah is by nature a contrarian, she intuits that for whatever she advises him, he will take the opposite course. Rose ends up helping him to establish touch with a girlfriend who can finally and lovingly touch him back. She truly is an ensorcelling ghost, and though she claims she is just a voice from Jonah's unconscious, I would suggest that she is more: that she is a classical ghost. She knows too many things that Jonah would have no way of knowing to be just a part of his subterranean mind (including the constantly hungry state ghosts are in, what the world of the dead really is, and how it felt to fall out of the tower in flames and on to the plaza). Scholars should have different ideas of what her role is: some could see her as a demonic agent summoning Jonah to bad deeds. I see her more of an advocate arguing for a variety of positions he could take, some of harm, some of help. He claims to suspect psychotherapy, especially psychoanalysis, and so Rose tells him to tell Jane so, get up, and turn his back on her. Yet, he stays: raptly listening to Jane's post-Freudian theories, loving her therapeutic questioning of him. Likewise, when Rose tells him to go ahead and throw a brick through the window of a new massive gas-guzzling SUV at the family inside, she is mostly testing how faithful he is to his angry pro-environment and anti-consumerist stances. He neglects to throw a brick in his hand at them. Instead, he waves at the materialistic family, and lifts a Starbucks coffee in salute—the product of yet another corporation he claims to despise, and that she urges him not to support. This moment when he refuses to throw a brick at a family Rose is raging on, will be the last time he ever sees or hears her. He thinks she just became "tired." I believe it is more than that: she may have felt her role fulfilled: that Jonah is growing and becoming more independent and less schizoid: he is going out with Jane and suggesting things that they could do. Rose is a challenger and fast-thinking skeptic: she seems to scoff at him with the attitude, *how much do you believe any of the ideas you espouse, Jonah*? I believe the unspoken question that she leads him to is *how much do you really need a ghost lover, and why do you have one—is it because death is an attraction? Why do you think a living lover is impossible for you*? Indeed, not long before she parts forever, Rose creeps into a conversation Jonah and Jane have on sex and mortality, again which only Jonah can hear.

"You have to face it—death is erotic," [Jane declared].
"I've never felt that way," Jonah said, feeling the heat of Jane's hand on his leg and an uninvited erection beginning to unfurl in his pants.

"I knew it," said Rose [silently], enjoying his discomfort. "I knew you wanted to fuck her. And you are getting off on it. Death. You're a regular necrophiliac."
"I've never gotten off on death," he said out loud.
"Sure you have," Jane insisted. (Hansbury 2012)

Such episodes of Jonah in a three-way argument become more comical as the book develops because Jane cannot here the wisely intrusive ghost Rose. Rose could be dismissed as jealous and petty at times, but perhaps these qualities mask her actual role which is an instigator and prodder to one who desperately needs a shove, and who is longing for love. The problem Jonah faces is that Jane has a boyfriend, and the unknown question is whether she will stay with him. In the meantime, Jonah must keep on his quest, he must bring back the elixir (Of self-confidence? Of freedom from the haunting of death? Of easing of his guilt over perversions? Of Oedipal resolutions and a release from the fear of the punishing father?), and that involves some dangers to body and soul.

## CASTRATION ANXIETY

Haunted by death around him, Jonah Soloway is still concerned principally for the fate of his penis. Considering how seldom it is invited out, readers may find the worry unwarranted. His last name not only hints to his loneliness in life and his melancholy finding of his own unpartnered way in life but also reliance upon masturbation (which he admits). Still, if we make assumptions about how Jonah's mind works that are based on psychoanalytic theory, as well as post-Freudian theorists including Camille Paglia, then we may posit that some of his wrenching insecurity is based on a disabling castration complex. Novels and novellas with some Gothic themes that feature the castration complex and a vagina dentata are not as uncommon as we may first guess, and range from Neal Stephenson's *Snow Crash,* Dan Simmons's *Hyperion,* Stephen King's *Christine,* Yoshiaki Kawajiri's *Yoju Toshi* (*Wicked City*), K. W. Jeter's *Dr. Adder,* Carlos Fuentes' *Christopher Unborn,* Russell Hoban's *Riddley Walker,* to Mario Vargas Llosa's *The Way to Paradise.* In the case of beleaguered Jonah, he has fear coming from *both* directions: fear of men castrating him, and the fear of women devouring him.

His one-eyed monster, which the novel refers to, becomes now in Gothic-horror terms a bisected worm. Paglia in her bestselling and first book, the 712-page tome *Sexual Personae* (1990) based on her PhD dissertation written in the early 1980s, discussed at length the "tormented fragility of male sexual identity—which most feminist theory, with its bitterly anti-male premises, seems incapable of recognizing" (Paglia 2018: xi). She probed into this supposed vulnerability, suggesting that "too often, women fail to realize how much power they have over men, whose ambition and achievement in the public realm are often wedded to remorseless anxiety and insecurity" (Paglia 2018: xi). Even more revealing to *The Nostalgist*, we could apply her idea that "The toothed vagina is no sexist hallucination: every penis is made less in every vagina, just as mankind, male and female, is devoured by mother nature" (Paglia 1990: 41). I would say that Jonah's sexual behavior, before he securely unites with Jane, is tied to two words: rejection and abjection. He is confused, frightened, embarrassed, full of failure, and unable to keep boundaries between order and the abject. One mocking look at him by any man or woman destroys his sexual presence and brings back all the intimidation and disdain from his father. He would like to dismiss his oppressors and detractors, but he is too attracted to them and wonders what he would have to do to take them home for the night: he embodies ambivalence itself.

That dread reaches scary depths in the book that have humiliation at their edges. He is visited by a flood of memories: of schoolyard taunts about what will happen to him from playing doctor on the playground, remembered visions of his father glowering at him like Saturn every time he and his mother bonded at the supper table, old wounds of how his father gave up on little Jonah building a telescope of his own for a school project. The father made the telescope for him, thrusting his superior skill with getting this phallic object up to the stars in young Jonah's face—the father was an astronomer, after all. This telescope Jonah carries with him as an adult, a kind of substitute and acceptable penis object, that of his superior father. Curiously, Jonah later uses the telescope to spy on lovely women undressing in their condos or women meeting handsome men for dinner and exchanging kisses. His contact of women is through this long, but cold physical object, rather than his own skin. Skin is the part of us that Freud so vividly identified with the ego in, writing in *The Ego and the Id* from 1923 that "The ego is ultimately derived from bodily sensations, chiefly from those springing from the surface of the body." Thus, a psychoanalytic theorist might intriguingly argue that if the ego is mostly an effect of how we perceive our skin, whether by touch or mirror or photography, and that Jonah feels that he cannot touch his skin against a woman's, then for most of the book Jonah's ego is a tiny and fragile thing, an almost unfunctioning construct. To dare to at least partially understand Jonah through Freudian spectacles, we may have to revisit the dark cave that represents the varieties of castration experience for those certain men of Jonah's deep-set fears and guilt. Indeed, Freud "considered castration to be one of the two major anxieties of human life" (Taylor 2016: 40). If the castration complex is underrepresented in current discourse, and consequently our awareness is lowered as we read a novel like this, still many psychoanalysts, including a leading University of Toronto psychology professor and psychiatrist Dr. Graeme Taylor still treat and write on many cases of castration anxiety in adult men. Jonah seems to be one of these men, as yet unmediated, of course.

When Jonah abruptly quits his copyeditor job at Omnimedia after another clash with his Medusa-likened boss over her desire for the company to market products that image the destruction of the WTC, he storms out of the office armed only and oddly with his Daddy's telescope. It may be as Freud argued in 1922 in his short piece that "Medusa's Head" that "to decapitate = to castrate," or that both the "Medusa's head takes the place of a representation of the female genitals," and in this case somehow stiffens Jonah without turning him to stone. As for the imagined snakes in his dreaded boss's hair, "however frightening they may be in themselves, they actually serve as a mitigation of the horror for they replace the penis, the absence of which is the cause of the horror" (Freud 1922: "Medusa's Head"). Jonah might feel this mitigation of horror, for he hits the Manhattan streets with bravado, after turning his back on that unartistic job, promptly entering an Eighth Avenue brothel and peep-show called the Clam Buffet that still impossibly has some of what was once called the "Devil's Playground" in it, some bit of the old seedy and not-yet-Disneyfied Times Square that Mayor Giuliani banished in the 1990s. In the Clam Buffet, still poised with his Daddy's upright-angled telescope, he settles into a an old-school peep-show's self-pleasuring room with rising door, plexiglass, an insert for money, an un-Lysoled stool, and a strong and shapely dancer dressed only in thigh-high leather books named "Virgina Dentata." Ms. Dentata dances in a way that consumes Jonah. It compares favorably to the languorous, slithery way Amanda Donohue moves and bites unsuspecting village men's members clean off as Lady Sylvia Marsh in Director Ken Russell's cult-classic adaptation of Bram Stoker's *The Liar of the White Worm* (1988). Long and serpentine Ms. Dentata, who flashes an Ouroboros tattoo and slit contact lenses that give her reptilian eyes, has a mouth that conjures a constrictor's. Her vagina dentata is both below, then, and above: and the fear is visible in poor Jonah's eyes who looks like he will not survive. He seems to sense that her mouth would open, bite him with its fangs and drug her with venom, then swallow him neatly whole just as an overgrown python sups on a monkey. I would argue that this symbolic devouring is the stylized and parodic punishment that he has wished for, from desiring the mother's breasts and wanting the father dead, and then suffering the twist of fate of his mother dying instead, all of which he runs from and blocks out, just as he blocks out those moments of seeing the towers burn. Note how much desire he is experiencing in his punishment, which is because he welcomes it, and feels he deserves it: "He was hard now, and managed, twitchingly, to unzip. The girl's torso looked like a giant face, the nipples staring at him, wide-eyed, the mushroom cloud like a terrible nose, the genital tongue in its tangled beard twirling against the window. He tried to follow it, watching the body-mouth whirl, twirling the lacteous smear into artful spirals, like a hypnotist's spinning disk" (Hansbury 2012). This passage (particularly in a debut novel) astonishes in its frenetic and lustful immediacy, the claustrophobia in the booth, the sense there is no escape, and all the associations that become psychoanalyst's dream case.

The formidable stripper's act and her tattoo associates to the atomic bomb dropping, which associates with Jonah's father's study of atoms, to the destruction of buildings falling and dust, fires, and to smoke rising. It conjures, moreover, the fall of the WTC, and the dust that is left from many who were inside or below it. Moreover, Ms. Dentata's high-octane act brings to mind blood, a body of an automobile-hit woman Jonah just saw on the street, and his own mother's death. Somehow desire, guilt, the erotic, and death merge in a dance macabre, and all that thanks to Ms. Dentata and just a twenty-dollar bill. Somehow our Jonah, who though himself so week before, endures. But where or what is this satirical portrait of a questing-hero's secret power source?

Jonah's strength and resistance to another victimhood comes, I believe, from his desire for Jane and a pride in her attraction for him, a desire to live that smashes against his father's degradations, against the prohibitions against worshipping the maternal breast as an adult, against all who are insisting he conform, all who have judged him a failure without knowing him. He sinks deeply and proudly into what he desires, and comes out on the other side:

> The girl's hands squeezed her breasts and worked their way down to part the snarled patch of hair. He thought with distaste of the term "meat curtains." . . . It made him think of the thick plastic curtains in meat-packing. He thought of blood. Of the woman dead on Broadway with her tender head broken open. He thought of his mother. He shook these thoughts as the girl pressed herself against the Plexiglas, sliding open to show pink flesh smearing a viscous, pelagic substance. (Hansbury 2012)

In a scene with so much abjection (the vaginal fluids smearing the plexiglass, the saliva spread from each of their mouths, and the eventual ejaculate splatting from Jonah), it is easy to overlook the blood. In fact, the blood is the life of this scene: the association of his Mother to blood is the most abject that she ever becomes for Jonah. Ironically, as she is becoming more abject, we will see he is becoming closer to finding the way to honor her life and her death, along with the ghost Rose, which forms the mourning and memorialization that is often the focus of trauma studies.

## CONCLUSION

*I am dead, I know what I'm talking about from where I am, and I'm watching you.*

—Jacques Derrida, *Ghost Dance* (1983)

As Barbara Creed sees it, integrating Kristeva's concepts into her own interpretation of women in horror, "the ultimate in abjection is the corpse" (38). That is what Jonah's dear mother is made into here: the ultimate abjection. She is associated with a middle-aged woman's pedestrian death Jonah just saw on the street. We need the abject to have order, to find our place that is away from it: we need the abject to show a physical representation of what we have not yet fully collapsed into ourselves. Despite all that in Ms. Virginia Dentata's salacious and lubricious performance causes him distaste, he is aroused—and, at some point, Daddy's telescope must have fallen. It is lost, it is vanquished, it is replaced in that sticky-floored room with Jonah's flesh. Tellingly, Jonah will know the telescope is gone, but he will not return for it. He does not need it anymore: he is his own man, and not Daddy's shadow. Jonah has come as close as he ever will to being devoured by a vagina now, he will suffer the compression and the swallowing, he will return to the womb, and then he will (unlike his first birth where forceps where used) not resist coming back to our world, coming out having gone through a devouring. Indeed, as he gazes as Ms. Dentata's vagina pressed so close to his eyes, "he saw his own face reflected in the Plexiglas, his own ghost hovering before him in the darkness, his own eyes looking back at him. His face transposed over the rheumy glaze, over the bubblegummy flesh that kept on spinning, seemed strangely unfamiliar and yet. If he could just name it. There were so many layers. His face, his ghost, the window, the smear, the flesh. The womb, the tomb. The bomb, the flash" (Hansbury 2012). This is the truest Freudian uncanny of a homecoming, this is the old home Freud wrote of, our Mother's womb. Having survived all this, Jonah is never the same. And his first longing after the visit to the Clam Buffet peep-show seems to be for his Mother's breasts, swollen nipple, and milk. He is like a newborn baby again and has the infant's first instinct to breathe the new air, cuddle, and feed. He has a dream, and in it are "white pillows surrounding him. A bull's eye hovering near, a target at which he aimed all of his yearning. It was good, so good. Like nothing else in this world. Like all the vanilla ice cream you could eat" (Hansbury 2012). While he births out of the vagina again, it is a close call: "He gulped for air, his mouth briny with the tang of salt, as deeper the [peep-show] box plunged [into some abyss]. And still the vulval mouth swam toward him, gulping in its frenzied hula dance, singing in its mermaid tongue" (Hansbury 2012). By not staying in this room, he is leaving the womb, breaking the lock of his blissful relationship with the mother and accepting separation from her. Like the classic stages of the hero's journey, so well known, Jonah, in his lampooning way, has crossed the threshold, approached and entered the inmost cave, and returned with the "elixir." In a book whose lead character is Jonah, we had to expect he might be face refuse the call for a time, face ordeals, be swallowed and then be expelled at some point. I think his recovered magic potion is actually greater knowledge, acceptance of his strength, the freedom to openly be the masochist he is, a release of pointless guilt, and a determination to meet Jane again and wrest her from a loathsome boyfriend who has put together a show called *Celebrity Death Wish*, which he does. I believe that his elixir is finally the elixir of love. He accepts that his lovemaking with his sweet Jane would not be a one-time miracle or strangely ecstatic hallucination, but could evolve into a deep relationship, could even grow into them living together.

Stuart Voytilla rephrases and reflects clearly on Joseph Campbell's famed formulations when he says that "Story lines [start to be] resolved, balance has been restored to the ordinary World, and the Hero may now embark on a new life, forever influenced by the Journey traveled" (Voytilla 1999: 6). This does seem to reflect Jonah's and New York City's new life: Jonah will soon have Jane move in with him, and he soon will finally sprinkle the ashes of the two ghosts whose urns sit side by side in his apartment: his lover and his mother, his Rose and his Teresa. Rather than keeping these dead women inside his house and letting them run his mind and ruin his chances for love among the living, he is finally letting them go. Moreover, Rose's ghost teaches him how being dead is much lonelier and hungrier and more desperately sad than being alive. As he is alive and able, he should seek out what community he can—with Jane, Rose's surviving family, and the victims' families at the Ground Zero memorial site. He should talk to the travelers on the ferry that carries him and his Mother's ashes, in that boat that moves her like Charon's boat moved souls upon the River Styx, and he does—conversing with the famed New Yorker "Cross Man" who carries a life-scale wooden crucifix serious on his back, who tells Jonah, "Don't be stupid. You've got your own nothing to do," to junkies, and to mothers' nursing babies who are sheltering on the ferry as they have nowhere else to go. America is there along with him for the ride. Jonah's longtime problem, like that of his Jewish namesake, was that he could only accept people from afar: in Jonah's exact case, from looking at a telescope at them, from floating over them like the speaker in Walt Whitman's "The Dreamers." By the end of the book on that Staten Island ferry he is connecting with New Yorkers, he is engaged in his community of fellow victims and mourners. After releasing the cremains of his mother at book's end, Jonah tenderly comes back up to the ferry deck, and Jane took his hand and Vivian put her arm in his. In one of the tenderest scenes of the novel, "they stood like that, not saying anything. Up ahead, its glass and steel glinting in sunlight, the city came back to Jonah. It looked the way it had that day when he blotted out the towers with his thumb, the way he'd wanted it to look. But he knew this had nothing to do with him. . . . Jonah consoled himself by imagining the many paths on which his mother was embarking" (Hansbury 2012). He has found that, in the words of a defeated presidential candidate from nine months before 9/11 whose loss would cause many to wonder how the post-9/11 realities may have been brighter, that "defeat might serve as well as victory to shape the soul and let the glory out" (Gore 2000). The compassion of this scene recalls Rollo May opinion that "The purpose of psychotherapy is to set people free" (qtd. in Hansbury 2020). In Jonah's openness to change as encouraged by a psychoanalyst-in-training (living) girlfriend, in his acceptance of social and personal responsibility as a trauma witness (by spreading the ashes: by commemorating their lives, instead of hiding their cremains in his kitchen and avoiding acceptance of their deaths), and in his shedding of his irrational guilt in the fall of the towers, Jonah has been freed at last.

## NOTE

1. As his memorist alter-ego, Jeremiah Moss, the fiction writer Griffin Hansbury has written lyrically of the shabby sexiness of old Times Square. Another great source for how it used to be is Meagan Drillinger's "I Went to One of Time Square's Last Remaining Peep Shows" from The Thrilllist posted on May 8, 2015.

*Chapter 5*

# Patrick McGrath's *Ground Zero* (2005)
## Abandoning and Angering the Dead

### CRITICAL RECEPTION

I believe that we read a book forever differently after a parent dies, or at least that is so my case, and it seems to be the situation for motherless Jonah Soloway and our next protagonist whose mother has also died, Daniel Silver in Patrick McGrath's *Ground Zero,* from McGrath's time-hopping collection of novellas, *Ghost Town: Tales of Manhattan Then and Now.* I perceive that we talk about ourselves and we write differently, too, after the death of our mother or father. There is a recognition of certain times and chances that we never will have back, and there is no clear sense of how to negotiate this absence of them. Ghosts may return, and Derrida stresses that the nature of a specter is to return again and again, but such chances with our living parent never do. Opportunities to talk and understand what is secret or unknown, yet vital, have all vanished with their last breaths. We may have the unnerving experience of seeing a parent in a video talk about death, or believing in ghosts, or in the messages of spectral returns. Derrida experienced this himself (though not with a parent) at a Texas university watching *Ghost Dance* with students long after its premiere and witnessing his costar, the young actress Pascale Ogier (of *Full Moon in Paris* fame) who had died at age twenty-five of a heart attack in the interim, gaze at him from the theater screen and ask, "Do you believe in ghosts?" During the movie Ogier and Derrida had for hours "looked into one another's eyes which is an experience of strange and unreal immensity, . . . prolonged and passionately repeated" in the movie and between takes (Derrida *Ghost Dance*: 1983). Derrida, in the most emotional passage I have read of his outside his memorials for other culture critics and philosophers including Roland Barthes, mentions that this nearly romantic bond made the dead Ogier's image surreal for him once she was dead. Hers, he remembers, was the "eye-line of a gaze that fixes and looks for the other, its other, . . . in an infinite night," actually looking for her own ghost and her subconscious inside the living body of Derrida himself (Derrida 1983: *Ghost Dance*). But moments for parents and grown sons and daughters to talk of metaphysics or experience wonderment together in real time—almost like becoming children again—by wandering somewhere faraway and perhaps sublime, whether the Grand Canyon or the Great Barrier Reef, are all gone. A new sensibility, finality, frailty, and regret settles upon us as evening creeps into our lives, and our minds drift to a lost parent. There is something unfulfilled in every day afterward. Moreover, the sensation is one of being bereft, almost of having lost a sense that was essential to us, or as Hilary Mantel (who has written Gothic stories her own, including "Sorry to Disturb") imaginatively describes its reflection in Nicholas Royle's memoir, *Mother*—"What we lose: the touch, the tone, the gaze of the past as it fades." Easily some of us would give up years of our lives for a few impossible hours that are not to be granted anymore with parents. In the middle of writing this book, my father died. I can appreciate how both Jonah and Daniel, though both adults, still feel like they are crying orphans crouched in an empty street with nobody left to hear them once their mothers are gone forever.

Because I write in the raging time of a virus named SARS-CoV-2 and a disease called COVID-19, all meditations on 9/11 seem new again. We can probably remember the first months after 9/11, and how any kind of terror—the knowable and the unknowable—could kill us. Indeed, more than any other words of the novelists covered herein, the psychological insight of the final novelist we cover ring truest: "One trauma always hides another, and can therefore function to uncover it" (McGrath 2017: "Afterword"). Another English contributor to one of my anthologies of short stories, Neil Gaiman, and a writer of books where a child's parents die (*The Graveyard Book* being just one Caldecott Award-winning example) said in the first days of his COVID-19 blog (May 2020) that he hadn't experienced the same loneliness of roads, planes, and airports since 9/11, as he tried to get around in a days after those attacks. Such an immediate and automatic reached-for comparison helps answer the question of how 9/11 is remembered and referenced by an author twenty or more years later. Everything we learned and felt and were wounded by from 9/11 comes back to us now: fear of disorder, of economic disarray, of loss of job and of shortages, of government abuses to civil liberties, of a police force out of control, and of death coming to old and young though a novel virus. Gaiman's English countryman McGrath wrote me much from New York City similar feelings from May 2020 when *The New York Times* was reporting one in four New Yorkers was going hungry, "Very pleased to know you're writing about *Ground Zero*. I've just been looking at it again, and it's hard not to recognize the dim outlines of the crisis we're enduring now, the various 'biohazards' that seemed to threaten us then, and the vaccines being stockpiled, even as civil life as we knew it was being so grossly disrupted. The air of unreality, with the Twin Towers down and lower Manhattan a smoking ruin" (McGrath Email: 12 May 2020). In May 2020 with the COVID-19 outbreak, New York, cursed once more, was the epicenter of infection, leading the country in overwhelmed hospitals and beleaguered makeshift morgues hastily put up in parking lots. It is New Yorkers, as it was with 9/11, who again felt early the greatest terror in the country and a staggering body count from an attack whose end is unknown.

Like *The Nostalgist* (and an exception to most of the books we have covered before in this study) and perhaps because of its authentic and detailed conjuring of McGrath's aforementioned "unreality," I could not find a negative appraisal of *Ground Zero* in the popular press at its release. Todd McEwen for *The Guardian* found that McGrath's novella is literally a ghost story "and once or twice the 'gothic' gets a little lurid" (appropriately so for our analysis) and notes how thought-provokingly this novelistic "study in a loss of power and confidence captures America's great city in its "decline into material and moral confusion, bereft of purpose" (McEwen 2005). Reviewing for the same newspaper, Tim Adams offered acclaim for McGrath's "sexual adventure . . . [which] plunges you into the heart of this horror with some gusto and relives it in vaguely antique prose" (Adams 2005). This fiction of lust during the atrocity investigates with "quietly disturbing perception" how Daniel's "desire somehow linked to her [Kim Lee's] grief at the loss of her partner who died in the towers" (Adams 2005). Staff at *Publishers Weekly* appreciated McGrath's resonant compassion as he "sets these stories against the burgeoning city and its stew of sublime aspiration, corrupt failure, and sexual and class antagonisms, . . . complicat[ing] each with a subtle, empathetic humanism" (Staff at *Publishers Weekly* 2005). Two more reviews concentrate on the menace and malice of characters in the novella. Staff at *Kirkus Reviews* detected a crueler and more manipulative Kim Lee than I do in the "over-the-top but compelling" *Ground Zero*: "The therapist/narrator is fighting for the soul of her patient Danny, who has become ensnared by Asian-American prostitute Kim in the wake of 9/11. The evil of the terrorist assault is replicated in Kim's evil sex games, previously inflicted on a lover who died during the attack. (She's seen his ghost.) . . . Strange bedfellows, but good company" (Staff at *Kirkus Reviews* 2005) The same threat of exploitation of a man colors the review from Michael Antman in *Bookslut* of McGrath's "painstakingly detailed and powerful prose . . . [of] anguish." Antman finds Daniel's "obsession with the prostitute is itself of secondary interest to the prostitute's own chillingly manipulative behavior. True, the psychiatrist's account, which unfolds in a way that makes it clear that she has a few obsessions of her own, yields some effective ironies" (Antman 2005).

We will explore later the critics' curiosity toward the women and how they "ensnared" Daniel.

As for the newspaper of his adopted home, *The New York Times* finds the eerie motions of *Ground Zero* "powerfully original" (Byrd 2005). With

> a voyeuristic narrator, erotic obsession, a painter, another domineering father, an ashy landscape of phantoms and wreckage, . . . the literary props have a chilling plausibility. The ghost the prostitute sees feels like a projection of real hopes and fears. In a series of beautifully linked metaphors, psychological abstractions grow almost unbearably physical. Under attack, the towers of New York seem suddenly human. When the story's final betrayal takes place, McGrath finds an image faithful at once to history and to felt experience. Gothic becomes tragic. (Byrd 2005)

Of all the reviews, this finely detailed latter one out of Gotham effused the most over *Ground Zero*, despite coming from the city where the highest expectations for covering their trauma often mean a disastrous critical panning for our previously covered 9/11 novels, as Michelle Kakutani has demonstrated. Byrd understands the implicit and fundamental Gothic conceit of a ruin standing for the broken people surrounding it.

If *Ground Zero* has a curious power over initial readers garnering positive reviews, then its power to entrance also extends to academics writing searching chapters on the novella's psychic indications, Gothic inklings, and its art. Inside scholarly articles, *Ground Zero* is touted for its search into the recesses and agonies of trauma. John Kuo Sheng sustains a resonant argument that McGrath potently uses the Gothic mode to reveal what were "certain invisible dimensions of the pre-and-post-9/11 culture" (Sheng 72). Georgiana Banita, expertly applying and enlarging Cathy Caruth's concepts on trauma over the years, finds McGrath's ghost story closes the "gap separating the world-historical trauma from the embodied trauma of personal relationships" (Banita 2011: 20). Fascinating unfoldings on the "Real" and on racism come through the insights of Jerrold E. Hogle, as well. Hogle contends that the

> Gothic is still helping us recognize, even after 9/11, how much our desire to both rejoin and avoid the Real is configured in our longings for objects of desire that are always no more than signs for the specters of still other objects that themselves recede almost infinitely back toward other specters, all so that the Real can be intimated in them but can never finally reabsorb those of us who are still alive. Perhaps one way to finally protect oneself from this endless regression is another deeply Gothic device employed by the *Ground Zero* psychiatrist, her climatic projection of monstrosity, to avoid her own, on Kim

Lee, as though this mixed "oriental" could justify even [Attorney General] John Ashcroft's . . . call for more racial profiling before and after 11 September 2001. (Hogle 2014: 78)

The psychiatrist is allied, then, with high legal offices in America to discriminate and even deny the rights of those who look somehow "foreign," a syndrome of racism and xenophobia present to this day. Hogle closes with the idea, which should be examined, that this novella encourages meditation on "how much the interpersonal/racial hatreds that both caused 9/11 and were exacerbated by it are in fact forces of history too outside individual control to be cured or are matters of very individual choice, such as the psychiatrist's racist suggestions prompted by her own unconscious and personal agenda" (Hogle 2014: 78). This is what Fiona Tolan helpfully calls the design of much of 9/11 fiction: its "genre? school? corpus? thematic preoccupation? the pattern of aggression, reaction, response and counter-response played out with such blood effect . . . [and] penetrated and interrogated by writers (and indeed artists and filmmakers) in a manner quite distinct from the discourse on terror conducted by both politicians and the press" (Tolan 2012: x). In the same study where she observes this, another contributor, Robert Duggan, argues that *Ground Zero*'s "hostility to Kim's ethnic difference . . . and her thirst for vengeance and her possessive and dismissive attitudes towards Danny all produce a portrait of a personality moving towards aggression and intolerance, with 9/11 acting as a catalyst. . . . The story creates a circulation of influence between personal and civic disaster, with trauma figuring prominently" (Duggan 2012:134). Duggan's observation leads us to equate Silver with some of the American public postdisaster, with a hope to go on after the fall of the towers and keep and nurture whatever peace they could, while the unnamed psychiatrist evokes the U.S. government's descent into suspicion, dubious rounds of surveillance, leaked and widely publicized interrogation missteps and trials, and forever wars. Gérald Préher herds readers back to Daniel's parenthood. He reflects on Marc Amfreville's statement on McGrath's earlier novel of an alcoholic and incestuous painter, *Port Mungo*, that "a trauma always hides another" (qtd. in Préher 2012: 116). Amfreville suggested to Préher (at a McGrathian fiction conference in Perpignan, France, that McGrath himself attended) that "trauma is always retroactive. In the case of 9/11, seeing the second plane hit the other tower confirmed that what had happened was not an accident and forced people to see that the country was under attack" (Préher 2012:116). Préher would apply the concept, and then insightfully take it farther: "I am tempted to add, that one trauma can expose another since the second event always comes as an explanation of the first. Dan . . . feels that the catastrophe [as the novella says,] 'brought back everything he had suffered after his mother's death'" (Préher 2012:116).

## GHOST SIGHTINGS

If one trauma in a disturbed psyche always hides yet can reveal an earlier trauma, we have a method to investigate Danny's suffering and release from mental torture. All this opens Derrida's wise insight from "Living On," that "One text reads another. . . . Each 'text' is a machine with multiple reading heads for other texts" (Derrida 1979: 107). In *Spectres of Marx*, he similarly confirms that insight in a supernatural way allied to our interpretive quest on the spirits in McGrath, "Everyone reads, acts, writes with *his* or *her* ghosts" (139). To this point, it is fascinating and revelatory how one book on terror can develop its own perceptive analysis on another, just as *The Nostalgist* reveals greater depths to the trauma and most desperate healing attempts in *Ground Zero*.

Like Hansbury's novel, McGrath's novella also features a psychoanalyst (this one is also a psychiatrist, yet never prescribes Daniel any medicine) who suffers a too-strong countertransference with her client. This unnamed therapist-narrator has been seeing her client Daniel Silver twice a week for the last seven years in her living room. She narrates her account of entanglement after Daniel has already left her treatment and gives a back story in the tone of "here is where Danny made his fateful mistakes—here is where he left me!" It is a book (like the *Nostalgist*) of ethical lapses: a psychotherapist is in love with her patient, and works for ways to involve preventing his love for other woman; she steers her vulnerable client's conversation back to why he needs to keep up the counseling with only her; she divulges what was said in privileged and protected therapist-client conversations. It is mysterious to me, then, how many critics assail the artist/prostitute Kim Lee and then defend this exploitative and manipulative psychiatrist. All I can offer is that the compressed distance in the story between this psychological-professional narrator and we the readers blurs our objectivity. Meanwhile, her client, a lawyer who often works pro bono to protect clients from civil rights abuses and landlord misdeeds, has his own professional-ethics lapses: he finds himself having sex in his office with a client of his own.

The similarities and even the oppositions to *The Nostalgist* are engrossing. Daniel's mother has died, and he had an as unusually intense and constricting relationship with her as did Jonah. Daniel inherited her house on Manhattan's Upper West Side, where he grew up in an affluent world close in distance but far in socioeconomic reality from Jonah's Lower East Side. Continuing to live for most of the novella in this emotionally haunted house where his mother died and two marriages perished, Daniel languishes as he is shackled to the dreary past. The anonymous therapist senses his problems are largely sexual, stemming from an overbearing mother, and like any psychoanalyst, she listens, asks, and jots notes. However, her classical Freudian spin—that the problems "originated in a suffocating maternal relationship which created conflicts that ran like fault lines deep in his psyche, becoming visible only when he tried to sustain intimacy with a woman" (McGrath 2005: 261)—seems very narrow. In a worrisome tendency for alert readers, she starts to tell him things bonding him ever closer to her and away from the memory of his mother, and any romantically available women. A second red flag rises when his psychoanalyst calls him her lost son. A third red flag waves, and strong evidence for an unreliable narrator who is more interested in having him as her pet than as an improving client with a mature and lasting relationship with a partner, when she encourages him to purchase women for his sexual needs. Raising our eyebrows, the therapist confesses with detectable pride: "I was aware Dan used prostitutes, nothing new there. In fact, I encouraged it" (McGrath 2005: 262). Why would any mental health professional advise this? Indeed, Daniel under her sanction has been seeking whores for seven years, yet his therapist cannot link this destructive behavior with "the frowns, groans, and sighs, . . . from [his] darkly bagged eyes that teemed with complicated anxieties" (McGrath 2005: 262), or even guess that his depressed look has anything to do with having a steady stream of prostitutes come to his abode with never a lasting relationship. If not one woman he has had sex with in the last seven years has done it for anything but dollars, then we can obviously see why he would have trust issues.

But one of the escorts he meets (from the back of *New York Magazine* where they still advertise in real life) is primarily a painter, a bold and unconventional conversationalist, and someone who says she needs protecting, Kim Lee. For this woman, contrary to what reviewers and scholars note, the paid sex is a side gig. She actually does sell her art, and Ms. Lee "wanted him to help her, or at least listen to her and not just write her off as a crazy person" (McGrath 2005: 264). Kim Lee wants what Jonah Soloway and Jane Lipschitz want, along with Daniel himself: someone to listen and to ask, and then love in a therapeutic and cathartic way. His therapist bans the love, says the "little Chinese hooker" will wreck him, and insists like a tormented and jealous lover for him to bring in Lee to her. The psychoanalyst is threatened by Daniel's description of the new woman who he clings to four days after the terrorist attack: "About forty. On the small side. Black hair, good body-very intense woman—little cleft chin that juts out" (McGrath 2015: 262). That offer refused, our narrator insists on being at least allowed to glimpse her and spy upon the lovers' conversation. Daniel buckles under the ill-advised idea, the therapist gets her look at a restaurant at the highly attractive Kim, but then is detected by her. This leads to a verbal explosion by Daniel's lover calling him "You stupid fuck," and she storms off (McGrath 2005: 277). After days of the begging on his part, contrite Daniel restores the relationship to Lee, but he feels he must abandon his therapist. Connections to *The Nostalgist* are not just the intense relationship and transference and countertransference grown to a towering degree in patient and analyst but also the ghost sightings and guilt to come. Kim Lee (like Jonah Soloway) actually feels responsible for the Twin Towers falling. She feels haunted, too, by her business client-cum-lover on the 108th floor, who left her warm bed that disastrous Tuesday morning, talked to her by phone during the first minutes of the attack. With Kim in her apartment looking toward WTC 1 and Jay inside the burning tower, they "had to shout to make themselves heard, but even as he grasped the enormity of his predicament he remained steady and calm, in fact he was comforting her. He told her he loved her" (McGrath 2005: 265). Falling over 1,000 feet from his jump, his remains are never recovered.

How two books so alike can start suddenly veering apart we notice next, for Jonah needs a psychotherapist to question him and to experience transference and move beyond his unfinished Oedipal relationship with his mother, but Daniel needs to break the transference that is so disabling and selfishly restraining him from any hope and healing. The inner and outer story of *Ground Zero* is of removing ruins and rebuilding, and all the courage it takes to lift the wreckage (physical and mental) as New York City would and begin again. The three supernatural presences or references that arise in the text are that Lee keeps seeing apparitions of dead lover Jay Minkoff every time she and Daniel have sex (at least three times), that Lee "is the Devil" (for prostituting herself to Jay's father while romancing the son), and that "evil" is emanating from "The Hole" (as perceived by the narrating psychiatrist who never believed in evil before the Al Qaeda attack). This is slightly unexpected as a psychiatrist would typically be empirical, tending to see human character as a matter of acquired traits and learned behavior. "Evil" would be, for someone schooled in psychiatry which claims scientific status, a religious or moral concept, irrelevant to her work. But as McGrath added to me, when prompted of her strange behavior and fallback on the paranormal, "Her own belief structures collapse in the face of the events of 9/11, and she falls back on ideas of good and evil, which would earlier have had no place in her thinking. It is an index of how deeply she has been shocked by the destruction she observed at Ground Zero" (McGrath Email: 12 May 2020). Throughout this novella, then, and repeatedly reflective of the other novels we have investigated so far, the outside destruction to Manhattan structures is reflected in the ravaged architecture of their minds. An opening to magical thinking, naturally, is self-protective: it may help to serve the narrator because as it gives a diversion strategy. Nothing is blamed on her by herself, and all guilt is projected on other people or "presences." Though critics continue to see Lee as the villain of the story, and of course she has her faults, I would side with McGrathian tradition where dangerous therapists like this narrator hold sway and abuse their considerable powers. In this chapter, we ask how trauma creates empathy, and encourages one lost soul to break free of some of his mind-forged manacles and comfort another lost soul.

## WHORES AND PSYCHIATRISTS

*Whores and psychiatrists—who sees clearer the true shapes and shades of men?*

—Patrick McGrath, *Ground Zero* (2005)

If we survey McGrath's doctors (he being the son of the longest-serving medical superintendent of England's storied Broadmoor Hospital and growing up in the doctor's family residence next to the admittance gate of what was called in the Victorian epoch "The Broadmoor Lunatic Asylum"), we

Figure 5.1 **Daniel's Unnamed Psychiatrist Walks Alone at Night to Ground Zero and Believes She Has an Encounter with the Traces of "Evil."** In real life, French documentarians Jules and Gedeon Naudet accompanied the firefighters of Engine 7, Ladder 7, and captured the only live footage inside WTC1 and later photographed Ground Zero, all looking like the day after a space attack against New York City from aliens. One of the firemen they interviewed captured the despair eloquently: "Our first shift was twenty-four hours, and in all that time, there was one person pulled out alive: *one*." Screenshot from *9/11: The Filmmakers' Commemorative DVD Edition*, Directors Jules and Gedeon Naudet, Goldfish Pictures/Silverstar Productions/Paramount, 2001.

find few of them that are morally or ethically or professionally dependable. Whole articles have been written in psychological and psychiatric journals in protest of McGrath's visions of cruel health professionals, with perhaps too much worry of how those portrayals are harming the reputation of the practice (cf. Jacqueline Hopson's "The Demonisation of Psychiatrists in Fiction and Why Real Psychiatrists Might Want to Do Something About It" in *The Psychiatric Bulletin*). Indeed, McGrath wrote to me on this question of his depictions of doctors and admitted that

> They are usually deeply flawed! But I think Charlie Weir in *Trauma* suffers from a deep-buried trauma that only surfaces late in his story, and at the end he willingly gives himself over to a doctor, Joan Bachinski, who is coming to take him into hospital, where he knows he belongs. I think there's also a benign psychiatrist in *Spider*, the old superintendent who discharges him because he "needs his bed." Can't think of any others who might qualify, other than maybe Stella's husband Max, in *Asylum*, who is not so much cruel as blind to his wife's frustration. (McGrath Email: May 12, 2020)

One of the great sadnesses about Daniel is that he seems to get in worse mental shape as the therapy drones on, from doctors that, as McGrath notes above, are either cruel, flawed, or blind, a bit similar at times to the doctor of the famed Wolf Man.

One of the most famous cases in psychoanalysis, and one that helped Freud to further his Oedipal formulation, is the Wolf Man (a wealthy Russian named Sergei Pankejeff, 1886–1979). In interviews in the 1970s, six decades later after his psychanalysis, the Wolf Man would say that Freud was brilliant, but that as a patient he himself never felt cured or highly relieved of his neurosis, though Freud announced him as "cured," and then even asked for a gift—the one given was, perhaps suggestive of the Wolf Man's fateful, regal, and forever missing sister: a "princess, Egyptian statuary, quite tall" (Pankejeff qtd. in Olbhozer 1982: 43). Something that has never made emotional sense until reading *Ground Zero* is why the Wolf Man would continue with psychoanalysis long after it was clear that it would not "cure" him. Pankejeff had his first appointment with Freud starting in 1910 (four years after his sister Anna died, and three years after his father perished—both of them by suicide) and would see psychoanalysts until his own death when so many other psychological treatments were available, but without tremendous or even recognizable results. Though psychoanalysis would seem palliative at times, and his psychoanalysts would seem like curious and fascinating characters for him to analyze himself, Pankejeff found there was no resolving his problems as Freud would declare. Pankejeff often complained of the fortune he spent on psychoanalysis in the interview, and admitted it was hard to afford even for him late in life, but he could not stop seeking its therapy. He found psychoanalysis's free-association talks could release some pressure in him, but the whole had many problems to go with it, as in his view it was a practice whimsical and indulgent, its dream analysis often having no two psychoanalysts to interpret the night visions in the same way, that it was an endless therapy, and that harmful and judgment-impairing transferences could often result. More of an impressonistic art than a science, it lacked any kind of scientific method, seldom able to replicate the same results, and the practice collapsed when scrutinized objectively, in this famous patient's mind. The Wolf Man's first revealing comment to the interview journalist Karin Obholzer registers such despair: "You know, I feel so bad, I have been having such terrible depressions lately. . . . Freud was a genius, there's no denying it! All those ideas that he combined in a system . . . even though much isn't true" (Pankejeff qtd. in Olbhozer 1982: 25). Treated far more in hours than the New Yorker Daniel Silver, Der Wolfsmann had appointments with Freud "every day except Sundays." This meant "every day for one hour, an hour every day for four years" (Pankejeff qtd. in Olbhozer 1982: 34). But the wonder of whether it was worth it is obvious in the conversation with the Russian: "In my story, what was explained by dreams? Nothing, as far as I can see. . . . No one had any idea that it would take all that time. I had assumed it would go very fast, and that everything would be alright afterward" (Pankejeff qtd. in Olbhozer 1982: 30, 35). One dark side of psychoanalysis could be this potentially exploitative aspect: the patient keeps coming, like some poor credulous gull coming back to a greedy fortune teller, and is strung along with questions and pledges that more time is needed to excavate all the traumas. Trust has developed, and the patients cannot tear themselves away. There is little financial incentive for the psychoanalyst to have a patient leave the couch forever. But what is of key interest in the Wolf Man's view of the patient-therapist relationship is not the sense that clients are emotionally entrapped in care that is long term and expensive and not obviously helping them (from their own vantage point). Instead, it is the attraction Pankejeff holds for his therapist. He finds that Freud had eyes that looked to the bottom of his soul, and that the charisma was irresistible, yet "too strong a transference ends with your . . . believing them uncritically. And that happened to me, to a degree. So transference is a dangerous thing" (Pankejeff qtd. in Olbhozer 1982: 31). Always there is this ambivalence toward Freud in him: waves of returning reverence and then waves of doubt: "If you look at everything critically, there isn't much in psychoanalysis that will stand up. . . . And it's also clear that he overestimated his work. . . . Well, actually I worshipped him" (Pankejeff qtd. in Olbhozer 1982: 31). What becomes even more sinister is the kind of certainty or sureness Freud had, his words of such coldness and unquestioned belief. After Pankejeff's sister died, "my Father died and I had no [physical or spiritual] father at all and came to Freud. And then Freud said, 'You were lucky that your father died, otherwise you would never have become well'" (Pankejeff qtd. in Olbhozer 1982: 31). Perhaps Freud's rather arrogant judgment of Pankejeff's father induces the Wolf Man in hindsight to admit that "Psychoanalysis harms a person when he has to make a decision on his own and relies on it" (Pankejeff qtd. in Olbhozer 1982: 33). Thus, the patient has successfully come to some independent judgment of his psychoanalyst despite having been personally treated by one of the most influential and charismatic psychological thinkers of the twentieth century.

My background on Pankejeff sets up an analogy of Daniel and his therapist who sways him far too unhealthfully. So remarkably detached, emotionally blind, and unimaginative she is, that she considers Daniel simply a man "of emotional numbness" who more than anything else wants to feel pain, so that is why "he had acquiesced in this sordid story [of loving Kim Lee] . . . become complicit in it by not expressing his moral disgust—it was because he was taking pleasure in his own torment" (McGrath 2005: 290). This is not a sentiment to help an analysand and promote self-discovery and healing, but to paralyze him or her. She has no capacity to understand or admit that he might need a love outside of the one-sided one she is trying to fit onto him. For seven years, she has been exploiting his weaknesses, disabling any progress he might make. Critics have not noted this, but I would argue that she attends methods his mother developed to subdue him (and adopts them herself), to make him overdependent on our narrator, and to shoo away women who interested a younger Daniel. Understandably for Daniel Silver's psychoanalytic model to work, he would need to have transference to his analyst, where the analyst became the problem-agent in his life: in this case, Daniel's mother. We know that a psychoanalyst does not let clients escape from answering certain vital questions key to their early development and manifesting in their current psychic troubles. Daniel's psychotherapist not only does this but she also hides her motives behind a high-pressure, staccato, rapid-fire questioning that becomes more like an interrogation of a suspect. The psychotherapist has made a study of all the maternal controlling words, endearments, and actions that can bring Daniel under her emotional spell. Note how every time he shows agency, independence, or dissent before, she uses some of the Mother's taming words to get him back under control. A certain look in the eyes, a tone of voice, an angle of the head, and a reversion to childhood name of "Danny" over his adult name "Daniel," and he falls under her command. She becomes a quietly dangerous Mommy then: "At once I heard the resistance in his voice, . . . and I had to become crisp with him. Did he or did he not need my help" (McGrath 2005: 281). Like *Get Out*'s (2017) smiling but also "crisp," menacing hypnotherapist mom-of-the-girlfriend Missy Armitage, Daniel goes down to some "Sunken Place" just as Chris Washington did at her quiet yet loaded words, and is quickly and effectively disabled by fear, dread, and the never-gone past. He looks down, his feet shuffle, and he mumbles some assent to whatever observation, proposal, or order of the psychoanalyst's like a child, no matter how harmful to his mental health (like a plan to spy on his girlfriend, which we will discuss later). In her own way she is a female version of McGrath's male psychiatrist in "The Other Psychiatrist" who vows of his patient, "In my deepest despair of ever getting through, I would want simply to fall to my knees before her, and nuzzle my face between her knees, until her legs parted; or gently lift her, and carry her to my couch, and lay her down, and undo her blouse and plant soft kisses on her white throat and her breasts" (McGrath 2017: 224–225). This psychiatrist actually regrets that he did not molest his private mental home-committed client, Margaret Edgar, because he thinks he could have been therapeutic. She later kills herself with the Nembutal he prescribed. As McGrath succinctly captures it to me in conversation, "Of course, there are good therapists as well as bad ones, I just find the bad ones more interesting" (McGrath Interview 2017: 198).

Unexplored by both initial reviewers or later scholars is the curious way McGrath's novella cuts the strings to his ethically wayward and romantically fixated psychotherapist. In some ways, *Ground Zero* aligns with *The Writing on the Wall* as both are interested in how the caring for another can heal an afflicted protagonist. The overwhelming shock of 9/11 gives Daniel an allowance to change himself, to become someone else, to concentrate on something else for a time than his own disastrous marriages, and to start to make movements of autonomy from a menacing, even predatory psychoanalyst (who was mostly interested in keeping him her incapacitated plaything in lieu of an outside romance of her own). His trauma moves over when the planes crash into the towers and is replaced with another's trauma. Vitally, he gives himself over to being the amateur but sincerely caring therapist to another: in serving another, listening, and asking, his neuroses take a secondary place. Declaring his independence from a predatory psychoanalyst is a massive struggle for him, but it is one of those cases where the impossible becomes inevitable. Daniel is prioritizing another sufferer's pain. As McGrath told me in interview, "The story begins to reverse the roles of psychotherapist and client. He frees himself of his various neuroses whereas she begins to develop neuroses, and in that way they reverse positions" (McGrath Interview 2017: 198). I pointed out that Danny declares in his last words, "I don't think you're much use to me anymore." McGrath laughed, raised a glass of beer, and concurred—"That's right. I know. He's fixed. She's not!" This shows how variable characters' responses are to trauma in his works and beyond.

We recall that *The Nostalgist* was about, in part, the erotic pull of death and the sadomasochistic mastery of what brings us pleasure—or ironically killing the thing that both arouses and feeds us. But *Ground Zero* is about how the person that brings us pleasure through sex and dreams is being harmed mentally by a ghost each time they make love. Her helplessness before an angry specter sows a sympathy in Daniel that starts becoming a more tender love and sharing than he has ever experienced:

> —She wrapped herself in his robe and went out onto the balcony where he had stood watching the towers burn. He heard her cry out.
> —What is it? he shouted.
> He leaped from the bed and found her staring down at the street. She turned to him, her fingers spread across her mouth.
> —He must have been down there all night, she whispered.
> —Who?
> —Him. *Jay.* (McGrath 2005: 269)

In ghost sighting after sighting of hers (to which Daniel sees nothing, but wants to), Kim Lee finally sighs, "I'm so frightened. —Will you help me?—You remember the morning the towers came down, you remember thinking, this is not real but I'm seeing it? That's what's happening to me all the time now. He's not real, but I'm seeing him" (McGrath 2005: 275). And what was on that ghost-lover's face, that visage of a man that this artist Lee betrayed with his own father? It was "Grief and pain and sorrow and loss and anger. A terrible quiet sad anger, and it was directed not at the men who had murdered him, but at her" (McGrath 2005: 266). The ghost seems to hate her for moving on and starting some kind of closure, or is it something deeper and unknown? The worry for her, ironically, might even be greater if Daniel does not see the ghost—or will not acknowledge the presence of this Other. If Daniel could ever witness the ghost even once, it would suggest that she is merely haunted. If he never sees the ghost, but she continues to, it suggests that she grows madder daily by her trauma. She is still seeing what is not there.

Tracking the curious and circuitous ways that real-life trauma enters fiction in a transformed way, we can look more closely at the angry ghost afflicting Kim Lee. Not raised by other McGrath critics yet, I would like to venture the idea that some of the source material, if not the inspiration for the story, comes from an emergencies services friend of McGrath's named Mickey. Inquiring of the author, I am told by him that "that would have been the fall of 2001, [I met in real life] Mickey and his girlfriend" (McGrath Email: 18 June 2020). Mickey was a New York City fireman who had rushed to the burning towers on 9/11. His girlfriend had been told that the North Tower had fallen on him, killing him instantly, but she discovers later that day that he was alive. The woman is traumatized by this in the fashion of Kate Chopin's

"The Story of an Hour," though she does not have a heart attack like Chopin's Mrs. Louise Mallard, she does suffer mentally. McGrath recalls,

> What was interesting then was that the girlfriend was far more deeply traumatized than Mickey by what had happened that day. In her mind he had died. She had watched the planes go in and the Towers collapse. And, as you say, she had "seen" in her imagination her man die. And then she saw him come back. He was undamaged, physically and psychically as far as I could tell. She, however, went on to explain to me that it had all been very difficult for her since that day. "The problem was," she told me, "that they were still around." Who's still around?, I asked her. "You know, those guys." Who? "Those guys that came after us on 9/11. I see them on the subway. I hear them talking. You know, they're plotting some more." She continued: "I was on the subway just the other day—this has happened a few times—and there were three men just at the edge of the subway. And I know what they were talking about. They're talking about the next attack." (McGrath Interview 2017: 195–196)[1]

As we learn about this female acquaintance of McGrath's who confesses to seeing the same notorious Al Qaeda hijacking operatives after 9/11 on the subway platforms (who of course should already be dead), we come to realize how trauma distorts time and breeds ghosts.

Besides the novel's inspirations, another unresolved mystery of the book not engaged yet by scholars (beyond the puzzle of the father Paul Minkoff

**Figure 5.2    An Attack Sublime and Surreal Left Experienced Firefighters (Like the One McGrath Describes in Interview) Stunned and in Disbelief.** Within days, a total 343 firefighters perished responding to the WTC collapse. Screenshot from *World Trade Center*, Director Oliver Stone, Paramount, 2006. Courtesy of the artist Harry Brockway.

willingly coming out of his hiding spot in Kim's apartment, just so that his son could see him and send all into an emotional spiral) that lingers after several readings is why the ghost of Jay Minkoff scowls at Kim Lee as if he wishes to kill her? After all, the living Jay, though he must have been devastated, does not push guilt upon her, he resists long and angry accusations, or menacing stares; in short, he does not make her suffer terribly for "the moral responsibility for an evil action" (McGrath 2005: 291). He quickly resumes their love. It seems that, somehow in a superhuman fashion, Jay "in effect refused to absorb the pain his father attempted to cause him, and decided instead to try to understand the impulse behind the injury" (McGrath 2005: 295). Then he chooses to go back to Kim to "salvage their relationship" (McGrath 2005: 295). Indeed, in her last call to him as the North Tower dies, he seems so understanding and not at all concerned about himself: "he remained steady and calm, in fact he was comforting her. He told her he loved her. He told her to be happy. Then he said he had to call his father to say goodbye, and the line went dead" (McGrath 2015: 265). And that is the last she ever knows or hears of the living Jay. If the furious ghost now is simply Jay's soul, and he in life already made peace with her betrayal with his father, then why must the ghost be so enraged? McGrath himself has written me on this point: "I've gone back to the story and I would say simply that Jay Minkoff is reproaching Kim Lee, or at least that is what she projects onto his ghost, the guilt she feels at having caused him so much hurt" (McGrath Email: 17 June 2020). This raises the idea that what we and Kim see the ghost suggesting with his visage is our projection, based on what we think the deceased boyfriend's face would show; or that his soul has undergone some change, and he is less forgiving, and now glowers at her in the afterworld.

Derrida's reasoning on fearsome ghosts is far richer than mine, in that he supposes that we the living are "a sort of graveyard for ghosts. A ghost is . . . someone else's unconscious. It's someone else's unconscious that speaks in our place. . . . It is the unconscious of the other which plays tricks on us. It can be terrifying" (Derrida 1982: *Ghost Dance*). A third explanation is darker. My sense for why Jay is enraged in death, but not in life, is because she is continuing the affair with his father. In a novella where so much is explained, we never do find out what Jay's last words were to his father. Add to that, there are plenty of times post-9/11 when Kim is not with Daniel. She continues to need financial support because there are few if any art sales during the days after 9/11, and her landlord demanded rent during a time that she could not enter her building because of its 9/11-related damage, and she remains at a hotel. She admits that the sex with the father when her lover/his son had no idea of it was perversely fantastic. Possibly the passion was to her as scintillating as a Gothic romance novel, perhaps because the silverback Paul was rich and willful and sadistic, lust was illicit, and the combination took her to a pitch of fear and nervousness over potential discovery that her body and mind had never felt: "It excited her.... The idea of fucking the father.... Whether they would get clear of it, all three, without harm done.... He paid her, and she took the money. It was a sophisticated game" (McGrath 2015: 287, 291). And Kim's game may not actually be over, as shocking as that sounds. The greatest circumstantial evidence for an ongoing affair with the father, that of course would make the ghost of Jay furious and want to pursue and punish her, is when the psychotherapist asks Daniel, "Do you think she's still having sex with him [the father, Paul, post-9/11]?" (McGrath 2015: 293) All the narrator says of Daniel's reply is that "Again he would not reveal his thoughts to me" (McGrath 2015: 293). In a book where so much is certain, this seems revealingly vague. Daniel cannot be silent about this charge on this unless he is actually worried that Kim is still romantically linked with her dead lover's father, Paul. We are never told when or if, by Kim or anyone else, the affair ends with her lover's father. The protagonist Daniel loves Kim, counsels her, defends her, takes umbrage at her being called a prostitute—and yet he is silent right here in this perfectly ambiguous passage, which makes his masochistic devotion to her even more striking. It is because, perhaps, he knows that some sexual relations once begun are difficult to abandon no matter how perverted, and she might need not only the father's contact, his financial support, but also his resemblance—so faint or strong—to Jay. This is the father whose opportunism, wealth, dishonesty, ability to gain trust, and last name Minkoff evoke the vulturism of disgraced New Yorker Bernard L. Madoff, who guided the largest Ponzi-scheme fraud in U.S. history. Yet this dark possibility remains that she secretly stays with the living father because he reminds her of the dead son. Moreover, she might crave the kind of risky sex she had with pater Paul before 9/11 to make her feel something and to forget everything else post-9/11. A character from McGrath often splits our loyalties cleanly in half like this, making us sympathize as much as we might despise. Further, McGrath's innovative works enjoy casting shadows where we cannot precisely see what happens, which makes the emotional darkness darker still. Perhaps the ghost, who can know so much that the living cannot, knows her sensual secrets and his father's. Indeed, while in the tower, Jay's last words were with the father which we are not privy to: at the most darkly Gothic, the father could have refused, even as the flames grew high, to apologize for the affair his son's lover and even pledged to continue it. Later Daniel, so telling in his silence, can pause and shudder over such passions. The possibilities of what the ghost's presence means, the wonder over why Daniel is romantically involved with a woman whose Oedipal triangle may not be finished, the hope that he can help Kim mourn Jay as he mourns his mother—all of these questions are stored but not articulated by Daniel yet, not to his psychoanalyst and not to anyone else, but they make us crave to know what life there will be for the lovers beyond the novella's last page.

# CONCLUSION

In the interview, McGrath told me of his own night walks to "The Hole," and a revealing openness to ghosts: "I had this notion in my mind that the collapse of the Towers would have created a great many disaster-ghosts. It's perfectly logical to say that if a number of people independently of each other have experienced the same thing, then that thing is there to be perceived" (McGrath Interview 2017: 197). However, the psychoanalyst's take on this double trauma seems extraordinarily shallow, smug, and self-importantly overconfident: "I have encountered this before. In fact, it is not uncommon, the conviction that one is being reproached by a loved one who has recently died. It is a function of unresolved guilt, and in acute cases there may be features of psychosis. . . . I could have tidied her up in a couple of sessions, no great problem there, routine psychiatry" (McGrath 2005: 266–267). No one would want to have such an automatic and arrogant mental health caregiver, too pat in her diagnosis, too limited in her hearing of the trauma, too hubristic in her powers. What the therapist does not understand is how draining this is to witness this lover-now-ghost Jay Minkoff following Kim for most of the novella, looking aggrieved and furious, whenever she is with Daniel. For his part, Silver is like Soloway, wondering if New York City has gone mad in the post-9/11 days. Whitman once asked in *Leaves of Grass,* "Do you think a great city endures?" and we ask the same question as we read both books. Perhaps the answer is Whitmanesque, as well: the love is not only the "kelson of creation," but the only feeling and experience that can help people survive and cope, for love is what both Jonah and Daniel fall deeply into, and love for someone who also feels lost and is a victim of terror. Lee, on the edge of nervous collapse, forms in her outreach the breakthrough relationship for Daniel, no matter her secrets.

I have asked my college and university classes before why physicians make perfect villains in Gothic literature (as well as in True Crime, and other non-fiction subgenres), and they have a hundred answers that parallel the critics' ideas. The consensus is that doctors are traditionally afforded a large amount of trust and also an access to prescribing medicine, giving counsel for our bodies or minds, and conducting surgeries and long-range treatments. But if a healer is ethically damaged, insane, or even wicked, then the patient is obviously a vulnerable target and will not easily survive the trauma. Such seems the case of the doctor and Daniel here. Despite that pressure on Daniel, he must step up and face his fears and be Lee's defender because there is no one else to do it, and to do this he must break off relationships dismissive or actively hostile to Lee (those like his psychoanalyst who condemns her because of her social class, ethnic identity, younger age, sexual threat, and predatory relationship to the two Minkoffs). In the end, Daniel is the one he can help listen to and comfort such a degree of pathology and guilt and loneliness, finally Daniel can break free from the bondage of his psychotherapist's control—that substitute for his mother, one whom he could never satisfy, one who forbade him bonding with another woman, one for whom he had (as did Jonah) an unfinished Oedipal relationship that crippled his bonding to other women. I think that Daniel achieves the highest hope for a client: he is accurately diagnosing his state and current relationships, and he is deciding on an appropriate action for his future. Rather than let another direct what has been a rudderless life, he has become the captain of his own psychic journey. In her scorn and disapproval, the therapist is right about one thing—Daniel is now deciding for himself what to do with his life, whatever the perils. And he does this not through this psychoanalyst but in spite of her.

## NOTE

1. McGrath continues his gentle questioning of a real-life ghost-haunted woman who sees dead terrorists at subway stops, and then ends with a fascinating reveal.
"And what did the FBI say?" [McGrath asked].
"They thanked me very much. They asked me at what subway stop I saw them at. Then they told me they'd look into it. . . . So I think they're looking after it," [Mickey's unnamed girlfriend answered].
The patient FBI officials respectfully do not discount the real-life girlfriend's story, though they easily could have. Perhaps they had traumas and ghosts of their own, just as Kim Lee does. McGrath closes his letter with the unpredictable effect of traumata upon us: "There was this sharp contrast [in this couple] about what was going on post-911. She was seeing conspirators—terrorists everywhere—and he [Mickey the Fireman] was eager for another experience that had the intensity he had faced on September 11, 2001" (McGrath Interview 2017: 195–196).

Figure 5.3  Woodcut Illustration of the Protagonist Daniel Silver's Traumatized Lover, The Artist and Prostitute Kim Lee, From Her Apartment Balcony as Described in McGrath's *Ground Zero*, Watching the Still-Standing WTC Burn with Her Boyfriend Inside of It. Used with permission by its copyright holder and engraver Harry Brockway. Originally published in Patrick McGrath's *Writing Madness: The Short Fiction of Patrick McGrath* (Edited by Danel Olson, Centipede Press, 2017). Courtesy of the artist Harry Brockway.

# Conclusion

*Writing a novel is like chasing and catching spirits.*
—Anchee Min, *Pearl of China* (2015)

Few, if any, theorists of trauma have acknowledged the profound overlap between Trauma Theory and the Gothic, or the ways in which literary representations of trauma frequently resort to some of the most established conventions of the Gothic in order to articulate traumatic excess. Terrorists attack, civilians die, and survivors mourn—every critic agrees. But invariably in these fictions, as shown in this Lexington monograph, apparitions also arise, doppelgängers pass by, and the memories of trauma assume the shape of the impossibly monstrous. To penetrate the strange guises in which memory masquerades its distress and ask what those semblances may mean is to perform a traumagothic reading. Unhealing ordeals are like the intermittent appearance of masked phantoms, and a traumagothic interpretation pursues and interrogates such specters, finding post-Freudian concepts particularly helpful in its execution. Usually in these novels surveyed, the undeclared remains of the dead feed the unresolved mourning of the living. And the Gothic impulse moves through the survivors' terror sex and terror-fueled revenge; through the disaster-ghosts that possess the living; through the survivors' mind-destroying guilt; and through the resultant shame, rage, torture, madness, and soul sickness exhibited over the sudden live burial of friends, colleagues, and family at Ground Zero. And sometimes, as in the case with *The Writing on the Wall* and *The Nostalgist*, we needed to explore how talking with ghosts can help the living victims process their traumata.

As this book demonstrates, these five novels speak their "unutterable trauma"—their abject fear, sublime dread, wounded memory, and shattered world—often through Gothic utterances, means, figures, and meditations. A traumagothic formulation asks how the Gothic mode invests these texts with conspiracies of incest and murder; occurrences of possession and traumatic reenactment; flashes of the grotesque; and intimations of evil during nocturnal wanderings past Ground Zero's exoskeletons of towers that hold both darkness and fire. "The Hole" was where the bodies burned and stank, and the spirits appeared and then brooded. By steadily Gothicizing trauma, the terrorism texts are able to embody in the carnage and aftermath a secret language, which news commentators on 9/11 merely branded "unspeakable" and "unfaceable." The Gothic impulse enters these five fictions again and again as stealthily yet constantly as the smoke, ash, and dust of the WTC dead drifted into the residences of the New York City authors composing these fictional narratives. Admittedly, these novels may show no Gothic nature initially on the first pages, yet through a process of reading that is finely attuned to the Gothic mode, we eventually experience what the texts' uncountenanced or unstated traumas are. It is true that declarations of the texts' Gothic manifestations may be invisible from the publishers' online press kits, dust jacket descriptions, and even authorial interviews—and yet the Gothic becomes the mode that speaks the psychic stresses and dwells on the greater mysteries after terrorist attack. A traumagothic presence in a terrorism novel can often be signaled by a recurring apparition. And we have to ask why spirits, again and again, exist in novels that are otherwise described as literary realism interrupted by sudden cataclysm. I determined that the persistence of such ghosts is not just a spectral reminder of the instant vaporization of thousands at the WTC, or the decisions of hundreds from the North Tower and then the South Tower to take their lives by jumping, sometimes holding hands as they fell. The arrival of ghosts is perhaps the greatest externalized trace to a concealed but corroding vault of traumatic memory. The explosively public 9/11 trauma also summons earlier hidden personal traumas for the texts' characters (especially for Keith Neudecker, Thomas Schell Sr., Renata, Jonah Soloway, and Daniel Silver), blurring borders between the nightmare of the present and a past that never finishes and a future that holds an unknown threat.

A traumagothic analysis might also be applied to other 9/11 texts in order to determine if the same pattern of trauma's secrets surface with other novels' ghosts. Other American-born or American-naturalized writers have been dwelling on the same blows for the New York City survivor. Thus, a traumagothic elucidation could focus on, for example, ghosts in Ken Kalfus's *A Disorder Peculiar to the Country* (2006), which I only briefly analyzed before, and the possession of (yet another) living lawyer by a dead terrorist; terror sex in Jay McInerney's *The Good Life* (2006) and the revenants that wriggle out of body bags at Ground Zero; a burned and decapitated 9/11 jumper's head speaking like a god in Hugh Nissenson's *Days of Awe* (2005), while the Devil in that novel also speaks as a "spirit of self-annihilation"; and the mystical transport of objects of the dead that follow and "speak" to the living in Stephen King's ghost story "The Things They Left Behind" (2005). Beyond that, a traumagothic approach might also be fruitfully applied to American writers' novels on torture and the terrorist's and informant's point of view from roughly the same period, including, for instance, *Terrorist* from John Updike (2006) or *The Garden of Last Days* from Andre Dubus III (2008).

The notion of the traumagothic provides a useful way of approaching a number of fictions written and published within the last five years, too. "Thumbprint" (2007), a story from one of Stephen King's sons, Joe Hill, makes a transition to a new very contemporary subgenre whose PTSD and ghosts could be illuminated by a traumagothic interpretation. The movement in American fiction on terrorism in terms of newest book releases is increasingly away from the New York City victim's unhealable reaction to the loss of the towers, and toward the perspective of those who serve as U.S. military or private contractors in operations overt and covert within Iraq and Afghanistan, often motivated out of a rage over the loss of both life and symbolic power from the WTC fall. Some of these U.S. personnel at times torture and kill and are haunted themselves by the trauma-ghosts (frequently vengeful and soul-destroying ones) arising from the destruction that comes of military invasion and occupation. Hill's story is of a military interrogator, Private First Class Mallory Grennan, and an Iraqi professor of literature haplessly swept up in an American arrest on a Baghdad street. During interrogation, she smashes the professor's broken leg with her rifle butt and then asks "if he'd like the barrel of her gun in his ass" to go with that (Hill 2007: 231). In an addition to the ghost story we might expect, Grennan is not only haunted by the professor but also is stalked and tortured upon returning Stateside by a fellow interrogator suffering PTSD and rampant paranoia. The fellow soldier named Carmody (who took part in physical abuses of Ba'athist suspects and now collects human thumbs) is certain she was part of a conspiracy against him and his resulting demotion. The story leaves her in the midst of traumatic memoires strapped to a bed after being clubbed on the back of the head by Carmody. Whether her interrogator is real or merely a Gothic projection is left up for the reader to decide. David Wellington's story "Twilight in the Green Zone" (2007) premiering in *Exotic Gothic*, narrates more lawlessness: the taboo and serial hunger in an American official named Vyner working within the American safe zone in Baghdad. Ironically employed for the United Nations, he also seeks a woman to torment and kill. However, after nearly being shot and tortured himself as he drives through Baghdad, Vyner finds the victim-pattern reversed. His intended target will stand above him giving the orders while he will not again be able to raise himself from his knees. She is, if not a purely a Gothic projection on Vyner's part, a supernatural spirit of ancient vengeance from the desert.

Victimhood, as we discovered in five novels analyzed in the volume, is not monolithic: its other side is rage and disproportionate violence. Kevin Neudecker beats a man for staring at his paramour for a second too long at a mattress store, and his wife smashes another woman's face for playing Middle Eastern music too loudly. Oskar Schell (at least symbolically) destroys a bully with a theater-prop. The twin Renata (surname never known to readers) threatens to kill a perpetrator who was dying in a hospital bed. The lust for vengeance inhabits them all. Likewise, more recent terrorism fictions by American authors follow American citizens who were living far away from Ground Zero to fly abroad and exact their own terror on other nations. From the two such transitional short stories aforementioned by Hill and Wellington, we also notice that the most recent terrorism fictions focus on the retributive violence of a state, beginning with U.S. and Allied troops in Afghanistan and Iraq, causing refugee epidemics as civil wars emerge and engulf parts of Iraq and Afghanistan, and destabilize neighboring nations. Depicting those characters who embody the sleep of reason and the transformation into monsters, the following list of fiction awaits traumagothic analysis: the stories in Phil Klay's *Redeployment* (2014), in particular "Bodies," as well as such novels as J. Robert Lennon's *Castle* (2009); Ben Fountain's *Billy Lynn's Long Halftime Walk* (2012); and Kevin Powers's *The Yellow Birds* (2012). From Klay we observe Mortuary Affairs Marines in the theater of war who "thought the spirits of the dead hung about the bodies. It'd creep them out. . . . [They were] swearing they could feel spirits everywhere . . . [and] always talked about ghosts" (Klay 2014: 54–55). A similarly eerie involvement of the dead into the business of the living features in Lennon's novel *Castle*, in which a logistics expert and chief warrant officer in the U.S. Army ends up torturing to death a Baghdad boy named Sufian while in detention at Camp Alastor, Iraq. During interrogation, the boy had whistled in answer to one of the narrating officer Eric Loesch's questions, and after that "strange, frightening whistling," Loesch suffers a fevered "Tell-Tale Heart" reaction. Loesch utters: "Anything but this—this whistling, which felt as though it was boring into my head like an auger. . . . I could have recognized it anywhere: it had an identity, a personality" (Lennon 2009: 217–218). This mere whistling invites a traumagothic analysis of the uncanny because it has no melody, no repeated movement, no "theme or phrase," and yet Loesch knows it from somewhere and is "painfully tired of it." Despite that familiarity, it was strange: "It was foreign, far more than this place [Iraq]. It was alien" (Lennon 2009: 218). A mere whistle grows into an intolerable burden, and the narrator insists that sound is a clear and present danger to everyone. In his traumatized state of super-vigilance and heightened paranoia, Loesch insists that a boy's tune could "[en]danger the stability of the facility, the morale of the men and women under my command, and the pliability of [Sufian's] fellow detainees" (Lennon 2009: 219). Therefore, the boy must be killed. To the narrator, who felt he was a victim himself on 9/11, this act was one more unpreventable "casualty of war" and not an abuse of a prisoner (Lennon 2009: 228). A traumagothic reading of this novel seems invited by the text itself when it wonders: "how the tendency of memory [can] twist and reshape itself, especially the memory of dramatic moments." Loesch (whose last name means "fine leather" in German, and who indeed turns his detainees into mere dead skin) can barely remember how he kills the child, or how Sufian's last moments looked and sounded. Like a murder in a dungeon from a Gothic novel long ago, there seems to be little help from the living world to prosecute the crime. We must look instead to the ghosts who will come later to plague the interrogator Loesch when he returns to America before we can understand why he killed a child in an Iraqi cell, and what awaits him now. Even greater brutality lurks in Ben Fountain's *Billy Lynn's Long Halftime Walk*, where a Sergeant Dime, like an incarnation of *Apocalypse Now*'s Air Cavalry officer Bill Kilgore, insists to his men: "We like violence, we like going lethal! . . . If we didn't like killing people then what's the point [of being in Iraq]?" But after the extremes of violence that the Sergeant's soldiers commit and are subjected to, the narrator has to ask: "How much reality can unreality take? . . . The past is a fog that breathes out ghost after ghost, . . . which makes the future the ultimate black hole of futile speculation" (Fountain 2012: 307). A traumagothic reading could help illuminate this black hole and challenge some of the speculations. Last, in one more novel of Middle Eastern tumult and torture, Kevin Powers's *The Yellow Birds*, the American narrator glumly spends his time "with the same ghosts [that he killed] every night" (Powers 2012: 112). For the works of both Fountain and Powers, a traumagothic approach might assist in finding the unspoken injuries by investigating the nature, pattern of reappearance, and messages that the apparitions impart. As for Lennon's ominous novel *Castle*, the question that matters is not so much what the narrator asks—"What should be done with the boy's body?" (Lennon 2009: 219)—but rather the one that he never articulates: What should be done with the boy's reappearing ghost? Here, a traumagothic reading, as we have applied, defined, and formed it in the novels from the first chapters of this study, could be enlightening.

Besides developing the traumagothic interpretations in this volume, I have attempted a recuperation of 9/11 fiction, against the tide of popular opinion, for more serious consideration. Critics have contended that the 9/11 novels should have been "game-changing," offering a "new paradigm" and able to "subdue an event that seemed to defy representation," of larger "scope and harrowing drama" (Kakutani 2011). Instead, the novels were in reviewers' minds often "trivializing," "mercenary and narcissistic," "resistant . . . to artistic treatment," "flimsy," "cynical," and "solipsistic" (Kakutani 2011). From more scholarly quarters, Richard Gray's retrospective repeatedly found the 9/11 fictions unusually "close minded," unduly "domestic," and unable to fully grapple with geopolitical themes (Gray 2008). What these two critical evaluations do not consider (and Kakutani and Gray are emblematic of the whole), however, is what I contend is their greatest success: that the presence of the dead is not merely *felt* in terrorism texts, but that *the dead have agency*. With insights on possession by the dead post-disaster through separate studies from the medical psychiatrists Adler and Lindemann, I have established that some of the WTC dead inhabit the living. That is, behavior of the living in these novels—in terms of newly adopted speech patterns, clothing choices, hobbies, sexual proclivities, and even their change in vocations—manifest their dead friends' or relatives' natures. All of the fictions I have investigated here show this phenomenon to some degree. What is more, by noticing and analyzing the harm inflicted on the self or on others by these fictional figures in the days and months after the terrorist attack, we also see an uncanny mirroring with the self-destructive impulses and duality of many earlier Gothic characters. For in these examined novels, a once-prosperous WTC insurance lawyer rages and strikes people and disappears into smoky gambling dens; a fifth-grade boy-inventor assumes the persona of an avenging skull and punishes himself and others physically and mentally; a respected librarian of lost languages arranges her apartment with true-crime stories of murder and devotes herself full-time to "terror sex"; and two grown sons find that one trauma reopens another (the deaths of their mothers) after they survive the WTC collapse.

The question should not be only, as reviewers and scholars have asked, how does the work reflect the chaotic state of the world and threats to Pax Americana, once so securely held by military domination of neutral spaces of air, sea, and sky? The question to add is how could we establish what texts become canonical in 9/11 literature? Why should we be reading them? How does a 9/11 text fully and intimately register the haunting of trauma on an individual, in ways that psychologists, psychiatrists, and therapists themselves might find arresting? After all, fiction's province, in the memorable words of the 9/11 Memorial & Museum Director Alice Greenwald during my interview with her, is to provide "a form of access to interior realities that are not as evident in more documentary forms of expression . . . a sense of personal investment in the narrative, creating a sense of immediacy and fostering an awareness of the familiar" (Greenwald: Interview in Appendix). If these novels capably depict not only the despair over what has been done to us but also the dread for what we are becoming—with distinctions sometimes disappearing in the divide between terrorist and victim, and narrowing between the dead and the living—then they have captured an experience remarkable, unexpected, and controversial, a quality which alone makes them worthy of interrogation and wonder. Maybe we will find that the novels of 9/11 give hints as to what the rush of post-pandemic novels will look like in the coming decade. Perhaps, as novelist Chris Bohjalian notes, 9/11 novels will be instructive in their framing and focus, showing us how collective nightmare is turned into a personal story, adding the "randomness . . . and the heinousness," the confusion, grief, tears, and mourning that we remember facing (Bohjalian 2020).

As this monograph has demonstrated, the most coherent and productive theoretical armature for the reading of traumagothic is one derived from a broad range of cultural, linguistic, and psychological theorists, especially those from post-Freudian interpreters of psychoanalysis, in particular Jacques Derrida. Notions taken from Derrida (typically concentrating on a text's, ideology's, or government's contradictions and unstated, maligned, ironic, and left-out aspects) include that the terrorist and the victim have an unclear division; that the state's preemptive strikes and torture act as a disabling process like an autoimmunity reaction in a human body; and that television and Internet media amplify the power of terror, keeping it an ever-happening attack, and creating the worst terror. As Derrida perceives terrorism, the sense in our imaginations becomes that the worst is not over, that the violence toward us, in fact, will never be over and there is no shelter to find. Further, his concept that "honest" mourning is "impossible," just as the complete and disinterested forgiveness of wrongs is impossible in his thinking, assists in the crafting of a more nuanced interpretation of and commentary on characters' chronic suffering. I have demonstrated that these novels imagine that if one can open to another's pain, and acknowledge what one's trauma shares with another's (as do Oskar in *Extremely Loud and Incredibly Close* and Renata in *The Writing on the Wall*), then one can have a united, if still unfinished mourning with others. Such a character tends to stay in New York City despite all the reminders of loss, and keep his or her roots, maintain contacts, help others, and become one for whom others will someday mourn. If one is not open to others' pain (as with Keith in *Falling Man*), one tends to become physically violent toward others and oneself, leave New York City, and lose family and lovers. Such characters become lost in more ways than one. They become the contradiction of being dead, as the family of Keith says he is, while still beating with a pulse.

Beyond shedding light on relationships that might go unnoticed and broadening our understanding of a Gothic phenomenon in contemporary terrorist-realism, this volume criticizes abuses of political-military power, especially extraordinary rendition, torture, and murder of terror suspects. Without meaning to overgeneralize a conclusion, or exaggerate a parallel, or move into political invective, the monograph nevertheless finds some solid connections between these texts and discussions of the U.S. government's unproductive reaction to 9/11 at home and abroad (via the pathways in thought already cleared by Derrida, Žižek, Baudrillard, Chomsky, Butler, Faludi, and Punter). The sense, here, is that the United States lost a chance to empathize and understand how the rest of the world suffers terrors similar to 9/11.

Consequently, the United States's disproportionate retributive violence supplanted new American initiatives to understand and resolve the causes of conflict that fuel terrorism. As Susan Faludi notes with much sorrow and perhaps some righteous rage, "There are consequences to living in a dream" (Faludi 2007: 289). I take not waking from the "'dream" after the mass atrocity of 9/11 to mean the United States squandered chances for greater reflection on terror and more beneficial changes to its international response to violence, risking the provocation of another generation of terrorists. Many of the characters in the five novels are to some degree somnambulists, too, not awake to making productive changes in their relationships and destructive behaviors (especially the constant gambler Keith Neudecker).

This volume has explored people's continued suffering through PTSD and the resulting vexing challenges to mental health professionals stemming from an attack that killed almost 3,000 citizens of seventy-eight countries and which would destabilize world economic stability when the city in the sky that was the WTC fell to earth. I maintain the aforementioned to be vital areas for further research. But I would add that terrorism and trauma comprise a significant research problem because they together affect and involve many academic disciplines, from political science and war studies, to sociology, to psychology, and economics. Therefore, to make a reasoned argument about 9/11 texts often involves tapping readings from some or all of these disciplines. What is more, when President George W. Bush successfully plied 9/11 as an incident to change official American policy and institute the use of preemptive strikes, he would usher two wars and worrisome potential conflicts and refugee crises for the future. Thus, 9/11 is at the heart of tragic changes to the lives of millions, from those displaced in Iraq and Afghanistan and neighboring countries, to those killed in the initial American wars of Middle East invasion and the subsequent civil wars. The dark journey of this book has found that such innocent dead will be with us, showing their mortal wounds and inviting us closer, as cinema's most haunting pair of twins—from *The Shining*—once told me in an interview over dinner in a dim London restaurant, "forever and ever and ever" (Burns and Burns 2015: 447).

# Appendix 1
## *Further Reading*

Ackerman, Spencer. *Reign of Terror: How the 9/11 Era Destabilized America and Produced Trump*. New York, Viking, 2021.

Altheide, David L. *Terrorism and the Politics of Fear*. 2nd ed. Lanham, MD, Rowman & Littlefield Publishers, 2017.

Araújo, Susana. *Transatlantic Fictions of 9/11 and the War on Terror: Images of Insecurity, Narratives of Captivity*. London, Bloomsbury, 2015.

Balfour, Lindsay Anne. *Hospitality in a Time of Terror: Strangers at the Gate*. Lanham, MD, Rowman & Littlefield Publishers/Bucknell University Press, 2017.

Briefel, Aviva, and Sam J. Miller. *Horror After 9/11: World of Fear, Cinema of Terror*. Austin, University of Texas Press, 2012.

Crawford, Joseph. *Gothic Fiction and the Invention of Terrorism*. London, Bloomsbury, 2013.

Denzin, Norman K., and Yvonna S. Lincoln, eds. *9/11 in American Culture*. Lanham, MD, AltaMira Press, 2003.

Donn, Katharina. *A Poetics of Trauma After 9/11*. London, Routledge, 2016.

Dony, Christophe, and Warren Rosenberg. *Portraying 9/11*. Jefferson, NC, McFarland & Co., 2009.

Gheorghiu, Oana Celia. *British and American Representations of 9/11: Literature, Politics and the Media*. London, Palgrave, 2018.

Graff, Garrett M. "9/11 and the Rise of the New Conspiracy Theorists." *WSJ*, 10 September 2020, https://www.wsj.com/articles/9-11-and-the-rise-of-the-new-conspiracy-theorists-11599768458. Accessed 2 March 2021.

Gurski, Phil. *The Threat from Within: Recognizing Al Qaeda-Inspired Radicalization and Terrorism in the West*. Lanham, MD, Rowman & Littlefield Publishers, 2015.

———. *An End to the War on Terrorism*. Lanham, MD, Rowman & Littlefield Publishers, 2018.

Harnden, Toby. *First Casualty: The Untold Story of the CIA Mission to Avenge 9/11*. New York, Little Brown and Company, 2021.

Hoag, Trevor. *Occupying Memory: Rhetoric, Trauma, Mourning*. Lanham, MD, Lexington Books, 2019.
Höglund, Johan. *The American Imperial Gothic: Popular Culture, Empire, Violence*. Farnham, UK, Ashgate, 2014.
Houen, Alex. *Terrorism and Modern Literature*. Oxford, Oxford University Press, 2002.
———. "Novel Spaces and Taking Place(s) in the Wake of September 11." *Studies in the Novel (Terrorism and the Postmodern Novel)*, vol. 36, no. 3, Fall 2004, pp. 419–437.
———. *States of War Since 9/11: Terrorism, Sovereignty and the War on Terror*. London, Routledge, 2014.
Houen, Alex, and Dominic Janes, eds. *Martyrdom and Terrorism: Pre-Modern to Contemporary Perspectives*. Oxford, Oxford University Press, 2014.
Houen, Alex, and Jan-Melissa Schramm, eds. *Sacrifice and Modern War Literature: From the Battle of Waterloo to the War on Terror*. Oxford, Oxford University Press, 2018.
Jarmakani, Amira. "Shiny Happy Imperialism: An Affective Exploration of 'Ways of Life' in the War on Terror." *Affect and Literature*. Ed. Alex Houen, Cambridge, Cambridge University Press, 2020, pp. 373–390.
Kassab, Hanna Samir. *Terrorist Recruitment and the International System*. Lanham, MD, Lexington Books, 2019.
Kauffman, Linda S. "Bodies in Rest and Motion in Falling Man." *Don DeLillo: Mao II, Underworld, Falling Man*, Ed. Stacey Olster. New York, Continuum, 2011, pp. 135–151.
Keeble, Arin. *The 9/11 Novel: Trauma, Politics and Identity*. Jefferson, NC, McFarland & Company, 2014.
Knafo, Danielle, ed. *Living with Terror, Working with Trauma: A Clinician's Handbook*. Lanham, MD, Jason Aronson, Inc., 2004.
Kowal, Ewa. *The "Image-Event" in the Early Post-9/11 Novel: Literary Representations of Terror After September 11, 2001*. New York, Columbia University Press, 2012.
Lawson, Chappell, Alan Bersin, and Juliette N. Kayyem, eds. *Beyond 9/11: Homeland Security for the Twenty-First Century*. Cambridge, MA, The MIT Press, 2020.
Lioy, Paul J. *The Inside Story of its Role in the September 11th Aftermath*. Lanham, MD, Rowman & Littlefield Publishers, 2010.
Lopez-Gonzalez, Crescencio. *The Latinx Urban Condition: Trauma, Memory, and Desire in Latinx Urban Literature and Culture*. Lanham, MD, Lexington Books, 2020.
Matusitz, Jonathan. *Symbolism in Terrorism: Motivation, Communication, and Behavior*. Lanham, MD, Rowman & Littlefield Publishers, 2015.
Mayer, Jane. *The Dark Side: The Inside Story of How the War on Terror Turned into a War on American Ideals*. New York, Anchor, 2008.
Nacos, Brigitte. *Mass-Mediated Terrorism: Mainstream and Digital Media in Terrorism and Counterterrorism*, 3rd ed. Lanham, MD, Rowman & Littlefield Publishers, 2016.

Nance, Kimberly A. *Ethics of Witness in Global Testimonial Narratives: Responding to the Pain of Others*. Lanham, MD, Lexington Books, 2019.

Palmer, Monte, and Princess Palmer. *At the Heart of Terror: Islam, Jihadists, and America's War on Terrorism*. Lanham, MD, Rowman & Littlefield Publishers, 2004.

Petrovic, Paul. *Representing 9/11: Trauma, Ideology, and Nationalism in Literature, Film, and Television*. Lanham, MD, Rowman & Littlefield, 2015.

Philpott, Don. *Is America Safe? Terrorism, Homeland Security, and Emergency Preparedness*, 2nd ed. Lanham, MD, Bernan Press, 2018.

Pozorski, Aimee. "Traumatic Realism and the Ethical Witness: Abu Ghraib Torture Photos, 2004–2008." *Augenblick*, vol. 48/49, Spring 2011, pp. 133–140.

———. *Falling After 9-11: Art and Literature in Crisis*. New York, Bloomsbury, 2014.

———. "Rebuilding After 9/11: The Figure of the Tower and Poetics of the Future." *9/11: Topics in Contemporary North American Literature*. Ed. Catherine Morley. New York, Bloomsbury, 2016, pp. 83–104.

———. *AIDS-Trauma and Politics*. Lanham, MD, Lexington Books, 2019.

Ramadanovic, Petar. *Forgetting Futures: On Meaning, Trauma, and Identity*. Lanham, MD, Lexington Books, 2001.

Rekret, Paul. *Derrida and Foucault: Philosophy, Politics, and Polemics*. Lanham, MD, Rowman & Littlefield Publishers, 2011.

Rubin, Gabriel. *Presidential Rhetoric on Terrorism under Bush, Obama and Trump: Inflating and Calibrating the Threat After 9/11*. Cham, Switzerland, Palgrave Pivot, 2021.

Setka, Stella. *Empathy and the Phantasmic in Ethnic American Trauma Narratives*. Lanham, MD, Lexington Books, 2020.

Sprunt, Barbara. "Nancy Pelosi Announces Plans For 9/11-Style Commission to Study Capitol Attack." *NPR*, 15 February 2021, https://www.npr.org/sections/trump-impeachment-trial-live-updates/2021/02/15/968144630/nancy-pelosi-announces-plans-for-9-11-style-commission-to-study-capitol-attack. Accessed 1 March 2021.

The Newseum. *Running Toward Danger: Stories Behind the Breaking News of September 11*. Lanham, MD, Rowman & Littlefield Publishers, 2002.

Tribute WTC Visitor Center, Lee Ielpi, and Meriam Lobel. *9/11: The World Speaks*. New York, Globe Pequot/Lyons Press/Rowman & Littlefield Publishers, 2011.

Wetmore, Kevin J. *Post-9/11 Horror in American Cinema*. New York, Continuum, 2012.

Yeomans, Frank E., John F. Clarkin, and Otto F. Kernberg. *A Primer of Transference-Focused Psychotherapy for the Borderline Patient*. Lanham, MD, Jason Aronson, Inc., 2002.

# Appendix 2

## *Interview at the Opening of the National September 11 Memorial & Museum, New York City, with Its Executive Vice President and Director Alice M. Greenwald (June 16, 2014)*

To give a fuller idea of the anguish represented by 9/11 and help give context to the literature I was reading, I visited four sites of commemoration and collection in New York City and Washington, D.C., between 2014 and 2015 and studied the ruined artifacts there.

A month following its official dedication on May 15, 2014, I traveled to New York City to interview the director of The National September 11 Memorial & Museum, Alice M. Greenwald, in her office. I wanted to understand how trauma would be officially memorialized for 9/11; I wanted to know what role literature would play. As the founding director, she has had to make, *The New York Times* records, some creative and "contentious decisions." Namely, she has had to decide "what artifacts the museum will include, what narrative it will present, [and] what kinds of exhibitions and symposiums might be scheduled" (Pogrebin 2006). A few years later, she would be promoted at the 9/11 Memorial & Museum with the new title of President & CEO. She continues to serve in that role as of the summer of 2021.

Extremely long lines wound before the entrance to the 9/11 Memorial Museum when I arrived, and it was clear that her schedule was full. The hope for the interview was to gain more light on themes of trauma, mourning, memorialization, the return of what we repress, and the process of narrating catastrophe. What effect the 9/11 dead continue to have on the living was a fascination, as well. As Director Greenwald puts it, in coming to the 9/11 Memorial Museum, a lot of people think they will be descending into Dante's *Inferno*. By the interview's close, the director mused on some of the novels featured in this book and on some of the novelists herein who have shared their story to the 9/11 Memorial & Museum.

*Author:* Director Greenwald, do you have any questions that I have not asked in my present file, or any questions that magazines and newspapers have not posed, that you wish someone would ask you?

*Alice M. Greenwald (AMG):* [Raises eyebrows, smiles, head falls back slightly] Oh no . . . no [laughs fully]. Oh my god, that's so funny, No. No questions that I have been waiting to be asked, that's for sure [rubs eyes slightly; staff shares her grin].

*Author:* I was struck by the Dedication of the 9/11 Memorial Museum's opening last month where President Obama spoke, as well as the present and the former mayors of New York City and governors of New York State. It seemed both nonpartisan and not overly patriotic. It was one of the few events ever attended by politicians, that I can recall, where identification, love, and genuine sympathy emerged toward others with sincerity, all un-embittered by political rancor. Did it not have an exceptional unity? Could you sum up your reaction to the Dedication?

*AMG:* It was very positive [looks at staff]—including from all of us! [laughs slightly]. Not unlike what you wrote me before, people have responded to the Dedication with a sense of gratitude. People were so grateful that it was handled in a way that focused on the stories and on real people. The politicians did not use it as an occasion or platform to espouse points of view or to promote

**Figure 7.1 Author Standing at What Was New York City's Ground Zero and Now Is the National September 11 Memorial & Museum.** Photograph by Author, June 16, 2014.

themselves. It was a ceremony in the service of history, and as the Dedication to this institution. I think many people were both surprised and grateful for that. It had a dignity about it; it was humbling. You got a sense that this isn't about partisanship or political beliefs. It was about something that happened to us as a nation, that happened to human beings, and that needed to be the focus and that was the focus. I haven't heard anyone say other about it but that they were moved by it deeply.

*Author:* Artists, including writers, often have an interest in collaborating with museums on new projects. Have you been getting many offers to work with them? Have they been visiting? Have they been contacting you?

*AMG:* We tend to get less interest from writers, per se—although I am sure there are plenty of writers who come through the 9/11 Memorial Museum—than from artists who work with tribute art: quilting, painting, and music in tribute to the victims. We have a lot of that expression displayed in the museum. The communications we tend to get from artists is "Would you like my piece for the museum? I'd like to present it in the museum." Writers we've had not so much. But Jonathan Safran Foer, who wrote *Extremely Loud and Incredibly Close,* participated in a tour of the Memorial and a preview of the Museum spaces, and he participated in one of our media installations called "Reflecting on 9/11." He's been very engaged.

We're just now launching our Public Program series, and I think there will be more opportunity for authors (historians, novelists, storytellers, poets) to be more involved. There hasn't been a mechanism for that until now.

*Author:* So, the Public Program series will be held right here amid the ruins?

*AMG:* Yes, in our auditorium. We'll have daytime programming, but also evening programming. Author: I noticed tribute art as I left the end of the main historical exhibit, and I remember that a number of comic books were in it. Do you think you will have an exhibit solely of the 9/11 novels, stories, and poems, along with sequential art?

*AMG:* Sure, but I think the question is this with museums: "What is the nature of the exhibition visually?" True, obviously, the Morgan Library & Museum does this all the time, and they do it very well, so it's not impossible to have wonderful exhibits that focus on books.

We have not yet started our special exhibition program. When you open an exhibition of 110,000 square feet, there's a lot for people to see the first time they come [smile followed by laughter]. So, we're putting off down the road, probably to the end of 2015, when we would launch of series of temporary exhibits. And that's the kind of theme we would look at: the way 9/11 has refracted through contemporary literature, or perhaps film. That's entirely within the scope of what we do.

*Author:* It seems a tremendous idea, and I look forward to coming again soon and seeing the temporary exhibitions.

I am curious about how an experience of mass trauma like this registers itself in art: what is put in, what is left out, and why? Also why is it that some New York novelists chose not to write a novel about it, including the prolific Joyce Carol Oates? While we have many 9/11 novels now, nevertheless novelists often remark on their protracted writers' block over 9/11—the long time it took to come around and write of the catastrophe. People who usually would write 2,000 words a day or more suddenly could write no more.

*AMG:* Trauma can do that to people.

One thing I've noticed is that a lot of people come into the Museum, and they've not really been in touch with the emotional reality they felt at 9/11, and in the immediate aftermath of the attacks from the days after. We tend to put that stuff away. You don't want to live in that mindframe all the time. I think coming into the Museum brings this back in a safe way. It's here and now, and not there and then. The Museum is in the middle of lower Manhattan and all [the memories are] coming back, but there's a lot of emotional safety also involved. The Museum gives people that space to reencounter something very profound and begin to integrate it in a more coherent manner, not in terms of literature but in terms of peoples' personal narratives.

*Author:* Does fiction gives anything we need, in your mind, that photography, journalism, oral history, the display of recovered objects, and academic history might not?

*AMG:* As a lover of literature, I would say that fiction often provides a form of access to interior realities that are not as evident in more documentary forms of expression. This in turn provides a reader with a sense of personal investment in the narrative, creating a sense of immediacy and fostering an awareness of the familiar.

*Author:* Are there some 9/11 novels that have moved you, or approached this catastrophe and tragedy with something you have not seen or felt elsewhere, or have defined the 9/11 decade more clearly?

*AMG:* To be honest, I have tried to avoid reading 9/11 fiction. The reason is simple.

Being immersed day after day in this subject matter, when I choose to read on my own time, I choose non-9/11 subject matter as a form of escape. So, my reading of late has been de Waal's *The Hare with the Amber Eyes*, Hosseini's *And the Mountains Echoed*, and for nonfiction, Matthiessen's *The Snow Leopard*. Two 9/11 books I did read were DeLillo's *Falling Man* and Amy Waldman's *The Submission*. I thought DeLillo's book was compelling but also struggling itself to come to terms with the history and so not quite as powerful as his other works. And Waldman's book was an easy read, with a good storyline and some characterizations of individuals I knew from the Memorial jury process that were quite entertaining. I thought she was able to create a thoughtful commentary about prejudice and politics, using this subject matter.

*Author:* As you have meditated on how memory works and what memorializing does, I will share what I remember: I was making my one-and-a-half-year-old and three-year-old daughters' breakfasts when we three saw—live on television—the second plane slice through the South Tower. They asked me, "What is that? What is going on?"

*AMG:* Right. And you couldn't answer them?

*Author:* It was one of the earliest moments with them where I could not say anything. They just saw my tears. I took them to a carousel in a mall that morning, but nearly no one was there: it was all a bit like the abandoned set of an apocalyptic movie. They had their lonely ride on the gaily daubed horses, and I held them later as we glumly ate our ice cream in silence on a bench. Sometimes, now fifteen years later, when we three happen to pass that same carousel, an uneasy quietness comes, although I wonder what they could consciously remember. My hope is that when they walk through this Museum later today, it can articulate what then I could not.

*AMG:* Yes. We've thought a lot about that, in particular in our education staff, because we've heard this not only from parents especially on its anniversary, about what to say, what not to say—but also from teachers. It is hard for teachers to teach 9/11, particularly for individuals who lived through it themselves and have their own difficulty with it emotionally.

So early on, several years ago, we produced a set of guidelines for adults on how to talk to their children about 9/11, particularly when September rolls around and it's all over the news again. We wanted to help parents contextualize what their kids are seeing.

And for teachers we've now developed over ninety lesson plans at different grade levels, all to help teachers manage the way into the telling of the story. Tomorrow night we're kicking off a series of programs where schoolteachers can bring their classes in to participate based on their grade level, using the Museum as a classroom. The Museum becomes a jumping-off point for certain kinds of discussions.

*Author:* I'm also curious about how the Museum helps people who were physically trapped in either of the towers, who escaped, but could never explain to anyone (friends or family) the horrors they underwent, and how it makes them different now. How might the Museum help them with these unhealable wounds? Do you sense there is something the Museum is able to express, too, that they cannot articulate?

*AMG:* I'm sure. I mean, it would be a presumption on my part, because I haven't heard from anyone specifically about this. But there is the fact that you can bring your family in, and, in many cases, survivors share things in our oral histories project that they haven't shared before with their families because it's too painful. Then you're listening to people in alcoves in the historical exhibition, and we show you where they were in the buildings as they moved down and evacuated. So for some people, I think, there is the experience of hearing the story, in a way, for the first time: in the voice of your parent, or your cousin, or your neighbor, but hearing it in the space of the Museum. I'm sure that's happening.

I also think for people who've done oral histories, hearing themselves talk has to be very emotional. We all compartmentalize difficult things in our lives, but when you come into the Museum, you realize that your story is part and parcel of this greater history—you've actually contributed to the historical documentation. I think that is a very profound experience. And for some very difficult because they don't live in that place all the time.

*Author:* I know you were affiliated with the U.S. Holocaust Memorial Museum in Washington, D.C., for fourteen years, and for part of that time were associate museum director for Museum Programs. Do you find that some of the physical structure of that extraordinarily moving museum and its involving ways of narration now appear here at the 9/11 Memorial Museum?

*AMG:* Certainly, my experience at the U.S. Holocaust Memorial Museum trained me to think about the way one constructs an exhibition. I worked closely with Jesaja (Shaike) Weinberg [1918–2000; born in Poland, educated in Germany], who was the founding director there, and he was a very interesting individual in the museum world of the 1980s. He had come out of theater. He was the head of the Tel Aviv Municipal Theatre for a number of years [the largest theater in Israel]. He had been very interested in computers early on. And only came to museums serendipitously. He created in Tel Aviv around May 1978 the Beit Hatfutsot (The Museum of the Jewish Diaspora). When it opened, it was a museum without artifacts. It was entirely a theatrical set with computers. You were moving through 4,000 years of Jewish history, and periodically you'd be stopped at a computer monitor, and it would say: "Here you are—you are in Spain, it's 1492, it's the Expulsion, and are you going to convert? Go into hiding?" You would make a choice on the monitor, and the screen would give you the historical consequence of that choice. At the time, it was very innovative and new, but it was not a museum per se in the classical sense because there were no artifacts. When Shaike came over to head the U.S. Holocaust Memorial Museum, many of us were concerned because here was a man who really didn't appreciate artifacts and for those of us who classically trained museum people it sounded . . .

*Author:* Like a gamble with history?

*AMG:* Yes, but what he did was life changing for me (in terms of my understanding about what museums can do). As a theater person, he understood the power of story, and that the museum had to tell a story. He understood perspective visually, and he hired a film documentarian named Martin Smith (who had worked for the BBC, and did the World at War series), and Martin was in effect the visual curator of the museum. He was structuring the narrative. They had historians, they had curators with objects, they had all that, but it really was about creating a storyline that the visitor moved through. I think that we in many ways have adapted that modality here at the 9/11 Memorial & Museum, particularly in the historical exhibition, less so elsewhere in the Museum. We are very self-conscious about creating a structured narrative and using the artifacts as exemplars of certain moments in the history, rather than as icons themselves as in an art museum where you would look at art for its own merit. In the case of most history museums, and certainly this one and the U.S. Holocaust Memorial Museum, the artifacts become a way in to understanding the broader narrative of the historical period. They are both illustrative as well as expressive of that moment in time, and I think that absolutely came out of my training with Shaike.

*Author:* The story inside these walls is exceedingly powerful. As I moved through the exhibits, I felt the loss, disappearances, and terror of the day on walls, pedestals, monitors, and large floor spaces, especially from the damaged fire engines, bashed turbines, wrecked radio and television antenna, and the massive twisted steel support beams from the WTC Towers. It captures the confusion of that day and the sense that the world had fallen down upon thousands of helpless people.

*AMG:* It's not meant to keep you at a distance, that's for sure. It's really meant to bring you in as a witness, as if you were a witness that day. However, it's not meant to be an immersive recreation of 9/11, at all. And if that was what people were experiencing, I'd be very upset because we're not here to traumatize the public at all, obviously. But it is about encountering the history—as we may encounter it ourselves watching television or walking on the streets of lower Manhattan, or in the tidal basin of Washington, D.C., looking across and watching the Pentagon burning.

*Author:* You have been designing this Museum for eight years and have had to look at thousands of photos and objects connected to the deaths of almost three thousand people. How do you face these terrible realities without constantly reexperiencing trauma yourself, and not becoming overwhelmed or incapacitated by grief? In brief, what keeps you and the museum staff able to function, when every day you look on the things that broke the heart of the world?

*AMG:* I think there are several answers to that question. One is that there are different layers of engagement with the hardest material on a daily basis. For the most part, I am not that close to it on a day-to-day basis. I would ask this question of our oral historians because they are sitting in that same room day in and day out, hearing these heart-wrenching stories. And I think it's very difficult, when you are at that close a level to the content, to get a more distant perspective and to move out of it.

For me, I am focused on delivering a product, focused on the work that has to be done. And that work would have to be done whether we were a museum about 9/11 or Van Gogh or the American Civil War. There are steps that have to be taken, decisions that have to be made, designs that have to be reviewed. There's the work of creating and running a museum that is The Work. So, you focus in on that level of your intellect: Get the Job Done. Because of the nature of the material, not all that in frequently, there will be moments in the day when you just get stopped in your tracks. Then you have to regroup.

But as often as one is shocked by that kind of content, even more often it's the stories of people's generosity, their selflessness, their innate heroism. That's what stops you. When I cry . . . it's generally because of that kind of story.

And there are so many of them, these incredible stories about resilience, about people's ability to be responsive, and that is what was captured in the Dedication ceremony. It was focused not on the evildoers, but it certainly was focused on the victims—and through the lens of the generosity of spirit that was demonstrated. Consider the man with the red bandanna, a perfect example of that. Here was a person in that moment who had the wherewithal, emotional stability, and the compassion to respond to the needs of others. That's what gets you. And it doesn't depress you: it elevates you to hear these stories. That's what gives us the motivation to keep working on the Museum. Also, I would say there is a palpable sense of dedication among the staff. This is a very highly dedicated group of people who are emotionally invested in first creating the Museum, now in running it, making sure that people have the right kind of experience, and ensuring that everything is accurate. That is what keeps you going, and that is what we are here to do.

*Author:* I read in the July 30, 2011, *Wall Street Journal* that the original Twin Towers developer Larry Silverstein said: "I suspect that in ten years very few people will remember what Ground Zero was." I wonder if that is true at all?

*AMG:* Oh, I don't think that's true at all [laughter]. I think the whole point of the Memorial is so that won't happen.

I would understand that statement of his a little differently, though. He may have meant: there's no longer this gaping wound in lower Manhattan. There's no longer a hole in the ground. We have these fabulous new skyscrapers, and shortly we are to have this fabulous new transportation hub, and we have this Museum and this Memorial, and it doesn't look at all the way it looked for the first seven or eight years after 9/11 when it was nothing.

But I don't think people will not remember what happened, Danel, because we're here to make sure they don't.

*Author:* I so appreciate your time today, Director Greenwald.

*AMG:* It has been wonderful to meet you. Good luck with your work. Are you yourself a writer?

*Author:* I write occasionally on contemporary Gothic novels.

*AMG:* Interesting.

*Appendix 2* 183

*Author:* Speaking of the contemporary, I do not think I have ever been to a museum that records such a recent trauma.

*AMG:* Right, I agree with that. That was part of the challenge. Exactly, I mean, the U.S. Holocaust Memorial Museum comes half a century after World War II. No, I can't think of another museum . . .

*Staff Member:* There's the Oklahoma City National Memorial & Museum . . .

*AMG:* Right, the Oklahoma Museum opens five years after the event, or actually 2001.

But the difference is that, for Oklahoma City residents that is a very personal piece of history, yet, for the majority of the United States, that is not. With 9/11, you've got not just Americans but people around the world with a sense of

Figure 7.2 In 2014, One World Tower (Freedom Tower) Opened Six Months after the 9/11 Memorial & Museum, Becoming the Tallest Building in the Western Hemisphere (as of Publication), with Its 1,776 Foot Height as a Reference to the Year of the U.S. Declaration of Independence Signing and a Symbol of American Perseverance. Photograph by Author, June 16, 2014.

connection to this event that I think is unprecedented as a shared experience. A global moment. And that was not true of Oklahoma City. I happen to remember Oklahoma City vividly, but I don't think it rose to the level of the JFK assassination or the MLK assassination, where people really do remember where they were when those events happened, as they do with 9/11.

*Author:* Is the explanation for how the Murrah Building bombing and the WTC destruction scar our memory differently the fact that the New York City violence was seen as an attack on the West, on American military, political, and economic dominance?

*AMG:* Right, I'm sure. The Oklahoma bombing was horrible—I remember vividly how shocked I was when I heard about it—but somehow when you found out it was Timothy McVeigh, the public could say, "Oh, he was off balance. He was one of these crazies, one of these ideological people, one of these sociopaths." Somehow you could package it and put it away.

Now I think with 9/11 most of the Country and most of the world was not paying attention to Al Qaeda. So, you didn't know who the perpetrator really was. It literally felt like it came out of the blue to so many people around the world.

I think the struggle to make sense of the terror and to understand the world we live in—rather than the one that we thought we lived in—forced the issue of questioning in the way that the Murrah Building bombing did not.

*Author:* I sense you are right. Thanks so much again for these thoughts.

*AMG:* Oh, thank you, my pleasure truly, and let us know how your family's experience in the Museum goes.

*Author:* My family is inside the Statue of Liberty right now, but they will come to the 9/11 Memorial & Museum soon.

# Bibliography

*9/11: The Filmmakers' Commemorative DVD Edition*, Jules and Gedeon Naudet, Goldfish Pictures/Silverstar Productions/Paramount, 2001. Film.
Abbott, Shirley. *The Future of Love*. Chapel Hill, Algonquin Books, 2008.
Abraham, Nicolas, and Maria Torok. *The Shell and the Kernel: Renewals of Psychoanalysis, Volume 1*. Trans. and Ed. Nicolas Rand. Chicago, University of Chicago Press, 1994.
Abrams, Floyd. *Speaking Freely: Trials of the First Amendment*. New York, Penguin, 2005.
ACLU. "Fact Sheet: Extraordinary Rendition." *American Civil Liberties Union*, 2016, www.aclu.org/issues/national-security/torture/extraordinary-rendition. Accessed 11 September 2016.
Adams, Tim. "Bring Out Your Dead (Rev. of Patrick McGrath's *Ghost Town*)." *The Guardian*, 20 August 2015, https://www.theguardian.com/books/2005/aug/21/fiction.features2. Accessed 21 June 2020.
Adler, Alexandra. "Neuropsychiatric Complications in Victims of Boston's Cocoanut Grove Disaster." *Journal of the American Medical Association*, vol. 123, no. 13, 25 December 1943, pp. 1098–1101.
American Psychological Association. *Diagnostic and Statistical Manual of Mental Disorders* (DSM-III), 3rd ed. Washington, D.C., American Psychological Association, 1980.
———. *Diagnostic and Statistical Manual of Mental Disorders* (DSM-IV), 4th ed. Washington, D.C., American Psychological Association, 1994.
———. *Diagnostic and Statistical Manual of Mental Disorders* (DSM-IV-Text Revision), 4th ed. Washington, D.C., American Psychological Association, 2000.
———. *Diagnostic and Statistical Manual of Mental Disorders* (DSM-V), 5th ed. Washington, D.C., American Psychological Association, 2013.
Amfreville, Marc. "American Gothic Romance as Trauma in *Port Mungo*." *Patrick McGrath: Directions and Transgressions*. Ed. Jocelyn Dupont. Newcastle Upon Tyne, Cambridge Scholars Publishing, 2012, pp. 103–114.

Amis, Martin. "The Voice of the Lonely Crowd." *The Guardian*, 31 May 2002, www.theguardian.com/books/2002/jun/01/philosophy.society. Accessed 26 July 2014.

Andriano, Joseph. *Our Ladies of Darkness: Feminine Daemonology in Male Gothic Fiction*. University Park, PA, Penn State University Press, 1993.

Anker, Elizabeth S. "Allegories of Falling and the 9/11 Novel." *American Literary History*, vol. 23, no. 3, 2011, pp. 463–482.

Anolik, Ruth Bienstock. *Horrifying Sex: Essays on Sexual Difference in Gothic Literature*. Jefferson, NC, McFarland, 2007.

Antman, Michael. "Review of Patrick McGrath's *Ghost Town*." *Bookslut*, March 2006, http://www.bookslut.com/fiction/2006_03_008170.php. Accessed 21 June 2020.

Araújo, Susana. *Transatlantic Fictions of 9/11 and the War on Terror: Images of Insecurity, Narratives of Captivity*. New York, Bloomsbury, 2015.

Armstrong, Nancy. *How Novels Think: The Limits of Individualism from 1719–1900*. New York, Columbia University Press, 2006.

Associated Press Staff. "After Complaints, Rockefeller Center Drapes Sept.11 Statue." *The New York Times*, 19 September 2002, www.nytimes.com/2002/09/19/nyregion/after-complaints-rockefeller-center-drapes-sept-11-statue.html. Accessed 15 July 2013.

Baelo-Allué, Sonia. "9/11 and the Psychic Trauma Novel: Don DeLillo's *Falling Man*." *Atlantis: Journal of the Spanish Association of Anglo-American Studies*, vol. 34, no. 1, June 2012, pp. 63–79.

Baker, Rachel. "Terror Sex: Love (or at Least Lust) in the Ruins." *The Encyclopedia of 9/11*, New York Magazine, New York Media, 27 August 2014, nymag.com/news/articles/wtc/. Accessed 1 August 2014.

Balaev, Michelle. "Trends in Trauma Theory." *Mosaic*, vol. 41, no. 2, 2008, pp. 149–165.

———. *The Nature of Trauma in American Novels*. Evanston, IL, Northwestern University Press, 2012.

Banita, Georgiana. "Scapegoating in 'Ground Zero': Patrick McGrath's Allegory of Historical Trauma." *Textual Practice*, 2011, pp. 1–25.

———. "Sex and Sense: McGrath, Tristram, and Psychoanalysis from Ground Zero to Abu Ghraib." *Plotting Justice: Narrative Ethics and Literary Culture After 9/11*. Lincoln, University of Nebraska Press, 2012, pp. 109–164.

Barker, Clive. "Clive Barker in the Flesh." An interview with Dave Hughes, *Skeleton Crew (Special Double Clive Barker Edition)*, 1988, pp. 3–4.

Barrett, Devlin. "Some Seeking to Move Past 'Ground Zero.'" *The Wall Street Journal*, 30 July 2011, www.wsj.com/articles/SB10001424053111904800304576474314214110294. Accessed 1 June 2020.

Baudrillard, Jean. *The Gulf War Did Not Take Place*. Trans. P. Patton. Bloomington, IN, Indiana University Press, 1995.

———. *The Spirit of Terrorism: And Requiem for the Twin Towers 2002*. Trans. Chris Turner, Brooklyn, Verso, 2012.

Beck, Stefan. "Kinderkampf: Rev. of Jonathan Safran Foer's *Extremely Loud and Incredibly Close*." *The New Criterion*, June 2005, pp. 92–95.

Belau, Linda. *Encountering Impossibility: Trauma, Psychosis, and Psychoanalysis.* Binghamton, SUNY, 2000.

Beville, Maria. *Gothic-Postmodernism: Voicing the Terrors of Postmodernity.* New York, Rodopi, 2009.

Blake, Linnie. *The Wounds of Nations: Horror Cinema, Historical Trauma and National Identity.* Manchester, Manchester University Press, 2008.

Bohjalian, Chris. "What Will Post-Pandemic Fiction Look Like? The Novels That Followed 9/11 Offer Some Clues." *The Washington Post*, 21 May 2020, www.washingtonpost.com/entertainment/books/what-will-post-pandemic-fiction-look-like-the-novels-that-followed-911-offer-some-clues/2020/05/21/625a3bc8-99d7-11ea-a282-386f56d579e6_story.html. Accessed 21 June 2020.

Boss, P. "Ambiguous Loss Research, Theory and Practice: Reflections After 9/11." *Journal of Marriage and Family*, vol. 66, no. 3, pp. 551–566.

Botting, Fred. *Gothic Romanced: Consumption, Gender and Technology.* New York, Routledge, 2008.

Bragard, Véronique, Christophe Dony, and Warren Rosenberg, eds. *Portraying 9/11.* London, McFarland & Co., 2009.

Bromwich, Jonah Engel. "Marcy Borders, 'Dust Lady' Who Survived 9/11, Dies At 42." *The New York Times*, 26 August 2015, www.nytimes.com/2015/08/27/nyregion/marcy-borders-dust-lady-who-survived-9-11-dies-at-42.html. Accessed 1 June 2020.

Bruhm, Steven. *Gothic Bodies.* Philadelphia, University of Pennsylvania Press, 1994.

———. "The Gothic Body." *The Handbook of the Gothic.* Ed. Marie Mulvey-Roberts, 2nd ed. New York, New York University Press, 2009, pp. 250–251.

Burke, Edmund. *A Philosophical Enquiry into the Origin of Our Ideas of the Sublime and Beautiful.* 1757. Oxford, Oxford University Press, 2014.

Burns, Lisa, and Louise Burns. "Reminiscence." *Stanley Kubrick's 'The Shining': Studies in the Horror Film.* Ed. Danel Olson. Lakewood, CO, Centipede Press, 2015, pp. 437–447.

Butler, Judith. *Precarious Life: The Powers of Mourning and Violence.* New York, Verso, 2004.

Byrd, Max. "*Ghost Town*: Gothic Gotham." *The New York Times*, 4 September 2005, https://www.nytimes.com/2005/09/04/books/review/ghost-town-gothic-gotham.html. Accessed 21 June 2020.

Byron, Glennis, and Dale Townshend, eds. "Introduction." *The Gothic World.* London, Routledge, 2014, pp. xxiv–xlvi.

Canfield, Kevin. "The Worst Fiction about 9/11." *SALON*, 8 September 2011, www.salon.com/2011/09/08/embarrassing_9_11_novels/. Accessed 12 June 2020.

Carter, Angela. Afterword. *Fireworks: Nine Profane Pieces*, 1974. New York, Penguin, 1987, pp. 132–133.

Caruth, Cathy, special editor. *Psychoanalysis, Culture and Trauma.* Two Issues of *American Imago: A Journal for Psychoanalysis, Culture and the Arts*, Part I, vol. 48, no. 1, Spring 1991 and Part II, vol. 48, no. 4, Winter 1991.

———, ed. *Trauma: Explorations in Memory*, 1995. Baltimore, Johns Hopkins University Press, 2006a.

———. *Unclaimed Experience: Trauma, Narrative and History*, 1996. Baltimore, Johns Hopkins University Press, 2006b.
———. *Literature in the Ashes of History*. Baltimore, Johns Hopkins University Press, 2013.
———, ed. *Listening to Trauma: Conversations with Leaders in the Theory and Treatment of Catastrophic Experience (with Photographic Portraits)*. Baltimore, Johns Hopkins University Press, 2014.
Castricano, Jodey. *Cryptomimesis: The Gothic and Jacques Derrida's Ghost Writing*. Montreal, McGill-Queen's University Press, 2001.
Cauchon, Dennis, and Martha Moore. "Desperation Forced a Horrific Decision." *USA Today*, 2 September 2002, www.coursehero.com/file/46350367/Desperation-Forced-a-Horrific-Decision2docx/. Accessed 11 June 2020.
Chambers, Ross. *Untimely Interventions*. Ann Arbor, University of Michigan Press, 2004.
Chiasso, Mary Ann, Sabina Hirshfield, Michael Humberstone, Joseph DiFilippi, Beryl Koblin, and Robert H. Remien. "Increased High Risk Sexual Behavior After September 11 in Men Who Have Sex with Men." *Archives of Sexual Behavior*, vol. 34, no. 5, 2005, pp. 527–535.
Childers, Doug. "The Lonesome Ghosts of 9/11 (Review of *The Nostalgist*)." *Richmond-Times Dispatch*, 23 September 2012, https://www.richmond.com/entertainment/the-lonesome-ghosts-of-9-11/article_7b566a64-d31d-535c-a249-a55a5a896e28.html. Accessed 19 June 2020.
Chomsky, Noam. *9-11: Was There an Alternative?* 2001. New York, Open Media/Seven Stories Press Updated Edition, 2011.
CIA Staff. "Terrorism FAQs." *CIA.gov*, 19 April 2013, https://www.cia.gov/news-information/cia-the-war-on- terrorism/terrorism-faqs.html?tab=list-1. Accessed 10 January 2020.
Cixous, Helene. "Fiction and Its Phantoms: A Reading of Freud's 'Das Unheimliche' ('The Uncanny')." *New Literary History*, vol. 7, no. 3, Spring 1976, pp. 525–548.
Cockley, David. "Lynn Sharon Schwartz's *The Writing on the Wall*: Responding to the Media Spectacle." *Studies in American Jewish Literature*, vol. 28, 2009, pp. 14–27.
Cohen, Roger. "Rumsfeld Is Correct--the Truth Will Get Out." *The New York Times*, 7 June 2006, https://archive.nytimes.com/www.nytimes.com/iht/2006/06/07/world/IHT-07globalist.html?pagewanted=all. Accessed 11 January 2020.
Coleridge, S. T. *Biographia Literaria; or Biographical Sketches of My Literary Life and Opinions*. Chapter 3, 1817, *Online-Literature*, The Literature Network, 9 September 2008, www.online-literature.com/coleridge/biographia-literaria/3/. Accessed 12 June 2020.
Conrad, Joseph. *The Secret Agent*. 1907. Intro. M. Seymour-Smith. Hammondsworth, Middlesex, UK, Penguin, 1984.
Constant, Paul. "Review of *Falling Man*." *The Stranger: Seattle's Weekly*, Index Newspapers LLC, 2007, www.thestranger.com/archive/paul-constant. Accessed 20 June 2020.
Conte, Joseph. "Don DeLillo's Falling Man and the Age of Terror." *MFS: Modern Fiction Studies*, vol. 57, no. 3, Fall 2011, pp. 557–583.

Coolidge, Pres. Calvin. 17 Jan. 1925. "Address to the American Society of Newspaper Editors, Washington, D.C." *The American Presidency Project*, UC Santa Barbara, 2014, www.presidency.ucsb.edu/documents/address-the-american-society-newspaper-editors-washington-dc. Accessed 11 June 2020.

Cowles, Gregory. "Fiction Chronicle: *The Writing on the Wall*." *The New York Times*, 3 July 2005, www.nytimes.com/2005/07/03/books/review/fiction-chronicle.html. Accessed 20 June 2020.

Cumming, Chris. "Falling Men: On Don DeLillo and Terror." *The Paris Review*, 30 April 2013, www.theparisreview.org/blog/2013/04/30/falling-men-on-don-delillo-and-terror/. Accessed 20 June 2020.

Davis, Colin. *Haunted Subjects: Deconstruction, Psychoanalysis, and the Return of the Dead*. New York, Palgrave Macmillan, 2007.

Däwes, Birgit. *Ground Zero Fiction: History, Memory, and Representation in the American 9/11 Novel*. Heidelberg, Universitätsverlag Winter, 2011.

DeLillo, Don. *Players*. New York, Knopf, 1977.

———. *Running Dog*. New York, Knopf, 1978.

———. *The Names*. New York, Knopf, 1982.

———. *White Noise*. New York, Viking, 1985.

———. *Libra*. New York, Viking, 1988.

———. *Americana*. Boston, Houghton Mifflin, 1971, Rev. Ed., New York, Penguin, 1989.

———. *Mao II*. New York, Viking, 1991.

———. *Underworld*. New York, Scribner, 1997.

———. *The Body Artist*. New York, Scribner, 2001a.

———. "In the Ruins of the Future: Reflections on Terror and Loss in the Shadow of September 11." *Harper's Magazine*, December 2001b, pp. 33–40.

———. *Cosmopolis*. New York, Scribner, 2003.

———. *Falling Man*. New York, Scribner, 2007.

———. "I Don't Know America Anymore." Interview by C. Amend and G. Diez, Trans. Dum Pendebat Filius, *Die Ziet*, 13 August 2008, www. dumpendebat.net/static-content/delillo-diezeit-Oct2007.html. Accessed 1 November 2019.

del Toro, Guillermo. "Spanish Gothic." *The Devil's Backbone* Voiceover, minutes 4:13–7:06 Disc Two. Criterion Collection, 2013, DVD.

De Niro Robert, and Al Pacino. "Interview with Brian Williams." *Today*, NBC, 2008, www.youtube.com/watch?time_continue=9&v=XR0jnAqUD9A&feature=emb_logo. Accessed 20 June 2020.

Denis, Dixie L. *Living, Dying, Grieving*, London, Jones & Bartlett Publishers, 2008.

Der Derian, James. "9/11: Before, After, and In Between." *Terrorism, Media, Liberation*, Ed. John David Slocum. New Brunswick, Rutgers University Press, 2005, pp. 321–337.

———. *Virtuous War: Mapping the Military-Industrial-Media-Entertainment-Network*, 2nd ed. New York, Routledge, 2009.

DeRosa, Aaron. "Alterity and the Radical Other in Post-9/11 Fiction: DeLillo's *Falling Man* and Walter's *The Zero*." *Arizona Quarterly*, vol. 69, no. 2, 2013, pp. 157–183.

Derrida, Jacques. "*Fors*: The Anglish Words of Nicolas Abraham and Maria Torok." Foreword, *The Wolf Man's Magic Word: A Cryptonymy*, Nicholas Abraham and Maria Torok, Trans. Nicholas Rand, Minneapolis, University of Minnesota Press, 1986, pp. xi–xlviii.

———. *Memoires: for Paul de Man*. Trans. C. Lindsay, J. Culler, E. Cadava, and P. Kamuf. New York, Columbia University Press, 1989a.

———. "Psyche: Inventions of the Other." *Reading De Man Reading*. Eds. L. Waters and W. Godzich. Minneapolis, University of Minnesota Press, 1989b.

———. *Memoirs of the Blind: The Self-Portrait and Other Ruins*. Trans. A. Brault and M. Naas. Chicago, University of Chicago Press, 1993.

———. "Jacques Derrida and Deconstruction." Interview with Mitchell Stephens, *The New York Times Magazine*, 23 January 1994, www.nytimes.com/1994/01/23/magazine/jacques-derrida.html. Accessed 20 June 2020.

———. "Archive Fever: A Freudian Impression." Trans. Eric Prenowitz, *Diacritics*, vol. 25, no. 2, Summer 1995a, pp. 9–63.

———. *The Gift of Death*. Trans. D. Wills. Chicago, University of Chicago Press, 1995b.

———. *Politics of Friendship*. Trans. George Collins. New York, Verso, 1997.

———. *Adieu to Emmanuel Lévinas*. Trans. A. Brault and M. Naas. Stanford, CA, Stanford University Press, 1999.

———. "Hostipitality." *Angelaki: Journal of the Theoretical Humanities*, vol. 5, no. 3, December 2000, pp. 3–18, eText.

———. *The Work of Mourning*. Eds. A. Brault and M. Naas. Chicago, University of Chicago Press, 2001a.

———. *On Cosmopolitanism and Forgiveness*. 1997. London, Routledge, 2001b.

———. "Autoimmunity: Real and Symbolic Suicides—A Dialogue with Jacques Derrida." *Philosophy in a Time of Terror: Dialogues with Jurgen Habermas and Jacques Derrida*. Ed. Giovanna Borradori, Chicago, University of Chicago Press, 2003, pp. 85–136, Kindle.

———. "Living On: Border Lines." *Deconstruction and Criticism*. 1979. Ed. Harold Bloom, Trans. James Hulbert. Bloomsbury/Continuum, New York, 2004, pp. 62–142.

———. *Specters of Marx. The State of the Debt, the Work of Mourning and the New International*. 1993. Translated from the French by Peggy Kamuf, with Introduction by Bernd Magnus and Stephen Cullenberg. New York, Routledge Classics, 2006.

Desmet, Christy, and Anne Williams, eds. *Shakespearean Gothic (Gothic Literary Studies)*. Cardiff, University of Wales Press, 2009.

Diehn, Andi. "Rev. of *The Writing on the Wall*." *Curled Up with A Good Book*, 2005, www.curledup.com/writwall.htm. Accessed 21 June 2020.

Dobnik, Verena. "Scientists Still Working to ID Victims form 9/11." *The Post and Courier*, 9 May 2014, www.postandcourier.com/archives/scientists-still-working-to-id-victims-from-9-11/article_c0ab3dad-24c2-5bf4-a41a-14d8484c996e.html. Accessed 2 June 2020.

Doctorow, E. L. *Lamentation: 9/11*. Foreword by Former Secretary-General Kofi A. Annan and Photographs by David Finn. New York, Ruder Finn Press, 2002.

Donn, Katharina. *A Poetics of Trauma After 9/11*. New York, Routledge, 2016.
Dowling, Frank D., Gene Moynihan, Bill Genet, and Jonathan Lewis. "A Peer-Based Assistance Program for Officers with the New York City Police Department: Report of the Effects of September 11, 2001." *American Journal of Psychiatry*, vol. 163, no. 1, 2006, pp. 151–153.
Drakakis, John, and Dale Townshend, eds. *Gothic Shakespeares*. London, Routledge, 2008.
Dubus III, Andre. *The Garden of Lost Days*. New York, Norton, 2008.
Duggan, Robert. "Ghosts of Gotham: 9/11 mourning in Patrick McGrath's *Ghost Town* and Michael Cunningham's *Specimen Days*." *Literature, Migration and the "War on Terror."* Eds. Fiona Tolan, Stephen Morton, Anastasia Valassopoulos, and Robert Spencer. London, Routledge, 2012, pp. 127–139.
Duvall, John N., and Robert P. Marzec. "Narrating 9/11." *Modern Fiction Studies*, vol. 57, no. 3, 2011, pp. 381–400.
———, eds. *Narrating 9/11: Fantasies of State, Security, and Terrorism*. Baltimore, Johns Hopkins University Press, 2015.
Dwyer, Jim. "A Nation Challenged: The Vault—Below Ground Zero, Silver and Gold." *The New York Times*, 1 November 2001, www.nytimes.com/2001/11/01/nyregion/a-nation-challenged-the-vault-below-ground-zero-silver-and-gold.html. Accessed 19 June 2020.
Eaglestone, Robert. "'The Age of Reason is Over, an Age of Fury was Dawning': Contemporary Anglo-American Fiction and Terror." *Wasafiri*, vol. 22, no. 2, 2007, pp. 19–22.
Edwards, Justin D., and Rune Graulund. *Grotesque (The New Critical Idiom)*. New York, Routledge, 2013.
Egan, Jennifer. *The Keep*. New York, Knopf, 2006.
Erikson, Kai. "Notes on Trauma and Community." *Trauma: Explorations in Memory*. Ed. Cathy Caruth, Baltimore, Johns Hopkins University Press, 1995, pp. 183–199.
*Extremely Loud and Incredibly Close*. Directed by Stephen Daldry, performances by Sandra Bullock, Tom Hanks, Thomas Horn, and Max von Sydow, Warner Bros., 2011.
Faludi, Susan. *The Terror Dream: Fear and Fantasy in Post–9/11 America*. New York, Metropolitan, 2007.
Farrell, Stephen. "In 'Ceremonial Transfer,' Remains of 9/11 Victims Are Moved to Memorial." *The New York Times*, 10 May 2014, National sec., p. 18.
Farrell, Susan Elizabeth. "Chapter 4: 'A Hole in the Middle of Me': Shattered Homes in Post- 9/11 Literature." *Imagining Home: American War Fiction from Hemingway to 9/11*. Rochester, NY, Camden House, 2017, pp. 144–185.
Faulkner, William. *Light in August*. 1932. New York, Vintage, 2011.
Faust, Drew Gilpin. *The Republic of Suffering: Death and the American Civil War*. New York, Knopf, 2008.
Felman, Shoshana, and Dori Laub. *Testimony: Crises of Witnessing in Literature, Psychoanalysis, and History*. New York, Routledge, 1991.
Fischer, Kathleen. *When Grief Won't Go Away*. St. Mainrad, IN, Abbey Press, 1991.
Flynn, Kevin, and Jim Dwyer. "Falling Bodies, a 9/11 Image Etched in Pain." *The New York Times*, 10 September 2004, www.nytimes.com/2004/09/10/nyregion/

nyregionspecial2/falling-bodies-a-911-image-etched-in-pain.html. Accessed 12 December 2019.

Foa, Edna B., Terence M. Keane, Matthew J. Friedman, and Judith A. Cohen, eds. *Effective Treatments for PTSD*. New York, The Guilford Press, 2008.

Foer, Jonathan Safran. *Everything is Illuminated*. Boston, Houghton Mifflin, 2002.

———. "Everything is Interrogated." Interview by Gabe Hudson." *The Village Voice*, 22 March 2005a, www.villagevoice.com/2005/03/22/everything-is-interrogated/. Accessed 9 June 2020.

———. *Extremely Loud and Incredibly Close*. Boston, Houghton Mifflin, 2005b.

———. "Jonathan Safran Foer Discusses *Eating Animals*, *Everything Is Illuminated* and *Extremely Loud and Incredibly Close*." Interviewer Unnamed, *BookBrowse*, 2015, www.bookbrowse.com/author_interviews/full/index.cfm/author_number/1120/jonathan-safran-foer. Accessed 5 June 2020.

Follansbee-Quinn, Jeanne. *Literature After 9/11*. New York, Routledge, 2011.

Foucault, Michel. *Madness and Civilization: A History of Insanity in the Age of Reason*. Trans. Richard Howard. New York, Random House, 1965.

Fountain, Ben. *Billy Lynn's Long Halftime Walk*. New York, Ecco, 2012.

Franklin, Marcus. "Remains from WTC Site Found in Manhole." *Channel 13 KVAL News*, 19 October 2006, kval.com/news/nation-world/human-remains-found-at-world-trade-center-site. Accessed 13 June 2020.

Franklin, Ruth. "The Stubborn, Inward Gaze of the Post-9/11 Novel." *The New Republic*, 23 August 2011, newrepublic.com/article/94180/september-11-the-novel-turns-inward. Accessed 14 February 2020.

Frascina Francis A. "Advertisements for Itself: *The New York Times*, Norman Rockwell, and the New Patriotism." *The Selling of 9/11: How a National Tragedy Became a Commodity*, Ed. Heller Dana, New York, Palgrave Macmillan, 2005, pp. 75–96.

Freud, Sigmund. *Beyond the Pleasure Principle*. 1919a. The Standard Edition of the Complete Psychological Works of Sigmund Freud. Vol. VIII. Trans. James Strachey in collaboration with Anna Freud. London, Hogarth Press, 1962.

———. *The Ego and the Id*. 1923. Ed. J. Strachey, Trans. J. Rivière. New York, Norton, 1989.

———. *The Uncanny*. 1919. Trans. David McLintock. London, Penguin, 2003.

———. "Analysis of a Phobia in a Five-Year-Old Boy." *The Standard Edition of the Complete Psychological Works of Sigmund Freud, Volume X (1909): Two Case Histories ('Little Hans' and the 'Rat Man')*. Psychoanalytic Electronic Publishing, 2010, pp. 1–150, library.princeton.edu/resource/4038. Accessed 1 May 2020.

———. "Memorandum on the Electrical Treatment of War Neurotics." 23 February 1920. *Freud Museum London, The Freud Museum*, 2014, www.freud.org.uk. Accessed 11 June 2020.

Frost, Laura. "*Falling Man*'s Precarious Balance." *American Prospect*, 11 May 2007, www.prospect.org/cs/articles?article=falling_mans_precarious_balance. Accessed 18 June 2020.

———. "Still Life: 9/11's Falling Bodies." *Literature after 9/11*. Eds. Ann Keniston and Jeanne Quinn Follansbee, Abingdon, Oxon, Routledge, 2008, pp. 180–206.

Garner, Dwight. "The Ashes." *The New York Times*, 18 May 2008, https://www.nytimes.com/2008/05/18/books/review/Garner-t.html. Accessed 1 June 2020.
*Ghost Dance.* Dir. Kenneth McMullen. Perfs. Pascale Ogier, Leonie Mellinger, Robbie Coltrane, and Jacques Derrida, Channel Four, 1983, Film.
Gordon, Avery F. *Ghostly Matters: Haunting and the Sociological Imagination*. Minneapolis, MN, University of Minnesota Press, 1997, Kindle.
*Gore Vidal: The United States of Amnesia*. Directed by Ian Honeyman, performances by Gore Vidal, Burr Steers, and Christopher Hitchens, IFC Films, 2013.
Gray, Geoffrey. "Gold: Recovery of the Towers' Buried Treasure." *The Encyclopedia of 9/11*. New York Magazine, New York Media, 27 August 2011, www.nymag.com/news/articles/wtc/. Accessed 1 June 2020.
Gray, Richard. "Open Doors, Closed Minds: American Prose Writing at a Time of Crisis." *American Literary History*, vol. 21, no. 1, 2009, pp. 128–151.
———. "'Passion on All Sides': Lessons for Planning the National September 11 Memorial Museum." *Curator: The Museum Journal*, vol. 53, no. 1, January 2010, pp. 117–125.
———. *After the Fall: American Literature Since 9/11*. Hoboken, Wiley-Blackwell, 2011.
Hagedorn Jessica. "Notes from a New York Diary." *110 Stories: New York Writes After September 11*, Ed. Baer Ulrich. New York, New York University Press, 2002, pp. 134–137.
Haggerty, George. *Queer Gothic*. Urbana, IL, University of Illinois Press, 2006.
Halberstam, Judith. *Skin Shows: Gothic Horror and the Technology of Monsters*. Durham, NC, Duke University Press, 1995.
Hamid, Mohsin. *The Reluctant Fundamentalist*. New York, Houghton, 2007.
———. "Writing *The Reluctant Fundamentalist*." *The Guardian*, 13 May 2011, https://www.theguardian.com/books/2011/may/14/mohsin-hamid-reluctant-fundamentalist-bookclub.
Hansbury, Griffin. *The Nostalgist*. Petaluma, CA, MP Publishing, 2012, Kindle.
———. Interview with Matthew Tanner. *Fiction Advocate*, 20 March 2013, fictionadvocate.com/2013/03/19/interview-griffin-hansbury/. Accessed 17 May 2020.
———. "About Me & My Practice." 2020, www.griffinhansbury.com/bio/. Accessed 20 June 2020.
Hartman, Geoffrey H. *Saving the Text: Literature/Derrida/Philosophy*. 1981. Baltimore, John Hopkins University Press, 1982.
———. "*Shoah* and Intellectual Witness." *Partisan Review*, Winter 1998, pp. 37–48.
Hawking, Stephen, and L. Mlodinow. *The Grand Design*. New York, Bantam, 2010.
Hegel, Georg Wilhelm Friedrich. "Zeitgeist." *The Hegel Dictionary*, Ed. George Alexander Magee. New York, Continuum, 2011.
Hemmings, Jo. Interviewer unnamed. *Amy Winehouse: The Untold Story*. Channel 5 Documentary, 2011.
Henry, Vincent E. "The Police, the World Trade Center Attacks, and the Psychology of Survival: Implications for Clinical Practice." *Psychoanalysis and Psychotherapy: The Journal of the Postgraduate Center for Mental Health*, vol. 21, no. 1, 2004, pp. 7–62.

herman, Judith. *Trauma and Recovery.* 1992. New York, Perseus Books, 1997.
Hill, Joe. "Thumbprint." *Postscripts 10*, Ed. Peter Crowther. Hornsea, UK, PS Publishing, 2007, pp. 225–245.
Högland, Johan. *The American Imperial Gothic: Popular Culture, Empire, Violence.* Abingdon, UK, Ashgate/Taylor & Francis, 2014.
Hogle, Jerrold E. "History, Trauma and the Gothic in Contemporary Western Fictions." *The Gothic World*, Eds. Glennis Byron and Dale Townshend. New York, Routledge, 2014, pp. 72–82.
Hopson, Jacqueline. "The Demonisation of Psychiatrists in Fiction (and Why Real Psychiatrists Might Want to Do Something About It)." *The Psychiatric Bulletin*, August 2014.
Horner, Avril. "Heroine." *Handbook of the Gothic*, Ed. Marie Mulvey-Roberts, 2nd ed. New York, New York University Press, 2009a, pp. 180–184.
———. "Unheimlich (The Uncanny)." *The Handbook of the Gothic*, Ed. Marie Mulvey-Roberts, 2nd ed. New York, New York University Press, 2009b, pp. 250–251.
Horner, Avril, and Sue Zlosnik. *Gothic and the Comic Turn.* New York, Palgrave, 2005.
*Inside 9/11: Zero Hour*, Supervising Producer Nicole Rittenmeyer, National Geographic, 2011. Film.
Interlandi, Naaneen. "How Do You Heal a Traumatized Mind?" *The New York Times Magazine*, 25 May 2014, pp. 42–58.
Irom, Bimbisar. "Alterities in a Time of Terror: Notes on the Subgenre of the American 9/11 Novel." *Contemporary Literature*, vol. 53, no. 3, Fall 2012, pp. 517–547.
Jacoby, Mary. "Qatar Contract Offers Glimpse into Giuliani Firm Dealings Have Potential for Trouble if Ex-Mayor Receives Nomination." *The Wall Street Journal*, 7 November 2007, https://www.wsj.com/articles/SB119440640166884884. Accessed 1 June 2020.
Johnson, Chalmers. "Blowback: US Actions Abroad Have Repeatedly Led to Unintended, Indefensible Consequences." *The Nation*, 27 September 2001, https://www.thenation.com/article/archive/blowback/. Accessed 10 June 2020.
Johnson, Samuel. *The History of Rasselas, Prince of Abissinia.* 1759. Oxford, Oxford University Press, 1999.
*Joker.* Directed by Todd Phillips, performances by Joaquin Phoenix, Robert De Niro, Zazie Beetz, Warner Brothers, 2019.
Jones, David. "Why The Hell Should I Feel Sorry, Says Girl Soldier Who Abused Iraqi Prisoners at Abu Ghraib Prison." *Daily Mail*, 13 June 2009, https://www.dailymail.co.uk/news/article-1192701/Why-hell-I-feel-sorry-says-girl- soldier-abused-Iraqi-prisoners-Abu-Ghraib-prison.html. Accessed 11 January 2020.
Jones, Kevin T., Kenneth S. Zagacki, and Todd V. Lewis. "Communication, Liminality, and Hope: The September 11th Missing Person Posters." *Communication Studies*, vol. 58, no. 1, 2007, pp. 105–121.
Kacandes, I. "The Changed Posttraumatic Self." *Trauma at Home: After 9/11*, Ed. Judith Greenberg, Lincoln, University of Nebraska Press, 2003, pp. 1168–1183.

Kahane, Claire. "Uncanny Sights: The Anticipation of the Abomination." *Trauma at Home: After 9/11*, Ed. Judith Greenberg, Lincoln, University of Nebraska Press, 2003, pp. 107–116.

Kakutani, Michiko. "A Boy's Epic Quest, Borough by Borough (Rev. of *Extremely Loud and Incredibly Close* by Jonathan Safran Foer)." *The New York Times*, 22 March 2005, https://www.nytimes.com/2005/03/22/books/a-boys-epic-quest-borough-by-borough.html. Accessed 5 June 2020.

———. "A Man, a Woman, and a Day of Terror (Rev. of *Falling Man* by Don DeLillo)." *The New York Times*, 9 May 2007, https://www.nytimes.com/2007/05/09/books/09kaku.html. Accessed 15 June 2020.

———. "Outdone by Reality. The 9/11 Decade: Artists Respond to Sept. 11." *The New York Times*, 1 September 2011, https://www.nytimes.com/2011/09/01/us/sept-11-reckoning/culture.html. Accessed 11 June 2020.

Kalfus, Ken. *A Disorder Peculiar to the Country*. New York, Ecco, 2006.

Kastenbaum, Robert J. *Macmillan Encyclopedia of Death and Dying, Vol II: L-Z*. New York, Macmillan Reference, 2003.

———. "9/11/01 and Its Consequences." *Death, Society, and Human Experience*, 10th ed. San Francisco, Pearson, 2008.

———. "Violent Death: Murder, Terrorism, Genocide, Disaster, and Accident." *Death, Society, and Human Experience*, 11th ed. San Francisco, Pearson, 2011.

Kauffman, Linda S. "The Wake of Terror: Don Delillo's 'In the Ruins of the Future,' 'Baader-Meinhof,' and *Falling Man*." *MFS: Modern Fiction Studies*, vol. 54, no. 2, Summer 2008, pp. 353–377.

———. "World Trauma Center." *American Literary History*, vol. 21, no. 3, 2009, pp. 647–659.

Kazdin, Cole. "Remember 'Terror Sex'? What Happened to the Relationships Kindled or Rekindled in the Aftermath of Sept. 11?" *Salon*, 11 September 2002, https://www.salon.com/2002/09/11/terror_2_2/. Accessed 11 June 2020.

Kelleher, Kathleen. "Perhaps the Most Primal Post-Disaster Reaction: Sex." *The Los Angeles Times*, 1 October 2001, https://www.latimes.com/archives/la-xpm-2001-oct-01-cl-51893-story.html. Accessed 12 June 2020.

Keniston, Ann, and Jeanne Follansbee Quinn. "Introduction: Representing 9/11: Literature and Resistance." *Literature After 9/11*. New York, Routledge, 2008, pp. 1–15.

Khakpour, Porochista. "The Top Ten Novels About 9/11." *The Guardian*, 17 December 2014, https://www.theguardian.com/books/2014/dec/17/top-10-9-11-novels-porochista-khakpour. Accessed 1 June 2020.

Kiely, Eugene. "Trump, Carson on 9/11 'Celebrations.'" *FactChecker.org*, 25 November 2015, https://www.factcheck.org/2015/11/trump-carson-on-911-celebrations/. Accessed 19 January 2020.

King, Stephen. *Danse Macabre*. 1981. New York, Simon & Schuster, 2010.

———. "The Things They Left Behind." *Transgressions: Ten Brand-New Novellas*. Ed. McBain. New York, Forge, 2005, Kindle.

———. "Stephen King is Sorry You Feel Like You're Stuck in a Stephen King Novel." Interview with Terry Gross, *Fresh Air*, NPR, 8 April 2020, https://www

.npr.org/2020/04/08/829298135/stephen-king-is-sorry-you-feel-like-youre-stuck-in-a-stephen-king-novel, Accessed 8 April 2020.
Klay, Phil. *Redeployment.* New York, Penguin, 2014.
Kohari, Alizeh. "Is There a Novel That Defines the 9/11 Decade?" *BBC News*, 27 August 2011, https://www.bbc.com/news/entertainment-arts-14682741. Accessed 27 May 2020.
Kostova, Elizabeth. *The Historian.* New York, Little, Brown, 2005.
Kristeva, Julia. *The Powers of Horror: An Essay in Abjection.* Trans. L. S. Rouidiez. New York, Columbia University Press, 1982.
Kunka, Andrew. "Re: Modernist Literature." Received by John Watts, 15 November 2000.
Kuo, John Sheng. "9/11 as American Gothic: Terror and Historical Darkness in Patrick McGrath's *Ghost Town.*" *Concentric: Literary and Cultural Studies*, vol. 33, no. 1, March 2007, pp. 53–73.
Lacan, Jacques. *The Four-Fundamental Concepts of Psycho-Analysis*, 1973. Trans. Joseph Sheridan. New York, Norton, 1981.
LaCapra, Dominick. *Writing History, Writing Trauma.* Baltimore, Johns Hopkins University Press, 2001.
Langmade, Lynn. "The Wilson Duplex: Corporatism and the Problem of Singleton Reading in Poe's 'William Wilson,' (or Why Can't You See Twins?)." *Poe Studies: History, Theory, Interpretation*, vol. 45, October 2015, pp. 5–39.
Lennon, J. Robert. *Castle.* St. Paul, MN, Graywolf, 2009.
Leonard, John. "Books: Best Literary Fiction." *New York Magazine*, 8 December 2005a, https://nymag.com/nymetro/arts/cultureawards/15295/index3.html. Accessed 22 June 2020.
———. "Culture Awards." *New York*, vol. 38, no. 45, December 2005b, p. 60.
Leps, Marie-Christine. "*Falling Man:* Performing Fiction." *Terrorism, Media, and the Ethics of Fiction: Transatlantic Perspectives on Don DeLillo*, Eds. Peter Schneck and Philipp Schweighauser, New York, Continuum, 2010, pp. 184–203.
Lewis, Matthew G. *The Monk*, 1796. Introduction by Patrick McGrath, Illustrations by David Ho. Lakewood, CO, Centipede Press, 2013.
Leys, Ruth. *Trauma: A Genealogy.* Chicago, University of Chicago Press, 2000.
———. *From Guilt to Shame: Auschwitz and After.* Princeton, NJ, Princeton University Press, 2009.
Library of Congress. "Life-Report Board." *Library of Congress*, 11 September 2001, /www.loc.gov/item/lcwaN0019810/. Accessed 11 May 2020.
Liénard-Yeterian, Marie, and Agnieszka Soltysik Monnet. "The Gothic in an Age of Terror(ism)." *Gothic Studies*, vol. 17, no. 2, November 2015, pp. 1–11.
Lifton, Robert Jay. "Tugging Meaning Out of Trauma (an Aftermath Conference Panel with Harvard Pres. Drew Gilpin Faust, Robert Jay Lifton, and Jacki Lyden)." *Neiman Foundation for Journalism at Harvard*, The President and Fellows of Harvard College, Winter 2009, https://nieman.harvard.edu/articles/tugging-meaning-out-of-trauma/. Accessed 11 June 2020.

Limbaugh, Rush. "The Rush Limbaugh Show." *Premiere Radio Networks*, 3 May 2004, www.premierenetworks.com/Pages/The-Rush-Limbaugh-Show.aspx. Accessed 29 May 2020.

Lindemann, Erich "Symptomatology and Management of Acute Grief." *American Journal of Psychiatry*, vol. 101, 1944, pp. 141–148.

Lowenstein, Adam. *Shocking Representation: Historical Trauma, National Cinema, and the Modern Horror Film*. New York, Columbia University Press, 2005.

Luckhurst, Roger. *The Trauma Question*. London, Routledge, 2008.

———. "Beyond Trauma: Tortuous Times." *European Journal of English Studies*, vol. 14, no. 1, 2010, pp. 11–21.

———. "Psychoanalysis." *The Encyclopedia of the Gothic*. 2013. Eds. William Hughes, William, David Punter, and Andrew Smith. Oxford, Wiley Blackwell, 2016, pp. 526–531.

Lukacher, Ned. *Primal Scenes: Literature, Philosophy, Psychoanalysis*. Ithaca, NY, Cornell University Press, 1988.

Manning, Doug. *Don't Take My Grief Away*, 3rd ed. Oklahoma City, OK, In-Sight Books, 2011.

Mantel, Hilary. "Ghost Writing." *The Guardian*, 28 July 2007, https://www.theguardian.com/books/2007/jul/28/edinburghfestival2007.poetry. Accessed 11 May 2020.

Marra, Lt. Frank, with Maria Bellia Abbate. *From Landfill to Hallowed Grounds: The Largest Crime Scene in America*. Dallas, Brown Books, 2015.

McCarthy, Rory. "They Abused Me and Stole My Dignity." *The Guardian*, 12 May 2004, https://www.theguardian.com/world/2004/may/13/iraq.rorymccarthy1. Accessed 10 January 2020.

McEwen, Todd. "The City that Ate the World (Rev. of Patrick McGrath's *Ghost Town*)." *The Guardian*, 23 September 2015, https://www.theguardian.com/books/2005/sep/24/featuresreviews.guardianreview18. Accessed 21 June 2020.

McGrath, Patrick. *Trauma*. London, Bloomsbury, 2008.

———. "Afterword." *Writing Madness*. Ed. Danel Olson, Lakewood, CO, Centipede Press, 2017a.

———. "Ground Zero." *Ghost Town: Tales of Manhattan Then and Now*, 2005, *Writing Madness*. Ed. Danel Olson. Lakewood, CO, Centipede Press, 2017b.

———. "Patrick McGrath: The Brewery Interview." Interview by Author, *Weird Fiction Review*, vol. 8, 2017c, pp. 189–214.

———. "Re: _Ground Zero." Received by author, 12 May 2020a.

———. "Re: Quick Question on _Ground Zero." Received by author, 18 June 2020b.

McInerney, Jay. "The Uses of Invention." *The Guardian*, 16 September 2005, https://www.theguardian.com/books/2005/sep/17/fiction.vsnaipaul. Accessed 19 June 2020.

———. *The Good Life*. New York, Alfred A. Knopf, 2006.

———. "The Devil Wears Nada." *The New York Times*, 22 June 2008, https://www.nytimes.com/2008/06/22/books/review/McInerney-t.html. Accessed 15 June 2020.

McNally, Richard J. *Remembering Trauma*. Cambridge, MA, Harvard University Press, 2003.

———. *What is Mental Illness?* Cambridge, MA, Harvard University Press, 2011.
McPherson, James M. *Crossroads of Freedom: Antietam*. New York, Oxford University Press, 2002.
McWilliams, Peter. *How to Survive the Loss of a Love*. Los Angeles, Prelude Press, 1993.
Merullo, Roland. *In Revere, in Those Days*. New York, Vintage, 2002.
Messud, Claire. *The Emperor's Children*. New York, Knopf, 2006.
Michael, Magali C. *Narrative Innovation in 9/11 Fiction*. Amsterdam, Brill/Rodopi, 2015.
Miles, Robert. *Gothic Writing 1750–1820: A Genealogy*. London, Routledge, 1993.
Miller, Kristine A. *Transatlantic Literature and Culture After 9/11: The Wrong Side of Paradise*. New York, Palgrave Macmillan, 2014.
Miller, Laura. "Why We Haven't Seen a Great 9/11 Novel." *Salon*, 10 September 2011, https://www.salon.com/2011/09/10/9_11_and_the_novel/. Accessed 9 June 2020.
Mishra, Pankaj. "The End of Innocence." *The Guardian*, 18 May 2007, https://www.theguardian.com/books/2007/may/19/fiction.martinamis. Accessed 31 March 2020.
Mishra, Vijay. *The Gothic Sublime*. Albany, NY, SUNY, 1994.
Moffatt, Gregory K. "Working with Sexually Abused Children." *Counseling Today*, American Counseling Association, 25 November 2013, ct.counseling.org/2013/11/working-with-sexually-abused-children/. Accessed 13 June 2020.
Morgan, Matthew J. *The Impact of 9/11 on the Media, Arts, and Entertainment: The Day that Changed Everything?* London, Palgrave, 2009.
Morley, Catherine, ed. *9/11: Topics in Contemporary North American Literature*. London, Bloomsbury, 2016.
Morrison, Toni. *Beloved*, 1987. New York, Knopf, 2006.
Mulvey-Roberts, Marie, ed. *The Handbook of Gothic*, 2nd ed. New York, New York University Press, 2009.
Munson, Sam. "In the Aftermath." *Commentary*, May 2005, p. 80.
Murray, Timothy. *Like a Film: Ideological Fantasy on Screen, Camera, and Canvas*. London, Routledge, 1993.
Myers, D. G. "Literary Commentary: Complete Annotated Guide to 9/11 Novels." *Commentary Magazine*, 24 August 2011, https://www.commentarymagazine.com/d-g-myers/911-novels/. Accessed 12 June 2020.
Napoleoni, Loretta. *10 Years That Shook the World: A Timeline of Events from 2001*. New York, Seven Stories, 2012.
Nash, Julie Blandon. "Play Therapy: Basic Concepts and Practices." *Foundations of Play Therapy*, 2nd ed., Ed. Charles E. Schaefer. London, Wiley, 2011, pp. 3–15.
National Commission on Terrorist Attacks upon the United States (Philip Zelikow, Executive Director; Bonnie D. Jenkins, Counsel; Ernest R. May, Senior Advisor). *The 9/11 Commission Report*. New York, W.W. Norton & Company, 2004.
National Institutes of Health. "Shaking Out Clues to Autoimmune Disease." *NIH*, USA Gov., 18 March 2013, https://www.nih.gov/news-events/nih-research-matters/shaking-out-clues-autoimmune-disease. Accessed 9 June 2020.

NFPA. "Key Dates in Fire History." *National Fire Protection Association*, 2020, https://www.nfpa.org/News-and-Research/Publications-and-media/Press-Room/Reporters-Guide-to-Fire-and-NFPA. Accessed 1 June 2020.

Nietzsche, Friedrich. *Untimely Meditations*, 1876. Ed. Daniel Breazeale, Trans. R. J. Hollingdale, 2nd ed. Cambridge, UK, Cambridge University Press, 1997.

Nissenson, Hugh. *Days of Awe*. Naperville, IL, Sourcebooks, 2005.

Oates, Joyce Carol. "Words Fail, Memory Blurs, Life Wins." *The New York Times*, 31 December 2001, https://www.nytimes.com/2001/12/31/opinion/words-fail-memory-blurs-life-wins.html. Accessed 14 June 2020.

———. "Strange Fruit and Weird Girls: A Conversation." Interview by Danel Olson. *Weird Tales*, vol. 7, no. 2, Spring 2014, pp. 103–109.

Obama, Pres. Barack. "A Sacred Place of Healing and of Hope." *The White House Blog*, The White House, 15 May 2014, https://obamawhitehouse.archives.gov/blog/2014/05/15/president-obama-speaks-911-museum-dedication-sacred-place-healing-and-hope. Accessed 17 May 2020.

Obholzer, Karin. "Freud the Father: Interview with Sergei Pankejeff." 1971. *The Wolf-Man Sixty Years Later: Conversations with Freud's Controversial Patient*. London, Routledge, 1982.

Office of the Armed Forces Medical Examiner. "CIA Copy of Autopsy Report: Manadel Al Jamadi, Abu Ghraib Prison, Iraq (Homicide)." *The Torture Database, ACLU*, 14 January 2014, www.thetorturedatabase.org/document/cia-copy-autopsy-report-manadel-al-jamadi-abu-ghraib-prison-iraq-homicide?search_url=search/apachesolr_search&search_args=filters=im_cck_field_doc_detainees:996%26solrsort=tds_cck_field_doc_release_date%20desc. Accessed 21 June 2020.

O'Gorman, Daniel. *Fictions of the War on Terror: Difference and the Transnational 9/11 Novel*. New York, Palgrave, 2015.

O'Hagan, Andrew. "Racing Against Reality." *The New York Review of Books*, 28 June 2007, https://www.nybooks.com/articles/2007/06/28/racing-against-reality/. Accessed 7 May 2020.

———. "Don DeLillo, *Underworld* and *Falling Man*." *The Good of the Novel*, Eds. Liam McIlvanney and Ray Ryan, London, Continuum, 2011, pp. 21–41.

Olbermann, Keith. "Memories of 9/11" *JWR. The Jewish World Review*, 11 September 2003, www.jewishworldreview.com/0903/olbermann091103.asp. Accessed 4 May 2020.

Oldfield, Molly. *The Secret Museum*. New York, Collins, 2013.

Olson, Danel. "Introduction." *21st Century Gothic: Great Gothic Novels Since 2000*. Ed. Danel Olson, Lanham, MD, Scarecrow Press, 2011a, pp. xxi–xxxiii.

———. "In Praise of She Wolves: The Native American Eco-Gothic of Louise Erdrich's *Four Souls*." *21st Century Gothic: Great Gothic Novels Since 2000*. Ed. Danel Olson. Lanham, MD: Scarecrow Press, 2011b, pp. 226–241.

———. "9/11 Ghosts." *Ghosts in Popular Culture and Legend*. Santa Barbara, Greenwood/ABC-CLIO, 2016a.

———. *Guillermo del Toro's 'The Devil's Backbone' and 'Pan's Labyrinth': Studies in the Horror Film*. Lakewood, CO, Centipede Press, 2016b.

Orwell, George. "Revenge is Sour." 1945. *In Front of Your Nose, 1946–1950*. Ed. Sonia Orwell. Boston, Nonpareil Books, 2000.

Padilla, Mariel. "CDC Warns of 'Aggressive' Rats Searching for Food During Shutdowns." *Boston Globe*, 25 May 2020, https://www.boston.com/news/animals/2020/05/25/cdc-warns-of-aggressive-rats-searching-for-food-during-shutdowns. Accessed 9 June 2020.

Panetta, Leon. "Message from the Director of the CIA: Justice Done." *CIA.gov*, 2 May 2011, https://www.cia.gov/news-information/press-releases-statements/press-release-2011/justice-done.html. Accessed 4 January 2020.

Parry, Richard Lloyd. "Ghosts of the Tsunami." *London Review of Books*, vol. 36, no. 3, 6 February 2014, pp. 13–17.

Pederson, Joshua. "Speak, Trauma: Toward a Revised Understanding of Literary Trauma Theory." *Narrative*, vol. 22, no. 3, October 2014, pp. 333–353.

Peeren, Esther, and Maria del Pilar Blanco. *Popular Ghosts: Haunted Spaces of Everyday Culture*. New York, Continuum, 2010.

Perrault, Charles. "The Blue-Beard." 1697. *The Classic Fairy Tales*, Eds. Iona Opie and Peter Opie. New York, Oxford University Press, 1980, pp. 133–141.

Phelps, Jordyn. "Donald Trump Again Says He Saw Cheering in New Jersey on 9/11." *ABC News*, 22 November 2015, https://abcnews.go.com/Politics/donald-trump-cheering-jersey-911/story?id=35355447. Accessed 10 January 2020.

Poe, Edgar Allan. "Annabel Lee." 1849. *Edgar Allan Poe: The Centipede Press Library of Weird Fiction*, Ed. S. T. Joshi, Lakewood, CO, Centipede Press, 2014a, pp. 766–768.

———. "The Fall of the House of Usher." 1839. *Edgar Allan Poe: The Centipede Press Library of Weird Fiction*, Ed. S. T. Joshi, Lakewood, CO, Centipede Press, 2014b, pp. 385–406.

Pogrebin, Robin. "Alice Greenwald, 9/11 Museum Director, Girds for Challenge." *The New York Times*, 22 April 2006, www.nytimes.com/2006/04/22/arts/design/alice-greenwald-911-museum-director-girds-for-challenge.html. Accessed 20 June 2020.

Powers, Kevin. *The Yellow Birds*. New York, Little, Brown, 2012.

Pozorski, Aimee L. "Trauma's Time (including Interview with Cathy Caruth)." *Connecticut Review*, vol. 28, no. 1, 2006, pp. 71–84.

Préher, Gérald. "Journeys to Selfhood in Post 9/11 New York: Reynolds Price, Patrick McGrath, and Jay McInerney." *Patrick McGrath: Directions and Transgressions*. Ed. Jocelyn Dupont, Newcastle Upon Tyne, Cambridge Scholars Publishing, 2012, pp. 115–126.

Punter, David. *Gothic Pathologies: The Text, the Body and the Law*. Bassingstoke, UK, Macmillan, 1998.

———. "Terrorism and the Uncanny; or, The Caves of Tora-Bora." *Uncanny Modernity: Cultural Theories, Modern Anxieties*, Eds. Jo Collins and John Jervis, London, Palgrave Macmillan, 2008, pp. 201–216.

———. "Terror." *The Handbook of the Gothic*. Ed. Marie Mulvey-Roberts, 2nd ed., New York, New York University Press, 2009, pp. 243–249.

———. "Trauma, Gothic, Revolution." *The Gothic and the Everyday: Living Gothic*, Eds. L. Piatti-Farnell and Maria Beville, London, Palgrave, 2014, pp. 15–32.

Punter, David, and Elisabeth Bronfen. "Gothic: Violence, Trauma, and the Ethical." *Essays and Studies 2001: The Gothic (Volume 54)*, Ed. Fred Botting, Suffolk, The English Association/D.S. Brewer, Ltd., 2001, pp. 7–21.

Radcliffe, Ann. *The Mysteries of Udolpho*. 1794. Ed. Bonamy Dobrée, Oxford, Oxford University Press, 2008.

Radcliffe, Mary Ann. *The Female Advocate; or, An Attempt to Recover the Rights of Women from Male Usurpation*. 1799. New York, Gale ECCO, 2010.

Radstone, Susannah, Janet Walker, and Noah Shenker. "Trauma Theory: Contexts, Politics, Ethics." *Paragraph*, vol. 30, no. 1, 2007, pp. 9–29.

———. "Trauma Theory." *Oxford Bibliographies*, 2013, https://www.oxfordbibliographies.com/view/document/obo-9780199791286/obo-9780199791286-0147.xml. Accessed 12 June 2020.

Rand, Nicholas T. "Introduction: Renewals of Psychoanalysis." *The Shell and the Kernel: Renewals of Psychoanalysis: Vol. 1*, Trans. Nicolas Abraham and Maria Torok, Ed. Nicholas T. Rand. Chicago, University of Chicago Press, 1994, pp. 1–22.

Reagan, Brad. "Meet the New Supercops: Protecting America's Cities, Ports, Borders and Airports Requires New Technology and New Tactics." *Popular Mechanics*, June 2006, www.PM.com. Accessed 25 January 2019.

Reuther, Bryan. "Posttraumatic Fragility." *Encyclopedia of Trauma: An Interdisciplinary Guide*, Ed. Charles R. Figley, Los Angeles, Sage Publications, 2012, pp. 275–276.

Rodi-Risberg, Marinella. "*The Nature of Trauma in American Novels (Book Review)*." *Journal of Literature and Trauma Studies*, vol. 1, no. 2, 2012, pp. 147–152.

Rothberg, Michael. "A Failure of the Imagination: Diagnosing the Post-9/11 Novel—A Response to Richard Gray." *American Literary History*, vol. 21, no. 1, 2009, pp. 152–158.

Royle, Nicholas. *Mother*. Brighton, Myriad Editions, 2020.

Rubinstein, Dana. "De Blasio Vows for First Time to Cut Funding for the N.Y.P.D." 7 June 2020, https://www.nytimes.com/2020/06/07/nyregion/deblasio-nypd-funding.html. Accessed 21 June 2020.

Sandoval, Edgar, Dan Friedman, and Rich Schapiro. "9-11 Museum Bosses Defend Party." *New York Daily News*, 21 May 2014, https://www.nydailynews.com/new-york/9-11-museum-bosses-defend-party-article-1.1800542. Accessed 6 June 2020.

Schingler, Michelle A. "Review of *The Nostalgist*." *Foreword Reviews*, 4 September 2012, https://www.forewordreviews.com/reviews/the-nostalgist/. Accessed 19 June 2020.

Shwartz, Lynne Sharon. "Near November." *110 Stories: New York Writes after September 11*, Ed. Baer Ulrich, New York, New York University Press, 2002, pp. 260–262.

———. *The Writing on the Wall*. New York, Counterpoint, 2005.

Schwartz, Pepper. *Everything You Know About Sex Is Wrong*. New York, Putnam, 2001.

Sedgwick, Eve Kosofsky. *The Coherence of Gothic Conventions*. New York, Arno Press, 1980.

Seeley, Karen M. *Therapy After Terror: 9/11, Psychotherapists, and Mental Health*. New York, Cambridge University Press, 2008.

Seow, C. L. *Daniel*. London, Westminster John Knox Press, 2003.

Sheng, Kuo John. "9/11 as American Gothic: Terror and Historical Darkness in Patrick McGrath's *Ghost Town*." *Concentric: Literary and Cultural Studies*, vol. 33, no. 1, March 2007, pp. 53–73.

Shivani, Anis. "Announcing the Death of the Post-9/11 Novel." *HuffPost Books*, AOL, 5 April 2010, https://www.huffpost.com/entry/announcing-the-death-of-t_b_525805. Accessed 29 May 2020.

Smith, Rachel Greenwald. "Organic Shrapnel: Affect and Aesthetics in September 11 Fiction." *American Literature*, vol. 83, no. 1, March 2011, pp. 157–158.

Snodgrass, Mary Ellen. *Encyclopedia of Gothic Literature*. New York, Facts on File, 2004.

So, Jimmy. "Reading the Best 9/11 Novels." *The Daily Beast*, 24 May 2011, https://www.thedailybeast.com/reading-the-best-911-novels. Accessed 9 June 2020.

Solomon, Jane, and Mosk, Matthew. "In Private Sector, Giuliani Parlayed Fame into Wealth: Candidate's Firm Has Taken on Controversial Executives, Clients." *The Washington Post*, 13 May 2007, https://www.washingtonpost.com/wp-dyn/content/article/2007/05/12/AR2007051201270.html. Accessed 9 June 2020.

Staff at *Kirkus Reviews*. "Review of Patrick McGrath's *Ghost Town*." *Kirkus Reviews*, 15 June 2005, https://www.kirkusreviews.com/book-reviews/patrick-mcgrath/ghost-town-3/. Accessed 21 June 2020.

Staff at *Publishers Weekly*. "Review of Patrick McGrath's *Ghost Town*." *Publishers Weekly*, 2015, https://www.publishersweekly.com/978-1-58234-312-9. Accessed 21 June 2020.

Staff of *The Encyclopedia of 9/11*. "9/11 by the Numbers." *The Encyclopedia of 9/11*, *New York Magazine*, New York Media, September 2012, www.nymag.com/news/articles/wtc/. Accessed 1 May 2020.

Staff of *The Garfield Book Review*. "Review of *Falling Man*." *The Garfield Book Review*, 30 April 2011, https://mybreadandjam.wordpress.com/2011/04/30/review-falling-man-by-don-delillo/. Accessed 29 May 2020.

Staff of *The New York Times*." *Extremely Loud and Incredibly Close*: Combined Print & E- Book Fiction." *New York Times Bestseller List*, 2005, https://www.nytimes.com/books/best-sellers/combined-print-and-e-book-fiction/. Accessed 19 May 2020.

———. "Nearly 1 in 4 New Yorkers Needs Food as Pandemic Persists." *The New York Times*, 21 May 2020, https://www.nytimes.com/2020/05/21/nyregion/coronavirus-ny-update.html#link-9a8c1d7. Accessed 20 June 2020.

Staff of *The Scotsman*. "FBI Shielded Me from Al-Qaeda Kidnap Plot, Says Crowe." *The Scotsman*, Johnston Publishing, 9 March 2005, www.thescotsman.scotsman.com/international.cfm?id=257242005. Accessed 4 April 2020.

*Standard Operating Procedure*. Dir. Errol Morris, Perf. Janis Karpinksi, Sabrina Harman, Lynndie England, et al. Sony, 2008. DVD.

Stewart, Garrett. "Digital Fatigue: Imaging War in Recent American Film." *Film Quarterly*, vol. 62, no. 4, Summer 2009, pp. 45–55.

Stock, A., and C. Stott. "Introduction: Narratives of Disaster." *Representing the Unimaginable: Narratives of Disaster*. Frankfurt, Peter Langer, 2007, p. 10.

Stoller, R. J. *Observing the Erotic Imagination*. New Haven, Yale University Press, 1985.

Taylor, Frederick. *Dresden: Tuesday, February 13, 1945*. New York, Harper Perennial, 2005.

Taylor, Graeme J. "Varieties of Castration Experience: Relevance to Contemporary Psychoanalysis and Psychodynamic Psychotherapy." *Psychodynamic Psychiatry*, vol. 44, no. 1, 2016, pp. 39–68.

The Bureau of Investigative Journalism. "Get the Data: Drone Wars Archive." *The Bureau Investigates*. London, City University, 2016, www.thebureauinvestigates.com/category/projects/drones/drones-graphs/. Accessed 11 June 2020.

*The Falling Man: The Story Behind the Richard Drew's Photograph*, Executive Producers Kira Pollack and Ian Orefice, TIME/Red Border Films, 2006. Film.

Thiemann, Anna. *Rewriting the American Soul: Trauma, Neuroscience and the Contemporary Literary Imagination*. New York, Routledge Interdisciplinary Perspectives on Literature, 2018.

Thomson, Douglass. "A Glossary of Literary Gothic Terms." *Saylor*, n.d., https://resources.saylor.org/wwwresources/archived/site/wp-content/uploads/2012/05/engl403-1.3.1-A-Glossary-of-Literary-Gothic-Terms.pdf. Accessed 2 June 2020.

Tolan, Fiona. "Editor's Note." *"Literature, Migration and the "War on Terror."* Eds. Fiona Tolan, Stephen Morton, Anastasia Valassopoulos, and Robert Spencer, London, Routledge, 2012, pp. x–xii.

Tóth, Réka. "The Plight of the Gothic Heroine: Female Development and Relationships in Eighteenth Century Female Gothic Fiction." *Eger Journal of English Studies*, vol. X, 2010, pp. 21–37.

Townshend, Dale. "Gothic and the Ghost of *Hamlet*." *Gothic Shakespeares (Accents on Shakespeare)*, Eds. John Drakakis and Dale Townshend, New York, Routledge, 2008, pp. 60–97.

Tracy, Ann B. *The Gothic Novel 1790–1830*. Lexington, KY, The University Press of Kentucky, 1981.

Trigg, Dylan. *The Memory of Place: A Phenomenology of the Uncanny*. Athens, OH, Ohio University Press, 2012.

Trump, Donald J. "Trump and Cruz Say They Would Bring Back Waterboarding—Video." *The Guardian*, 6 February 2016, https://www.theguardian.com/us-news/video/2016/feb/06/donald-trump-ted-cruz-waterboarding-torture-republican-debate-video. Accessed 10 June 2020.

Twain, Mark. *The Innocents Abroad*. Oxford, Oxford University Press, 1996.

Updike, John. "Mixed Messages: *Extremely Loud and Incredibly Close*." *The New Yorker*, 14 March 2005, https://www.newyorker.com/magazine/2005/03/14/mixed-messages. Accessed 12 May 2020.

———. *Terrorist*. New York, Knopf, 2006.

Versluys, Kristiaan. *Out of the Blue: September 11 and the Novel*. New York, Columbia University Press, 2009.
Voytilla, Stuart. *Myth and the Movies: Discovering the Mythic Structure of 50 Unforgettable Films*. Studio City, CA, Michael Wiese Productions, 1999.
Wakefield, Jerome C. "Max Graf's 'Reminiscences of Professor Sigmund Freud' Revisited: New Evidence from the Freud Archives." *The Psychoanalytic Quarterly*, vol. LXXVI, no. 1, January 2007, pp. 149–192.
Waldman, Amy. *The Submission*. New York, Farrar, Straus and Giroux, 2011.
Walpole, Horace. *The Castle of Otranto*. 1764, Ed. W. S. Lewis, Oxford, Oxford University Press, 2008.
Walter, Jess. *The Zero*. New York, Regan, 2006.
———. "About the Book: *The Zero* Journals." *The Jess Walter Homepage*, 1 August 2007a, www.jesswalter.com/. Accessed 1 April 2020.
———. "An Interview with Jess Walter." By Alice Grace Lloyd, *Playboy*, January 2007b.
———. "An Interview with Jess Walter." By Greg Olear, *Nervous Breakdown*, http://thenervousbreakdown.com/golear/2010/11/an-interview-with-jess-walter/. Accessed 10 November 2010.
Weber, Cynthia. *Imagining America at War: Morality, Politics and Film*. New York, Routledge, 2005.
Wellington, David. "Twilight in the Green Zone." *Exotic Gothic*, Ed. Danel Olson. Ashcroft, BC, Ash-Tree Press, 2007, pp. 46–60.
Whitehead, Anne. *Trauma Fiction*. Edinburgh, Edinburgh University Press, 2004.
———. *Memory*. New York, Routledge, 2009.
Williams, Anne. *Art of Darkness: A Poetics of Gothic*. Chicago, University of Chicago Press, 1995.
Willis, Deborah. "'The Gnawing Vulture': Revenge, Trauma Theory, and *Titus Andronicus*." *Shakespeare Quarterly*, vol. 52, no. 1, Spring 2002, pp. 21–52.
Wilson, Edmund. "A Treatise on Tales of Horror." *The New Yorker*, 27 May 1944, p. 72.
*Wish I Was Here*. Dir. Zach Braff, Perf. Zach Braff, Joey King, Pierce Gagnon, and Kate Hudson, Worldview Entertainment, 2014. Film.
Wood, James. "James Wood's Lighter Side . . ." Interview by Sarah Sweeney, *The Harvard Gazette*, 15 January 2013, https://news.harvard.edu/gazette/story/2013/02/james-woods-lighter-side/. Accessed 19 May 2020.
Woolf, Virginia. "Two Antiquaries: Walpole and Cole." *The Death of the Moth*, London, Hogarth Press, 1945, p. 51.
*World Trade Center*, Dir. Oliver Stone, Perf. Nicolas Cage, Michael Peña, Maria Bello, Michael Peña, Maggie Gyllenhaal, Stephen Dorff, Michael Shannon, Paramount, 2006. Film.
Wyatt, Edward. "Literary Novelists Address 9/11, Finally." *The New York Times*, 7 March 2005, https://www.nytimes.com/2005/03/07/books/literary-novelists-address-911-finally.html. Accessed 13 December 2013.
Yuan, Jada. "Ground Zero." *The Encyclopedia of 9/11*, *New York Magazine*, New York Media, September 2012, www.nymag.com/news/articles/wtc/. Accessed 7 June 2020.

Zaczek, Iain. "Keith." *The Book of Scottish Names*. London, CICO Books, 2007.
Zipp, Yvonne. "Still No Great 9/11 Novel?" *The Christian Science Monitor*, 8 September 2011, https://www.csmonitor.com/Books/chapter-and-verse/2011/0908/Still-no-great-9-11-novel. Accessed 15 May 2020.
Žižek, Slavoj. *Mapping Ideology*. New York, Verso, 1994.
———. "Between Two Deaths." *London Review of Books*, vol. 26, no. 11, 3 June 2004, p. 19.
———. *Welcome to the Desert of the Real: Five Essays on September 11 and Related Dates (Radical Thinkers Series)*. Brooklyn, Verso, 2013a, Kindle.
———. "*Zero Dark Thirty*: Hollywood's Gift to American Power." *The Guardian*, 25 January 2013b, www.theguardian.com/commentisfree/2013/jan/25/zero-dark-thirty-normalises-torture-unjustifiable. Accessed 1 June 2020.

# Index

Page numbers for figures are italicized.

9/11 Commission, 9
*The 9/11 Commission Report*, 20, 49n3

abduction, 92–93
abjection, 103, 129, 136, 138–39
abreaction, 101
Adler, Alexandra, 44, *46*, 91, 168
Adler, Alfred, 31, 44
Afghanistan, 11, 29, 170
airplanes, *2*, 17, 25, 32, 48, 60–61, 64, 74, 76n2, 83, 117, 121n10, 144, 147, 155, 157
alcohol, 40, 90, 118, 132, 147
*The Algerines, or, The Twins of Naples* (by William Child Green), 98
Al Qaeda and Jihadis, 1, 13, 20, 28, 32, 47, 59, 110, 150, 157, 184
Alfred P. Murrah Federal Building, 184
American diversity, 28
*American Pastoral* (by Philip Roth), 17
Amis, Martin, 22, 24n3, 27
amnesia, 67, 71, 73
anger, 66, 67, 95, 107, 115, 134, 156, 158
"Annabel Lee," 60, 62, 76n1
anthrax threat, 40, 107, 145
anti-Arab violence in America, 30–31

antiheros, 125–26, 132
*Apocalypse Now* (dir. Francis Ford Coppola), 167
architecture, 12, 123, 126, 150
archives and "archivization", 39, 107, 120n8, 121n8
*The Armies of the Night* (by Norman Mailer), 24n3
art forbidden, 103–5
artists, 16, 41, 103–5, 148, 150, 156
assassinations: JFK, 184; MLK, Jr., 184
ash and soot from the burned WTC, 33, 43, 83, 88, 106, 140–41, 146
Ashcroft, John, 147
Asian-Americans, 147, 149
Asperger's syndrome, 54
Atta, Mohamed, 25–26; and American University in Cairo, 49n3; and Kafr el-Sheikh, Egypt, 49n3

babies, 54, 74, 94, 98, 114, 118, 119, 126, 139; and babysitters, 101; death of, 108
Banita, Georgiana, 9, 11–12, 146
Barthes, Roland, 143
Basho, 50n5
Baudrillard, Jean, 170

*Between Two Rivers* (by Nicholas Rinaldi), 17
*Billy Lynn's Long Halftime Walk* (by Ben Fountain), 166–67
Blake, William, 107
Bloomberg, Michael, 3
"Bodies" (by Phil Klay), 166
*The Body Artist* (by Don DeLillo), 37
bonds and community between trauma survivors, 49n4, 118, 123, 140–41, 155, 160
bones, 3–5; and skeletons, 102
the Book of Daniel, 120n5
breasts, 19, 127–28, 130, 137–39, 155
Brockway, Harry, *162*
Brown, Charles Brockden, 14
burial, 62, 69, 120n6; live, 57
Bush, George W., 2, 3, 11, 116, 170
Butler, Judith, 31, 42, 71, 170

cadavers, 94, 102, 103, 106
Campbell, Joseph, 140
carnival, 81
Caruth, Cathy, 31, 32, 36, 42, 44, 55, 65, 69–71, 80, 82, 87, 92
"The Cask of Amontillado" (by Edgar Allan Poe), 114
*Castle* (by J. Robert Lennon), 166–67
*The Castle of Otranto* (by Horace Walpole), 38, 82, 85, 89
CDC, 2
China, 2
Chomsky, Noam, 170
*Christine* (by Stephen King), 135
*Christopher Unborn* (by Carlos Fuentes), 135
Chrysler Building, 126
churches, *124*, 132
Cixous, Hélène, 33, 35, 50n8
clash of civilizations, 28–29
closure, 5, 78n3, 123, 156
coffins and caskets: without bodies, 57, 60–62, 72, 88, 110, 132; breaking into, 62, 72
*In Cold Bold* (by Truman Capote), 100

collectors, 126
comic books and graphic novels, 1, 9, 10, 12, 13, 56, 127, 177
concentration camps, 42, 57, 74, 114–15
*The Condition* (by Jennifer Haigh), 19
confession, 64, 97, 108, 112
consumption, 13, 106, 134
Coppola, Francis Ford, 53
*Cosmopolis* (by Don DeLillo), 28
counselors and counseling, 25, 101, 148, 159, 160
countertransference, 123, 148, 150
COVID-19, 1, 118, 144–45
Crane, Hart, 82
Creed, Barbara, 139
cremains, 140–41
*Crimson Peak* (dir. Guillermo del Toro), 85
Crumb, Robert, 15, 127

*Danse Macabre* (by Stephen King), 90
*Days of Awe* (by Hugh Nissenson), 164–65
*Dear John* (by Nicholas Sparks), 19
DeLillo, Don, 6, 11, 14, 17, 22, 25–49, 49n1, 50n5, 53, 89, 92, 104, 178
del Toro, Guillermo, 58, 84–87
de Man, Paul, 92–93, 108
denial, 2, 70, 111, 117, 118
Derrida, Jacques, 14, 16, 93, 94, 107, 108, 169–70; and burial, 60; and forgiveness, 117, 121n11; and ghosts, 84, 88, 92, 95, 119n2, 139, 143, 144, 148, 158, 164, 166–67; and monsters, 115; and terrorists, 58–59, 83, 107, 120n8
the Devil, 63, 150, 165
*The Devil's Backbone* (dir. Guillermo del Toro), 58, 84–87
*Diagnostic and Statistical Manual of Mental Disorders* (*DSM*), 41, 44, 68
Didion, Joan, 80
disaster-ghosts, 31, 59, 160
*A Disorder Peculiar to the Country* (by Ken Kalfus), 40, 164

dissociation, 26, 27, 31, 44, 53, 70, 71, 73
divorce, 17, 69
DNA, 3, 130
"Don't Look Now" (by Daphne du Maurier), 98
doppelgängers and doubles, 15, 35, 49, 57, 80, 88–89, 98, 103, 109, 111, 112, 163
*Dracula* (by Bram Stoker), 128
*Dr. Adder* (by K. W. Jeter), 135
"The Dreamers" (by Walt Whitman), 140
Dresden, bombing of, 55, 60, 71–72, 74, 76n1, 76–77nn4–6
Drew, Richard, *37*, 104. See also art forbidden; photographs and photography
*The Drowned and The Saved* (by Primo Levi), 73
drugs, 40, 68, 112, 118
dybbuk, 97
dystopia, 1

economy: collapse of world, 144; halting of American, 1, 5; inequality in USA, 148
Egypt, 48n3, 152
empathy, 54, 112, 117, 151
*The Emperor's Children* (by Claire Messud), 17
Empire State Building, 56, 126
England, 151
the Enlightenment, 29
entombment (mental), 108; "psychic mummification" (Derridean term), 108
Erikson, Kai, 118
eroticism of death, 39–41, 134–35, 155
*Everything Is Illuminated* (by Jonathan Safran Foer), 54
evil, 7, 29, 98, 107, 145, 150, *151*, 158
*The Exorcist* (dir. William Friedkin), 96
*Exotic Gothic* (edited by Danel Olson), 165

*Extremely Loud and Incredibly Close,* 6, 14, 18, 19, 53–78, 166, 168–69
*Extremely Loud and Incredibly Close* (dir. Stephen Daldry), *66, 75*

*Falling Man* (novel), 25–52, 166, 168–70, 178
Falling Man (photograph), 104
"The Fall of the House of Usher" (by Edgar Allan Poe), 23, 98, 120n7; Madeline and Roderick Usher in, 23, 120n7
Faludi, Susan, 170
fantasy, 20, 66, 81, 90, 100, 114, 123, 128, 130. See also phantasy
father (threatening), 136–37
FBI, 2
fear, 3, 7, 9, 13, 36, 44, 47, 49, 53, 54, 56, 63, 65, 69, 70, 86, 102; of castration, 129, 135–37; and Derrida, 158; of falling, 49n1; and Freud, 99; and genocide, 42; of leaving indoors, 128; of Other, 4, 14; of prostitutes, 147, 148, 160; of romantic involvement, 107, 132; and sex, 38, 39, 41, 126, 159; of therapy, 128; and the unrepresentable, 96; and uncanny, 34
Felman, Shoshan, 36, 44, 71, 82
fetishes: bras, 131; breasts, 130; feet, 38; gloves, 132; hairbrushes, 131; panties, 131
*The Female Advocate* (by Mary Ann Radcliffe), 112–13
fire, 3, 6, 20, *37*, 44, 46, 55, 56, 60, 71, 72, 74, 76n1, 96, 100, 115, 128; Cocoanut Grove Nightclub Fire, *45*, 91
Fire Department of New York, 2, 3, 5, 39, 42, 106, 107, 120n8; as depicted in film, *151, 156, 157*
Fischel, Erick, 104. See also art forbidden
flashbacks, 32, 44, 47, 65, 71, 92, 94
Foer, Jonathan Safran, 6, 11, 14, 18, 23n2, 53–76, 76nn2–3, 79–80, 177

forgiveness, 32, 60, 74, 114–15, 117, 121n11, 158, 178
France, 29, 121n11, 147

Gaiman, Neil, 144
games, 96, 99; poker, 26, 30, 32, 96; sexual, 96, 145, 157–59; toy therapy, 99–101
*The Garden of Last Days* (by Andre Dubus III), 19, 20, 165
Germany, 25, 30, 44, 50n6, 77n6, 85, 108, 115, 130, 167, 180
*Get Out* (dir. Jordan Peele), 144–55
Ghost Dance (dir. Ken McMullen), 143–44
ghosts, 91, 124, 133, 164; of best friends, 31; of dead dreamgirls, 16, 125–26, 131–32, 134–35, 138–40; of dead lovers, 16, 145–46, 148, 150, 156, 158–60; of dead terrorists, 15; and del Toro, 85–87; and Derrida, 84, 88, 92, 95, 119n2, 139, 143, 144, 148, 158; of family, 75, 111; and guilt, 113; and *Hamlet*, 61, 102; and haunting, 32, 58; and possession, 46–49, 61, 89, 90, 92, 95–97, 108, 113, 115, 119n3; of soldiers in War on Terror, 59
Giuliani, Rudolph, 49n2, 103, 133, 137
*Gladiator* (dir. Ridley Scott), 20
*The Good Life* (by Jay McInerney), 19, 40; author's volunteerism and field research, 24n3, 164
Gore, Al, 141
*The Graveyard Book* (by Neil Gaiman), 144
Gray, Richard, 12, 18, 87–88, 168
Greenwald, Alice M., 5, 8, 22, 23, 29, 42, 168, 175–84
*Ground Zero* (novel) 6, 143–62, 164, 168
Ground Zero (former World Trade Center North and South Towers), 3, 4, *5*, 8, 12, 24n3, 43, 56, 124, 127, 131, 132, 140, *151,* 163–66, *176*, 182, *183*; as depicted in film, *151*

hallucination, 111, 129, 136, 140, 156
Hamburg cell, 20, 25
Hansbury, Griffin, 6, 15, 123–42
Hartman, Geoffrey, 87, 97, 99
Heart of Darkness (by Joseph Conrad), 21
*Here I Am* (by Jonathan Safran Foer), 23n2
Herman, Judith, 51n12, 70–71, 88, 114
The Hero's Journey, 140
Hill, Joe, 165
Hiroshima, bombing of, 7, 55
*The History of Rasselas, Prince of Abissinia* (by Samuel Johnson), 82
Hoepker, Thomas, 104. See also art forbidden; photographs and photography
Hogle, Jerrold E., 25–26, 63, 146–47
The Hole (Ground Zero), 150, 160
Holocaust, 49, 57, 73–74, 115
"The Holy Virgin Mary" (painting by Christopher Ofili), 103–5
humor, 19, 34–35, 49n1, 67, 135
*Hyperion* (by Dan Simmons), 135

Imperialism (American), 11, 55
*Inception* (dir. Christopher Nolan), 18
incorporation (psychological), 93, 95, 108, 117
interrogation, 42, 147, 154-55, 165–67
Iraq, 11, 29, 59, 165–66, 170
irony, 35, 111, 131–32

Janet, Pierre, 71
Japan, 47–48, 121n11
jealousy, 14, 134–35, 149
*Jerusalem Liberated* (by Torquato Tasso), 69
Jesus Christ, 132
Jonah (figure from the Bible), 140
jumping to death from the WTC, 16, 41, 51n10, 106, 116, 150, 164–65; art based on, 104; nightmares of, 65;

pictures of, 58, 68, 72; simulation of, 25, 30, 41, 49nn1–2

Kakutani, Michelle, 30, 49, 54, 146, 148, 167–68
Kristeva, Julia, 103, 105

Lacan, Jacques, 116
Las Vegas, 20, 26
Laub, Dori, 36, 44, 82, 115
lawyers, 7, 14, 16, 25–26, 30, 32–33, 53, 64, 147, 148; legal battles with New York City Mayor Rudolph Giuliani, 103; U.S. Attorney General, 147
*Leaves of Grass* (by Walt Whitman), 28
*Le Feu/Under Fire* (by Henri Barbusse), 21
*The Liar of the White Worm* (dir. Ken Russell), 137
lies, 15, 83, 102, 117, 128, 131
Lifton, Robert Jay, 7, 31, 36, 44, 82
liminal states, 89
Lindemann, Eric, 44, 168
*The Little Stranger* (by Sarah Waters), 96–97
London, 71, 170
lovers, 6, 16, 30, 38, 48, 51n13, 60–62, 69, 74, 76n1, 79–81, 108, 113, 116, 123, 125, 134, 140, 145, 149–50, 160; forbidden, 158–59
Lower East Side (of Manhattan), 130, 132, 148

Madoff, Bernard L., 159
MAGA, 1
magical thinking, 43, 110, 117, 123–24, 150
Mailer, Norman, 24n3
Maisel, Todd, 105. *See also* art forbidden; photographs and photography
Man in Red Bandana (Welles Crowther), 182
*Mao II* (by Don DeLillo), 28, 30

masochism, 154–56, 159
masturbation, 101, 132, 135
May, Rollo, 141
McEwan, Ian, 11, 17, 24n3, 79
McGrath, Patrick, 6, 80, 123–24, 143–62
McNally, Richard, 73
McVeigh, Timothy, 184
memorials and memorialization, 48, 56, 81, 97, 107, 110, 116, 120n6, 131–32, 138, 140, 143, 175, 179
memory, 4, 51n12, 66, 91–92, 129, 149; debates about its nature, 70–75; and film, 84–85, 87; of fires, *45*; and language, 12, 27; loss of, 31; and nostalgia, 50n8; and revenge, 114; sexual trauma, *84*, 100, 102*;* and violence, 8, 13–15, 36, 40, 49n2, 80–81, 102, 104–5 117
missing persons, 3, 15, 16, 36, 41, 55, 58, 60, 61, 83, 90, 91, 93, 94, 109–10, 112, 117, 120n5, 121n8, 130, *131*, 152; signs or posters for, 15–16, 94–95, 109, 120n5, *131*, 132; University of California-Berkeley website for, 110; unlikely discovery of or reunions with, 110–11
*The Monk* (by Matthew G. Lewis), 89, 128
"The Monkey's Paw" (by W. W. Jacobs), 110
monsters, 4, 17, 38, 51n9, 85, 102, 114–15, 129, 135
*Mother* (by Nicholas Royle), 144
mourning, 5–7, 11, 41, 47, 60–61, 68, 71, *75*, 81, 89, 91–96, 98, 102, 104, 106–8, 113, 116–17, 119–20n3, 120n6, 121n8, 124, 126, 129, 133, 138, 159, 161; by children, 14, 15, 56, 68, 71, 75, 131; by colleagues, 26, 51n13; and Derrida, 58–60, 91, 92, 108; and Freud, 14, 116, 119n34; and ghosts, 102, 113; by lover, 126, 129, 138, 140, 159; by Maria Torok and Nicolas Abraham, 92, 95; and

melancholia, 124; by parents, 3; and Shakespeare, 62, 63, 65, 66, 102, 120n6, 121n8; by siblings, 81, 89, 91, 94, 96, 117
mullahs, 28
"The Mutants" (by Joyce Carol Oates), 24n3
*The Mysteries of Udolpho* (by Ann Radcliffe), 82

*The Names* (by Don DeLillo), 28
National Guard, 25
nationalism, 1, 10, 12
National September 11 Memorial & Museum, 3, 4, 8, 23n1, 29, 42, 168, 175–84
Naudet, Gedeon and Jules, 2, 106, *151*. See also art forbidden; photographs and photography
Nazism, 54, 74; slave-worker and concentration camps, 42, 57, 74, 114–15
necrophilia, 126, 128, 134–35
*Netherland* (by Joseph O'Neill), 17
New York Police Commissioner, 103. See also New York Police Department
New York Police Department (NYPD), 3, 39, 120n8
Nietzsche, Friedrich, 48
*Night* (by Elie Wiesel), 73
night terrors, 71
nostalgia, 30–31, 50nn4–5, 68, 90, 124, 125
*The Nostalgist*, 123–42, 155–56, 163, 168

Oates, Joyce Carol, 24n3, 53, 178
Obama, Barack, 3, 176
Oedipal attractions and relationships, 16, 128–29, 135, 150, 152, 159, 161
Ogier, Pascale, 143–44
One World Tower (Freedom Tower), 183
Oklahoma City National Memorial & Museum, 183–84
orphanages, 85–86, *87*

orphans, 85–86, *87*
Orwell, George, 114–15
the Other (term from philosopher G. W. F. Hegel), 4, 10, 14, 15, 36, 49, 59, 93, 95, 105, 108, 144, 155

Parry, Richard Lloyd, 47–48
Patriot Act, 8
pedophilia, 99, 109, 111–12
peep shows, 139
penises, 129, 135–37
Pentagon, xii, 17, 39, 180
phantasy, 116–17
photographs and photography, 56, 58, 72, 86, 104–5, 110, 120n5, 121n9, 136, *151*
"Piss Christ" (photo-art by Andre Serrano), 104
Poe, Edgar Allan, 23, 60, 62, 120n7
Poland, 180
porn, 59, 112
Pozorski, Aimee L., xi, 36
pregnancy, 57, 60, 62, 74, 76n1, 82, 94, 97–98, 101–2, 112
psychoanalysis, 12, 51nn12–13, 134, 136; and cinema, 84; and dreams, 65; failure of, 16; and Freud, 31, 35, 44, 50n6, 152–53; and post-Freudian theorists, 135, 137, 138, 141; and uncanny, 50n8
psychoanalysts, 15, 16, 170; abusive, 16, 148, 149, 153–55, 159–61; novelists who are, 129, 133
PTSD, 13, 30–31, 41, 42, 44, 48, 51n13, 68, 128, 165, 170
punishment,; by father, 135; leading to death, 114; of Memorial & Museum staff, 181–82; seeking it, 88, 113; of self, 81, 119n3; sexual, 127, 128, 135, 159
puns, 32, 56
Punter, David, 7, 36, 170

*The Queen of the Damned* (by Anne Rice), 98

queer, 51n9
quests, 14, 53, 57, 60–62, 64, 118, 135, 138, 148
*The Quiet American* (by Graham Greene), 21

*Rabbit Run* (by John Updike), 20
racial profiling, 147
racism and racial hatred, 146–47, 161
RAF, 60, 72, 76n1
rage, 49, 53, 67, 83, 99, 101, 113, 158–60, 166
Rank, Otto, 35
rape, 18, 40, 99, 112
Rat Man (client of Freud), 49
*In Revere, in Those Days* (by Roland Merullo), 17
the Real (psychoanalytic concept of infinity and the absolute from Jacques Lacan), 4, 106, 116, 146
*The Recess* (by Sophia Lee), 98
Red Brigades, 25
*Redeployment* (by Phil Klay), 166
*The Reluctant Fundamentalist* (by Mohsin Hamid), 21
remorse, 107
renunciation, 93
repetition cycles, 7, 31, 41, 43–44, 50n7, 58, 69–70, 88–89, 99, 101, 106–7, 110, 120n8, 143, 150
repression (psychological) and the repressed, 4, 14, 43–44, 51n10, 56, 61, 83, 87, 113; from previous trauma, 80, 82, 88, 99, 102; and substitution, 43–44
revenge and retribution, 14–16, 63–67, 81, 89, 100, 112–15, 166, 170; fantasies of, 81
revenge tragedies: Elizabethan and Jacobean, 112; Gothic literature, 112–15
*In Revere, in Those Days* (by Roland Merullo), 17
*Riddley Walker* (by Russell Hoban), 135
ruins, 4, 5, 43, 150

"Ruins from the Future" (by Don DeLillo), 28
Russia, 153–53

Salinger, J. D., 54
*Saturday* (by Ian McEwan), 17
Schwartz, Lynne Sharon, 6, 15, 31, 79–122
secret, 15, 26, 31, 38, 56, 68, 81, 85–88, 95, 97, 100–101, 105, 107–8, 114, 117–18, 128, 143, 159; language, 119n1; muse, 130, 138, 160
*Secret Agent* (by Joseph Conrad), 17
self-harm, 53, 68
separation: familial, 95, 108, 140; marital, 17
sex, 4, 15, 19, 22, 31–32, 81, 82, 95–97, 107, 119, 126, 129, 145, 155–56; and death, 134–35; extra-marital affairs, 32, 116; and fathers, 115, 127–29, 131, 135–38, 143, 144, 146, 150, 152–54, 156–59, 161; and Freud, 97, 129, 132; incest, 85–86, 89, 95, 98, 102, 147, 164; and mothers, 50n7, 129, 132, 139, 148; prostitution, 145, 148–50, 156; return to the womb, 50n7, 139; sexually oriented businesses, 19–20, 124, 137–40, 141n1; strippers, 19–20, 137–40; terror sex, 14, 16, 17, 19, 38–41, 145; vagina dentata, 136–40; voyeurism, 126, 127, 136
sexual abuse and violence, 31, 50n9, 75, 81, 101
sexual identity, 129, 135
*Sexual Personae* (by Camille Paglia), 129, 135, 136
*The Shadow of No Towers* (by Art Spiegelman), 56
shellshock, 3
*The Shining* (dir. Stanley Kubrick), 108, 121n9, 170
Silverstein, Larry, 4, 182
skin (human), 61, 97, 109, 113, 136
skulls, 62–65, *66*, 66–68, 80, 99

*Slade House* (by David Mitchell), 98–99
sleep and somatic distress, 45, 57, 65, 67, 76n2, 107, 113, 118; and Ann Radcliffe, 82; nightmares, 65, 132; sex, 82, 105
"The Sleepers" (by Walt Whitman), 28
social work and social workers, 81, 91, 124
"Sorry to Disturb" (by Hilary Mantel), 144
South Africa, 121n11
Spain, 86–87, 180
spirit possession, 14, 31, 37–38, 43, 44, 47, 48, 61, 70, 95, 97, 115, 119n3, 164
Starbucks and its logo's symbolism, 125, 134
Staten Island ferry, 123, 140
Statue of Liberty, 184
Stephen King, 1, 90, 95, 135, 165
"The Story of an Hour" (by Kate Chopin), 157–58
*The Submission* (by Amy Waldman), 178
subways, 6, 24n2, 37, 38, 76n2, 127, 130, 157
suicide, 15, 16, 25, 51n10, 65, 79, 90, 102, 119
*The Sunflower* (by Simon Wiesenthal), 73
surveillance (governmental), 8, 11–12, 147
survivor guilt, 57, 81, 90
symbols, 41, 63, 65, 68, 99, 101, 104, 105, 132, 137

taboos, 50n9, 81, 88–89, 94, 99, 103; of touching the dead, 40
Taliban, 29
*Taxi Driver* (dir. Martin Scorsese), 109
technology, 28–29, 51n9, 88
teenagers, 79, 80, 90, 117, 127
"The Tell-Tale Heart" (by Poe), 166
terrorism-romances (fiction), 19
*Terrorist* (by John Updike), 19–20, 165

"The Things They Left Behind" (by Stephen King), 165
*The Thirteenth Tale* (by Diane Setterfield), 98
*This Way to the Gas, Ladies and Gentlemen* (by Tadeusz Borowski), 73
"Thumbprint" (by Joe Hill), 165
Times Square, 37, 137–38, 141n1
torture, 4, 148, 165–66; and extraordinary rendition, 11, 169; and Holocaust, 42
Townshend, Dale, 67, 92, 102, 120n6
transference, 123, 150, 153–54
transgender, 124; transitioning from female to male, 124
trauma-inflicted muteness, 15, 62, 79, 89, 94
Trauma Theory, 4, 6, 8–10, 13, 14, 16, 27, 44, 72, 76n4, 99; and being overwhelmed, 5; and dissident theories, 71, 72; and memory, 70, 74; and the past, 92; and reenactment, 41, 164; and revenge, 115; and the unrepresentable, 22
triage, 110
Tribute in Light, 131, 133
Trigg, Dylan, 36, 50n7
Trump, Donald, 2
tsunami, 47–48
TV, 27, 32, 82, 105
"Twilight in the Green Zone" by David Wellington, 165
*Twilight Zone*, 33
twins, 15, 79–85, 89, 91, 94, 97–99, 101, 117; death of, 103, 108, 112–13, 120n7; mythological, 98; from *The Shining*, 121n9; twin language, 102

Ukraine, 54
the uncanny (the unheimliche), 4, 6, 14, 30–31, 33–36, 43, 48, 50n6, 50n8, 53, 63, 70, 75, 89, 98, 103, 105, 109, 111, 119n1; and Freudian return to womb or "homecoming," 139; and revenge, 113; and substitution

for lost people, 116; and unfinished mourning, 113
unconscious and subconscious, 16, 95, 132, 134, 144, 147, 158
*Underworld* (by Don DeLillo), 28, 30
Updike, John, 18–20, 54, 56, 68
Upper West Side (of Manhattan), 148
USAF, 60, 76n1
U.S. Holocaust Memorial Museum, 5, 29, 180–81, 183; and Jesaja (Shaike) Weinberg, 180

vaginas, 124, 132, 135–39
van der Kolk, Bessel, 70–71, 73, 82
*Villa Incognito* (by Tom Robbins), 19
vulvas, 104, 139

war: of 1812, 2; Afghanistan, 11, 29, 166; Iraq, 11, 29, 165–66; Spanish Civil, 85–87; on Terror, 1, 10; Vietnam, 7, 24n3, 44; World War I, 31, 50n6, 53, 65; World War II, 14, 44, 46, 126
warnings, 2, 22, 57, 64
Washington, D.C., 5, 175, 180–81
*The Way to Paradise* (by Mario Vargas Llosa), 135
Whitman, Walt, 28, 82, 140, 160
*Why Are We in Vietnam?* (by Norman Mailer), 24n3

the Wolf Man (Sergei Pankejeff), 49, 92, 152–54
Woolf, Virginia, 92
World Trade Center, 1, 3–6, 8, 15, 17–18, 24n3, 32, 39, 41–42, 44, 53, 55, 62, 64, 75, 79, 92, 98, 116, *131*, 170; and attack planes, 82–84; business, 60, 137; crossing by wire, 59; digging out human remains, 108; dust, 51n11, 138; firefighters, *151*, *157*; and gold, 87; jumpers, 25, *37*, 56, 58, 68, 72; and lovers, 150; and miraculous thinking, 110, 122, *124*; and neighbors, 118; people missing from, 94, 168; photographs of, 104–6; and ruins, 57; and secrets, 88; and Tribute in Light, 133
*The Writing on the Wall*, 79–122, 163, 166, 168–69

xenophobia, 89, 147

*The Yellow Birds* (by Kevin Powers), 166–67
*Yoju Toshi* (*Wicked City* by Yoshiaki Kawajiri), 135

Zen, 47
Žižek, Slavoj, 14, 106–7, 170

# About the Author

**Danel Olson** is a three-time Bram Stoker Award finalist and the winner of a Shirley Jackson Award and World Fantasy Awards for his work on the Gothic. He conceived and edited a six-volume print anthology series, premiering stories from established and emerging Gothicists from 2007 to 2012, *Exotic Gothic*.

His three edited collections on film include *"The Exorcist": Studies in the Horror Film*, *Stanley Kubrick's "The Shining": Studies in the Horror Film*, and *Guillermo del Toro's "The Devil's Backbone" and "Pan's Labyrinth": Studies in the Horror Film*.

Danel's edited study on novels is *21st-Century Gothic: Great Gothic Fiction Since 2000*. His most recent project is a collection of all the short fiction to date from Patrick McGrath called *Writing Madness*, with an introduction by Joyce Carol Oates. Danel earned his PhD on the Gothic and terrorism from the University of Stirling, Scotland, in 2017, and has taught literature and film in the United States, Canada, Israel, and China.

www.ingramcontent.com/pod-product-compliance
Lightning Source LLC
Chambersburg PA
CBHW061712300426
44115CB00014B/2660